THE PEOPLE OF THE GREAT FAITH
The Highland Church, 1690-1900

For
Tamsin
Bryony and Rowan

DOUGLAS ANSDELL

THE PEOPLE OF THE GREAT FAITH
The Highland Church, 1690-1900

acair

The
People
of the
Great Faith

✿

iv

Text copyright © Douglas Ansdell

First published in 1998 by
Acair Limited
7 James Street,
Stornoway
Scotland
HS1 2QN

The right of Douglas Ansdell to be identified as the author of
the work has been asserted by him in accordance with the Copyright,
Designs and Patents Act 1988.

A CIP catalogue record for this title is available from the British Library.

ISBN 0 86152 198 6

Text and cover designed by Mark Blackadder
Printed by ColourBooks Ltd., Dublin

Contents

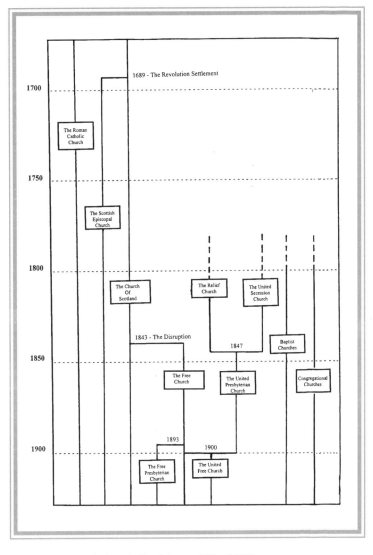

1689 - The Revolution Settlement

1700

The Roman
Catholic
Church

1750

The Scottish
Episcopal
Church

1800

The Church
Of
Scotland

The Relief
Church

The United
Secession
Church

1843 - The Disruption

1847

Baptist
Churches

1850

The Free
Church

The United
Presbyterian
Church

Congregational
Churches

1893

1900

1900

The Free
Presbyterian
Church

The United
Free Church

*The Scottish Church between 1700 and 1900 was more
fragmented than is shown here. This diagram depicts the
principal strands that shaped church life in the
Highlands and Islands.*

CHAPTER 1

Introduction

*The People of the Great Faith was the common epithet by which
they were mentioned in scorn . . . Their fame was spread far and wide as
a people that had gone distracted – that had committed the most extravagant
things, and ought to be shunned by every one as a pest to society . . .
These things were grievous to flesh and blood and not easily borne.*

Neil Douglas
JOURNAL OF A MISSION TO PART OF
THE HIGHLANDS OF SCOTLAND (1797)

There is a particular image of the Highland church which depicts
it as being gloomy, censorious and dictatorial. The church shares
this vulnerability to caricature with many other aspects of
Highland history. Examples which would support this can, of
course, be found. The reality, however, is more complex.

Within the period covered by this study there have been some
ministers who wanted to tear down the Government of their day.
Other ministers could barely separate loyalty to the state from
spiritual duties. Some ministers behaved more like landed gentry
while others tramped over countless miles and stood in wind, rain
and snow to take their message to isolated communities.

Some ministers shared the grief of their people when they were
dispossessed of their homes and lands and others imposed an
intolerable burden by claiming that such events were ordained by
God and were a just punishment for sin. Some church people
danced and sang in their communities while others condemned
such amusements as having no place in a believer's life. There are
many other examples that could be provided to demonstrate the
richness and complexity of Highland church life.

The story of the church in the Highlands is a fascinating and
absorbing subject. Indeed, without it, any understanding of
Highland history would be greatly impoverished. Throughout this

period the church was intimately associated with social change and had a central role in Highland history. It legitimately shares this with the other great themes of Highland history such as rebellion, eviction, famine, emigration, crofting, language, culture, clanship and land. Indeed, a study of any of these would be incomplete without some consideration of the role of the church.

The approach adopted in this study will be broadly chronological. The development of the Highland church will be traced from the Revolution Settlement in 1690 to the union of the Free Church and the United Presbyterians in 1900. In Highland history this was a period of immense social and religious upheaval and the story of the church will be firmly set within the context of Highland culture and society.

The scope of this survey is wide-ranging both in geographical, chronological and ecclesiastical terms. It, therefore, needs to be selective. It would clearly not be feasible to follow every tradition in every parish throughout the specified period. This would be an unmanageable project and one which might obscure the main developments of Highland church history. This study, therefore, offers a survey of the period that is selective by tradition and area yet seeks to highlight the significant developments.

An issue that has been approached with considerable caution in the following pages is the use of the term the Highland church. Although there were a number of strands of Christianity in the Highlands and Islands that can be collectively referred to as the Highland church there was, of course, no such thing as a monolithic institution which was known as the Highland church. In this study, particular developments have mostly been associated with particular strands of the church in the Highlands. At certain points it has, however, been considered appropriate to use the term 'the Highland church' when more general comments are required.

The major developments of this period which this study has highlighted are the legal establishment and the extension of presbyterianism, the success of evangelical Christianity, the Disruption and the fragmentation of the Free Church. These developments will receive appropriate consideration.

There are also certain themes that can be followed throughout this study. These include the church's efforts to extend a measure of social control in Highland and Island communities, the effect of religious and sectarian divisions on church life, the influence of forces external to the Highlands in shaping the church in the Highlands and the distinct nature of Highland spirituality.

Of these themes, the social control exercised by the church inevitably created a measure of tension between the church and Highland society and church divisions also produced a measure of conflict and controversy within the church. Both of these tensions will be explored in this study.

The interaction between external forces and indigenous developments can also be demonstrated at various points. Throughout the period of this survey the recognised centres of power and influence have consistently been outwith the Highlands. A common view expressed from the 'outside' was that the Highlands stood in need of the benefits of external wisdom. This perspective elicited a degree of external interest and activity. The Highlands, however, might have been lacking centres of political and religious authority but as a region it certainly was not lacking its own culture, history and traditions.

The dynamic relationship of these two forces, external influence and indigenous culture, at times complementary and consensual, at times imposed and contentious, resulted in the Highlands and Islands having their own distinct spirituality and provided a means of assisting social change.

A study of this nature needs to give due attention, not only to the events and personalities of Highland church history but also to those who have recorded the events and described the personalities. The writing of Highland church history has been a battleground of competing perspectives. Writers who have viewed the church as either a positive or negative force in Highland society have expressed this in their accounts of the past. In addition, church historians have used the writing of history in support of their own church position. Much church history has involved struggle and contention. These debates have frequently been continued into accounts of Highland church history which have been used for the purpose of affirming and perpetuating certain traditions.

It is, therefore, important not only to describe the main religious developments throughout this period but also to explain the competing perspectives that have been employed by commentators and participants in interpreting these developments.

Along these lines, there is a distinctly evangelical perspective on Highland church history. This has a number of themes that were held in common yet it also contains points of divergence. The points of divergence are represented mostly by the main presbyterian denominations. To an extent this exposes the tragedy of the Highland presbyterian churches. On the one hand they have shared a common view of the past, they have praised the same people, have exalted the same movements and have clung to the same principles. Yet these people who had so much in common were bitterly divided. In many cases they were divided by events that often had their origin outwith the Highlands.

The points of divergence have significantly reflected the main denominations, the Church of Scotland, the Free Church, the Free Presbyterian Church and the United Free Church. Those writing Free Church history in the nineteenth-century saw evangelicalism as a major turning point in Highland history and affirmed that this glorious tradition was secured within the Free Church at the Disruption in 1843. Their writing praises the heroes of this tradition and celebrates their faithfulness to its principles.

The United Free Church came into being in 1900. At this point the majority of the Disruption Free Church decided they could unite with the United Presbyterians, and this was regarded, by those remaining in the Free Church, as a betrayal of Free Church principles. The United Free Church, however, was quite unwilling to relinquish the spiritual high ground to the Free Church. Many Highland ministers, either facing union in the 1890s or writing after union, grafted the new United Free Church on to the Highland evangelical past and thereby established a continuity with the Disruption generation.

The Free Presbyterian historians, who had broken from the Free Church in 1893, stood in the same tradition as the Free Church and the United Free. They shared the same reformed and Disruption roots but considered the other churches' attachment to this tradition to be unsatisfactory. They claimed to represent a more complete adherence to the Disruption traditions.

The Church of Scotland is slightly more complex. In many Highland communities the Church of Scotland was reduced to the status of a minority institution following the Disruption. In accounting for the Highland Disruption some Church of Scotland writers explained it in terms of simple minded people being easily led astray by scheming demagogues.

In 1929, however, the majority of the United Free Church united with the Church of Scotland. The Disruption tradition that the United Free laid claim to thereby found itself back in the Church of Scotland. There were some Highland ministers who had been adamantly Free Church in the 1890s, yet found themselves in the Church of Scotland after 1929. They could still lay claim to the same Disruption tradition and, after 1929, the Church of Scotland could also share this heritage.

More recently social and economic historians have also made an extremely important contribution to Scottish Highland history. In so doing they have offered valuable insights into Highland church history. However, their preference for seeing the only significant social groups as being those defined in material terms carries the potential for limiting their treatment of Highland church history. Ideas and beliefs are quite capable of providing the common factors which define social groups and by which the particulars of Highland history can be better understood.

Although this survey is rich in information and detail, conflicting views of the church in the Highlands will remain. The church certainly exerted a powerful and formative influence on Highland and Island communities. This is arguably far in advance of the church's social significance in other areas of Scotland. The response to the church, whether attachment or antipathy, has consequently been much stronger.

For some their church is and will remain an object of affection that sustained Highland culture throughout two very difficult centuries. Others have seen it as an additional burden that undermined Highland culture. The following pages will not attempt to unravel this question. They will, however, attempt to present the Highland church in both its magnificence and its short-comings. The ambivalence is perhaps appropriate in what is essentially an account of people and communities. Despite being referred to as the 'People of the Great Faith' the following pages demonstrate that they held much in common with other peoples and with other communities.

CHAPTER 2
The Presbyterian Settlement

*'prelacy and the superiority of any office in the church above
presbyters is, and hath been a great and insupportable grievance and trouble
to this nation, and contrary to the inclinations of the generality of the people,
ever since the Reformation, and, therefore, ought to be abolished.'*

THE CLAIM OF RIGHT, 1689

1689 had far reaching consequences for religious life in Scotland. In that year, in what has been referred to as the Glorious Revolution, the crown passed from James VII to William III. In the Revolution Settlement which followed, a series of political and religious measures were adopted which, among other things, transformed the face of religion in Scotland. The fundamental change was that presbyterianism replaced episcopalianism as the lawful form of church organisation.

This transition was far from smooth in some communities. Inspired by the ideal of one national church, presbyterians advanced towards the goal of settling ministers throughout the Highlands. As they did this, presbyterian ministers were battered and wounded, stripped of their clothes, forced out of churches with guns at their heads and marched out of parishes surrounded by swordsmen. It certainly was not an easy or an instant transition and depended ultimately on the support of the law and the power of the state. Indeed, the resistance that was offered was undermined by the failure of two Jacobite uprisings and the consequent unwillingness of Jacobite episcopalians to maintain this resistance in an increasingly unfavourable political climate.

Power had now passed from one group to another and in recognition of this a number of measures were taken to support the new arrangements. The Westminster Confession of Faith was approved as the standard of the newly established Scottish church. The right of a patron, a landed noblemen or gentleman, to select ministers was transferred to the local parish heritors and the elders of the parish church, and the Act of Supremacy, whereby Charles II had asserted his authority over the church, was repealed. Ministers in Scotland were required to demonstrate their loyalty to William and Mary by praying for them publicly and by name. Also, in accordance with this switch in the balance of power, provision was made for those presbyterian ministers who had been deposed, after the restoration of Charles II, to be re-instated. They had been deposed for not conforming to new episcopal arrangements introduced in the 1660s.

Following the departure of James VII, affairs in Scotland were managed by the Convention of Estates. The initial resolutions of the Convention of Estates were contained in the Claim of Right. It was this document that offered the crown to William and declared that 'prelacy and the superiority of any office in the church above presbyters is and hath been an insupportable grievance and trouble to this nation' and that superiority of office 'ought to be abolished'.

The new arrangements were further supported by the requirement that the clergy should take an oath of loyalty to William and Mary. Faced with this the Scottish bishops and a number of the clergy refused to take this oath of allegiance. In 1693 an oath of assurance was added. This required subscribers to recognise William and Mary, not only as the actual sovereigns, but also as possessing the legal right to the throne. Later in that year subscription to the Westminster Confession and acceptance of the presbyterian form of church government were added to the two oaths.

Episcopalians who conformed to the above requirements could be protected in their parishes. If they failed to do this they faced the threat of being deprived of their position and having their parishes declared vacant. Those who had not conformed and who had been deprived of their position were the focus of a further piece of legislation in 1695. In this year deprived episcopalian clergy were forbidden from celebrating marriage or baptism and could be imprisoned for doing so.

These remnant episcopalians were later, under the Toleration Act of 1712, allowed to meet and worship but the toleration that was being offered was still conditional upon loyalty to Queen Anne and the renouncing of Jacobite sympathies. Although non-juring episcopalians might still be subject to repressive measures, the Toleration Act demonstrated that the state had little intention of imposing an ecclesiastical uniformity in which everyone belonged to the established church. There was further legislation which served to undermine Jacobite episcopalianism and they suffered again following the 1715 and 1745 uprisings. Despite these developments a number of non-juring episcopal clergy refused to recognise the new arrangements. Many of them were found in Highland parishes and their experience after 1689 varied considerably.

To many in the late seventeenth-century, church life would have looked very similar under episcopalianism and presbyterianism. To a great extent both systems were indistinguishable in the visible aspects of church organisation and forms of worship. Before 1689 presbyteries and bishops co-existed. The episcopal church had retained kirk sessions, presbyteries and synods. The moderators of these church courts were, however, chosen by bishops who also presided at synods. Ministers were chosen by the system of patronage, and ordination would normally take place in the bishop's cathedral.

There were also similarities in forms of worship. A similar order of public worship was followed by both systems as it was some time before the episcopalian church adopted the regular use of the liturgy. In episcopal services the Lord's Prayer was repeated, the doxology was sung and prayers were often unprepared. In the seventeenth-century and for long afterwards it was not common for the episcopal clergy to wear any distinctive ecclesiastical vestments and communion services were conducted in a similar fashion to those of presbyterians.

Despite such similarities the crucial distinction was that the episcopalian system was hierarchically arranged with superiority of office vested in bishops. Bishops, however, found themselves out of favour, with no place in the system of government in the church that followed 1689. In the first place they refused to co-operate with William and maintained their attachment to James VII. Bishops were also contrary to the levelling ethos of presbyterianism and they had the misfortune of representing an obvious similarity with the Roman Catholic Church. Furthermore, bishops were linked to the excesses of the thirty years before 1690. This left them with a reputation and an association that, from a presbyterian point of view, made their removal necessary. In a church that was never too far away from claims of spiritual independence, bishops also represented an erastian intrusion. As the balance of power had now shifted in favour of presbyterians, episcopacy had no place in the new arrangements.

The imposition of a new ecclesiastical order was not a straightforward undertaking at the end of a century that had witnessed periods of bitter conflict and division. As a result of this conflict, certain alliances had emerged in the Highlands. Highland clans that retained a loyalty to the Stuarts found that they shared a common cause with episcopalians. Both groups had little sympathy with presbyterians. In some areas of the Highlands where Jacobite episcopalianism prevailed after 1690 presbyterians long remained out of favour. One notable historian commenting on this situation has suggested that much of the north west Highlands was 'actively hostile or sullenly resentful' of whig politics and presbyterian religion.[1] As Highland Jacobitism had links with the episcopal church, the extension of presbyterianism became a matter of national security and concern. Episcopalianism, in Highland Scotland particularly, because of its associations with Jacobitism, was perceived as a threat to the security of the state.

HIGHLAND DIVERSITY

❄

The political and religious situation in the Highlands was clearly not conducive to one solution in 1690. The presbyterian settlement met with both opposition and acceptance. It is, however, not so easy to map out and account for the various responses. Religious preference could vary from one parish to the next. Nevertheless, it is possible to make some general comments about the strength of the two systems in the Highlands. After 1690 support for episcopalians can be found in Perthshire, Ross-shire, Inverness-shire, Caithness and northern Argyll. Presbyterian support can be found in Argyll, Sutherland and Easter Ross.

It is little surprise that the effort to extend presbyterianism in the Highlands was a slow process. There were a number of factors that ensured this. The previous century had contained considerable conflict which was fuelled by clan loyalties and religious antagonism. The presbyterian settlement endeavoured to impose a uniformity over this and found that many areas did not willingly fall into line. To an extent it was an imposed settlement but this was not true in all cases. Many areas in the north welcomed the move towards presbyterianism. Thus, this transition involved in some areas, coercion and resistance, in other areas a more consensual arrangement.

In 1690 episcopalian clergy had a few options. They could refuse to recognise the new arrangements and find themselves deposed and their parishes declared vacant. On the other hand episcopalians could approach their local presbytery and request that they be admitted to the established church. They could also take the necessary oaths, keep their stipends, and remain protected as episcopalians in their parishes. As parishes were vacated by episcopalians it was expected that presbyterians would be settled in their place. These were the acceptable alternatives for parish provision at this time. The reality was, however, even more complicated.

Indeed, the variety of religious provision in the Highlands is quite fascinating between the years 1690 to 1730. In some parishes presbyterian ministers were restored. These were ministers who had been removed after 1661. As a result of the distance in time there was not an abundance of ministers in this category. In some areas ministers with presbyterian sympathies had held positions before the revolution. Some episcopalians who renounced episcopacy were admitted into the new establishment but others were not accepted despite renouncing episcopacy, accepting the presbyterian form of church government and taking the necessary oaths. Episcopalian curates could also take the required oaths and remain protected as episcopalians in their parishes. Some who did this still managed to get into trouble with the local presbytery and found themselves deposed for other reasons. Then there were the episcopalians of the non-juring variety; some were deposed and others, even though deposed, continued to minister in their parishes. The latter were supported by the local heritors and parishioners. In some districts heritors appointed, or intruded, non-juring episcopalians for some time after 1690.

For the presbyterians a vacant parish and a presbyterian appointment to it was not the end of the matter. In some parishes presbyterian ministers were unable to exercise their ministry because of the level of resistance which they encountered. Gradually, presbyterian ministers gained the ascendancy and secured appointments to Highland parishes. Undoubtedly, the two unsuccessful Jacobite uprisings of 1715 and 1719 transformed the atmosphere in the Highlands and softened the assertive mood of Jacobite episcopalian heritors who subsequently offered fewer obstacles to the settlement of presbyterian ministers. In 1728, the Royal Bounty Committee's report to the General Assembly supported this assessment. They remarked that 'it is certain that before the late rebellion there was little or no access for ministers of the established church to do any service in these parts and when they attempted the same they were violently opposed and most inhumanly used'.

In 1724 much of the Highlands was organised by the Church of Scotland into four synods. These were Argyll, Ross, Glenelg and Sutherland and Caithness. Although not in existence in 1690 they are useful geographical areas for considering the responses to the settlement of 1689. In the Synod of Argyll twenty-three ministers were deprived of their charges and a further six demitted office; five moved into the presbyterian church, three appear to have had pre-revolution presbyterian sympathies, four episcopalians did not conform and one was a restored presbyterian.

A different picture emerges from the Synod of Ross in which thirteen ministers continued as episcopalians, eight were deprived of their position, one minister would appear to have already been presbyterian and another was a restored presbyterian. In the Synod of Glenelg ten ministers remained in their parishes, five were deprived and two were received into the presbyterian church. In the Synod of Sutherland and Caithness twelve ministers continued in their parishes after the revolution, six were deprived of office, one was a restored presbyterian, one was received into the presbyterian church and two others were pre-revolution presbyterians.[2]

There are a few qualifications which should be added to the above lists. In the first place not all of those who were deprived left their parishes; some remained. In addition, not all those deprived at this time were deprived for not conforming to the new arrangements. For some it was reasons such as immorality and profaning the Sabbath which led to their removal. Also there is a need for caution as to when the changes took place. It was not always the case that those who were deprived were removed in 1689 or 1690. Similarly the above figures might not include all those deprived or all who moved into the established church. This is because many of these changes were still happening in the early eighteenth-century; some time after the revolution Most of the gaps created were being filled by presbyterians but these figures do not reflect how quickly the local presbytery managed to get ministers into the churches. In some cases this happened in 1690; in some cases much later.

THE PRESBYTERIAN EXPERIENCE

✼

There were a number of presbyterian ministers in the Highlands and Islands who were treated with extreme violence and some came very close to losing their lives. Opposition came from Jacobite episcopalian chiefs, landowners and parishioners. In a number of instances they obstructed the efforts to settle presbyterian ministers in certain parishes. Such activity was not confined only to the years immediately following 1689.

In 1711 considerable difficulties were experienced in the attempt to settle Mr John Morrison as the minister of Gairloch. A colleague of his, Mr Thomas Chisholm, minister of Kilmorack, was appointed to serve the edict in the parish. He was denied access to the parish. He was also seized by a group of men and imprisoned for some time at Kinlochewe. It was here, after he was released, that he eventually managed to read the edict to a small group in a house.

In March 1711 the presentation of John Morrison took place in Kiltearn. Morrison encountered difficulties from the outset. He was unable to gain access to the parish and encountered violence frequently. At one point he did receive assurances of safety but Morrison and his servant were attacked and imprisoned in a byre without food or bedding. On the fifth day of his imprisonment he was taken to Sir John MacKenzie of Coull who informed him that 'no presbyterian should be settled in any place where his influence extended unless his majesty's forces did it by a strong hand'.[3]

In one unfortunate incident Morrison's treatment was slightly more humourous but no less unpleasant. On this occasion Morrison was apprehended at Letterewe, stripped of his clothes and tied naked to a tree. He was then left exposed to the full force of the local midges. He remained there until a woman took pity on him and released him.

Morrison complained that he had no manse and no glebe. Also, when he had taken a tack of land his crops had been destroyed. In the year 1715 his house was plundered and his provisions and cattle were taken away. Morrison moved on in 1716.

In the same year as Morrison's troubles began, 1711, John Grant was inducted to Knockbain. This seems to have passed off without incident but on the following Sunday, Grant was surrounded and attacked by about 200 men and women. Some of the men were in women's clothes, had their faces blackened and carried swords and staves. At this encounter Grant was badly cut and beaten. He was dragged by the crowd and then choked by some who intended to kill him. There were, however, others who intervened to spare his life. His attackers then ripped his clothes off and pinned and tied pieces to themselves as trophies of victory. Grant also moved away from the area.[4]

In the parish of Glenorchy Mr Duncan Campbell's appointment proved to be very brief. It was, however, terminated without violence. What Campbell's expulsion lacked in terms of violence was made up for in drama. Campbell was surrounded by twelve men with drawn swords and two pipers who played a death march. He was then escorted to the eastern boundary of the parish, warned never to return and asked to swear this on the Bible. Campbell consented and later described his ordeal as being 'verie undutiful entertainment'.[5]

Even safety in numbers would not guarantee presbyterian security in a hostile area. In 1721 the local presbytery along with members of their congregations visited Daviot parish. They were met by a stone-throwing crowd. The minister of Croy, Mr Farquhar Beaton, along with some of his congregation managed to gain access to the church. This was with the view of holding a service. This party were again attacked, stones were thrown, the pulpit was broken down and the presbyterians were assaulted and wounded by men and women with swords and staves. The presbyterian party then retreated, badly beaten and wounded.[6]

One of the more familiar accounts of this period is that of Aeneas Sage who was settled in the parish of Lochcarron in 1726. On the night before his induction an attempt was made on his life. He was sleeping in a barn which was set alight. Sage, however, managed to escape, chased and caught the man who was responsible for setting alight his overnight accommodation. Sage frequently found himself in fights with his parishioners. For this purpose he carried arms and often had to use his sword to defend himself. Sage was described as being both strong and tall and at times needed to depend on these qualities.[7]

Similar incidents happened in a number of other Highland parishes. In 1720 John MacKillican who was being presented at Lochalsh was driven out. In that same year, Mr Chisholm, the minister of Kilmorack, was chased naked out of his house. An armed mob were active in preventing a presbyterian service in Dingwall in 1704 and when the settlement of a presbyterian minister was attempted four years later, it was unsuccessful because of Jacobite episcopalian opposition. Similar events occurred in Avoch in 1712 when Mr Alexander MacBean could not get access to his church or manse, in Killearnan where Mr Hugh Campbell was assaulted in the pulpit and threatened with the loss of his life, and in Urray where the hapless Mr John Morrison, formerly of Gairloch, experienced continual opposition during his ministry.

THE EPISCOPAL EXPERIENCE

❋

At a national level presbyterianism had replaced episcopalianism. This, however, had not been fully implemented or enforced at a local level and episcopalian experience, in the Highlands and Islands, varied. It was not uncommon to find episcopalian clergy in their parishes long after 1690 and in some cases non-jurors, whose parishes had been declared vacant, remained active, ministering both in their former parish and in neighbouring parishes.

The General Assembly of the Church of Scotland expressed

some concern about this in 1703. They noted that both tolerated clergy and non-jurors often strayed beyond their parish boundaries for religious purposes. In 1730 the Synod of Glenelg was still bringing such matters to the attention of the General Assembly. In that year they raised the subject of a deposed curate who was active in the Presbytery of Gairloch and the following year the Synod reported that a non-juror was administering the sacrament to hundreds of communicants in the north-west. Even the Old Statistical Account which was compiled at the end of the eighteenth-century, includes references to the activity of non-juring clergy.

A significant number of episcopalian clergy were deprived of office but continued to minister in their parishes. Examples of this can be found throughout the Highlands. In such cases episcopalian ministers were deprived by the Privy Council for not reading the proclamation of the Convention of Estates, neglecting to pray for William and Mary, or refusing to take the required oaths.

Within this category the longest serving was Robert Cumming, episcopal curate of Urquhart and Glenmoriston. Cumming remained a Jacobite and an episcopalian and in 1724, when the Presbytery of Abertarff was created, it was noted that 'Mr Robert Cumming being of the episcopal persuasion it is not expected he should attend our meetings'.[8] Nevertheless, Cumming appears to have maintained acceptable relations with the local presbytery and collaborated with them in the spiritual oversight of the people and the restraining of Roman Catholicism in the locality. There were a number of other episcopalians who remained in their parishes for many years after the revolution. In Glenorchy, Dugald Lindsay, who had witnessed his presbyterian replacement marched out of the parish, remained until 1728. In Ardnamurchan, Alexander MacDonald was deposed for non-jurancy but continued to minister to the few protestants in Ardnamurchan until 1724. There were others throughout the Highlands and Islands who remained without conforming and yet were protected locally.

Other episcopalian clergy sought admission to the presbyterian church. In Glenaray, Argyll, John Lindsay was deprived of his parish in 1690. He renounced episcopacy and was promptly received into the established church. Similarly, in Strachur, Argyll, James Campbell demitted office in 1690, he renounced episcopacy and moved into the established church in 1692. Some

were not so successful. Three ministers in Caithness, John
Gibson, John MacPherson and George Oswald spoke of the evils
of prelacy and the rightness of presbyterianism. They sought
admission into the established church and to be given the liberty
to preach the gospel. They were, however, unsuccessful in their
bid. In some cases there was a measure of delay before decisions
were made. In the case of Allan Morrison, minister of Barvas, it
was 1722 before he moved from episcopalianism to presbyterianism. This, however, is probably attributable to the change of
mood that followed the Earl of Seaforth's failure in the 1715
campaign and his reluctance to engage in subsequent Jacobite
campaigns. Again, the Highland and Island parishes provide
many more examples of those who transferred successfully and
also of those who did not find acceptance with the new order.

Many episcopalians took the necessary oaths and remained in
their parishes until their deaths. A number of the clergy took this
route in Sutherland and Caithness. The last survivor, Alexander
Gray of Assynt, died in 1727. There are also examples of ministers
who, although protected by virtue of taking oaths, found
themselves deposed for other reasons. In 1699 Mr Donald Forbes,
minister of Kilmuir Easter, was accused of errors and gross
scandals and asked to preach before the presbytery. He refused
and was suspended. He continued to preach and was then charged
with a list of failings which included arminian errors, ante-nuptial
fornication, covetousness, breach of the Sabbath and the neglect of
discipline. Forbes was then deposed and his parish was declared
vacant. Mr Robert Ross, episcopal curate of Tain, received similar
treatment.

In areas where the heritors had Jacobite sympathies, episcopalians were still being intruded into parishes long after 1689. Mr
Finlay MacRae, who was the minister of Cumbrae, left at the
revolution and was intruded into Lochalsh in 1695 by Frances,
Countess of Seaforth. MacRae had not taken the oaths of
allegiance and assurance and in 1715 encouraged his parishioners
to join the Jacobite uprising. A similar progression was followed
by Mr Duncan Stewart who, as minister of Dunoon, was deprived
in 1690 and intruded in the parish of Blair Atholl in 1709. An even
later episcopal appointment was that of Alexander Nicolson to
Kilmuir, Skye, in 1715.

In 1689 the presbyterians were in the minority. However, even though a minority they had the upper hand as presbytery regulated church discipline and controlled appointments. Their eventual dominance was thus assured. Initially there was a measure of opposition to presbyterian appointments. Yet with the increasing unwillingness of Jacobite heritors to provoke the authorities after 1715 and 1719 the freedom of presbytery to make appointments went unchallenged.

The Highlands and Islands have always been an area of great regional diversity. This is clearly illustrated in the various responses to the presbyterian settlement of 1689. At this point presbyterianism replaced episcopalianism which was at this time deeply entrenched in a number of Highland communities. This religious divide was further complicated by the Jacobite sympathies that many episcopalians entertained. The Highlands, however, were not consistently episcopalian and a number of areas welcomed the changes.

The extension of presbyterianism throughout the Highlands and Islands was slowed down by local episcopalian loyalties and a shortage of suitable presbyterian ministers. Without the legally deprived but continuing episcopal ministers, some parishes would have been denied a measure of religious provision for some years. These difficulties were, however, being progressively overcome and addressed in the first half of the eighteenth-century. The establishment of a presbyterian minister in Highland parishes was not the end of the matter. There was much that still had to be done in order to extend religious provision to Highland and Island communities.

CHAPTER 3
The Extension of Presbyterianism

*'It would be hard that the children of men who have fought and died for the
maintenance of our institutions, both civil and religious, should be left so nearly
destitute of all benefit from those institutions which the blood of their
fathers has been shed to maintain'*

Dr John Inglis
MINISTER OF OLD GREYFRIARS,
EDINBURGH, 1819

In the early eighteenth-century the Church of Scotland was
confronted with a number of obstacles in its work in the Highlands.
These were in addition to the continued activity of illegal episcopalians and the stubborn attachment of some areas to the Roman
Catholic faith. Although these issues ensured that the Church of
Scotland focused attention on the Highlands, it also faced a
number of other difficulties relating to geography, language,
personnel and accommodation. These difficulties inhibited the
church's ability to extend itself adequately throughout the
Highlands and Islands. The resulting patchy provision heightened
the concern that catholicism and episcopalianism could remain,
thrive and expand. These obstacles, therefore, had to be overcome
in order to secure presbyterianism throughout the Highlands and
Islands. Only this, presbyterians and Government believed, would
have the effect of dispelling superstition, overcoming ignorance
and promoting loyalty throughout this region.

The fundamental unit of church management that would
secure these improvements was the parish. A minister should be
settled in every parish and, aided by his kirk session, should attend
to the spiritual needs of the people and exercise church discipline.
It was, therefore, the first task of the Church of Scotland to put in

place the structure, consisting of parish, presbytery and synod, that would facilitate this. It was also expected that, where possible, people would attend the church in the parish in which they lived. This arrangement was to be the basis from which the church hoped to extend religious provision in the Highlands.

There is a measure of debate as to when the Church of Scotland could claim to have successfully extended its influence throughout the Highlands. Some historians have regarded 1750 as a turning point and have claimed that at this stage the task of securing the presence of the Church of Scotland had been accomplished. Other commentators have considered this assessment too optimistic. They have argued that even by the end of the eighteenth-century the religious transformation of the Highlands was not complete and there was still room for new initiatives.[1]

The above views, however, need not be regarded as either antagonistic or incompatible. There are two different things being discussed; one relates to the development of the administrative structure of presbyterianism and the second to the church providing adequate religious instruction for all Highland communities. Thus, some historians have identified mid-century as the point at which they recognise that the structure was in place. Others have made the observation that the benefits which this structure was to deliver took a little longer.

In some places the presbyterian structure, once in place, was still not adequate to the task set before it. The settlement of a presbyterian minister in every Highland parish did not immediately secure adequate religious provision for Highland communities. The established church took the view that there remained areas of great need in the Highlands. There are a number of reasons for this which are mostly associated with the nature and size of Highland parishes. In terms of meeting this need an important contribution was made by the efforts of missionaries, catechists and school teachers. These individuals supplemented the work of the parish ministry by also providing religious instruction.

PROBLEMS OF PROVISION
❄

There is a measure of consensus among historians that the nature and size of Highland parishes was a major obstacle with which the

Highland and Adjoining Parishes in the Mid Eighteenth-Century

1	Thurso	51	St. Andrews Lhanbryd	100	Kilmartin
2	Olrig	52	Urquhart	101	Kilmichael Glassary
3	Dunnet	53	Birnie	102	North Knapdale
4	Cannisbay	54	New Spynie	103	Kilfinan
5	Bower	55	Rothes	104	Stralachlan
6	Watten	56	Speymouth	105	Strachur
7	Wick	57	Bellie	106	Kilmodan
8	Edderton	58	Rathven	107	Inerchaolain
9	Tain	59	Cullen	108	Dunoon and Kilmun
10	Tarbat	60	Deskford	109	North Bute
11	Fearn	61	Ordiquhill	110	Rothesay
12	Nigg	62	Grange	111	Kingarth
13	Logie Easter	63	Keith	112	Kilcalmonell
14	Kilmuir Easter	64	Cairnie	113	Saddell and Skipness
15	Rosskeen	65	Glass	114	Rosneath
16	Alness	66	Botriphnia	115	Lochgoilhead and Kilmorich
17	Kiltearn	67	Boharm	116	Arrochar
18	Fodderty	68	Mortlach	117	Cardross
19	Dingwall	69	Aberlour	118	Old Kilpatrick
20	Urquhart and Logie Wester	70	Knockando	119	New Kilpatrick
21	Resolis	71	Cabrach	120	Dumbarton
22	Cromarty	72	Inveraven	121	Bonhill
23	Rosemarkie	73	Glenbucket	122	Kilmarnock
24	Avoch	74	Towie	123	Aberfoyle
25	Knockbain	75	Strathdon	124	Port of Mentieth
26	Killearnan.	76	Abenethy and Kincardine	125	Kilmadock
27	Urray	77	Duthil and Rcthiemurchus	126	Balquhidder
28	Lochcarron	78	Moy and Dalarossie	127	Ardoch
29	Lochalsh	79	Arisaig and Moidart	128	Muthill
30	Kiltarlity and Convinth	80	Ardgour	129	Mozievaird and Strowan
31	Kirkhill	81	Kingussie and Insh	130	Crieff
32	Urquhart and Glenmoriston	82	Glenmuick, Tullich and	131	Fowlis Wester
33	Inverness and Bona		Glengairn	132	Logiealmond
34	Dores.	83	Logie Coldstone	133	Auchtergaven
35	Daviot and Dunlichity	84	Aboyne and Glentanar	134	Little Dunkeld
36	Croy and Dalcross	85	Birse	135	Weem
37	Petty	86	Edzell	136	Logierait
38	Ardersier	87	Lochlee	137	Dunkeld and Dowally
39	Nairn	88	Lothnot and Navar	138	Lethendy
40	Auldearn	89	Cortachy and Clova	139	Caputh
41	Dyke and Moy	90	Glenisla	140	Clunie
42	Ardclach	91	Kirkmichael (Perthshire)	141	Kinloch
43	Forres	92	Moulin	142	Blairgowrie
44	Kinloss	93	Glenorchy and Inishail	143	Rattay
45	Rafford	94	Ardchattan	144	Bendochy
46	Edinkillie	95	Muckairn	145	Alyth
47	Alves	96	Kilmore and Kilbride	146	Kingoldrum
48	Elgin	97	Kilninver and Kilmelfort	147	Glentrathen
49	Dallas	98	Kilchrennan and Dalavich	148	Kirriemuir
50	Spynie	99	Craignish		

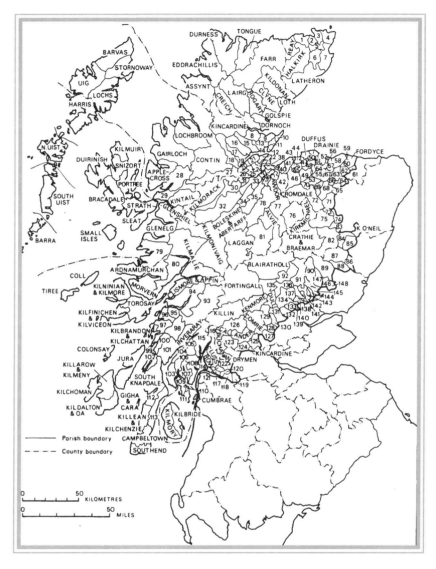

This map clearly shows the difference in size between parishes in the eastern Highlands
and those further to the north and west. Many Highland parishes covered large areas
of land and proved to be very demanding for one minister.
(Source: by kind permission, CWJ Withers: Gaelic Scotland, p 34)

established church had to contend in order to extend provision in the Highlands. A number of parishes were simply unmanageable as they could be up to forty or fifty miles long. Parishes such as Gairloch, Lochbroom, Kilmallie, Ardnamurchan, Glenorchy, Kilmonivaig, Kilmorack, Farr and many others were inordinately large and beyond the capabilities of one parish minister. These difficulties were exacerbated if a parish consisted of island territories. In the late eighteenth-century the parish of Harris consisted of seven inhabited islands, the small isles of Eigg, Rum, Muck and Canna formed one parish and the parish of Jura and Colonsay consisted of nine islands, of which six were inhabited. For much of the eighteenth-century each of these three combined parishes was managed by only one minister. Other parishes combined both mainland and island districts.

In addition to problems of size, the nature of the land provided obstacles; rivers, sea and inland lochs, mountains and marshes conspired to render ministerial duties more difficult. Parishes such as Lochbroom and Lochs were cruelly divided by sea inlets. Urquhart and Glenmoriston, Kilmallie and others contained formidable mountain ranges which added to the problems facing eighteenth-century ministers. Such physical features could often be compounded by poor communications as was noted by the parish minister of Applecross who commented in the 1790s that, in his parish, 'there is neither public road nor bridge from one extremity of it to the other' and this was a parish that contained 'rugged hills, rapid waters and deep marshy moors'.[2]

In some cases such difficulties were further complicated by population distribution and the location of the church within the parish. In large parishes it was quite possible for the church to be located at one end of a parish and yet the parish might contain two, three or four distinct and distant population centres. In the entry for Kincardine, contained in the Old Statistical Account, the minister noted that the parish church was within one mile of the eastern end of the parish yet the parish was thirty miles long. Similarly in Kiltarlity, the parish was estimated to be about the same size and again the parish church was located at one end.

In Barvas, Lewis, the minister observed that there were significant numbers of people at both ends of his parish and at certain times of the year it was extremely difficult and dangerous for the more remote parishioners to attempt to travel to the parish church. On a couple of occasions lives had been lost as distant parishioners had endeavoured to cross swollen rivers in order to attend church while poor weather prevailed.[3]

The situation that existed in the Highlands and Islands meant that many people were not within easy reach of a weekly church service which was enjoyed as a matter of course in the Lowlands. Indeed, many did not live within reach of a service each month. As a result of distant and scattered populations within a parish some ministers were obliged to hold infrequent services in remote areas of their parish. These were designated as preaching stations and it was quite common for such services to be held in the open-air. If the weather was poor, ministers often did not attempt the journey to these preaching stations. Thus the opportunity of attending a service would be lost until the minister's next visit.

Even in the 1830s in Uig, Lewis, the parish minister would not hold services in remote areas of his parish between the months of November and May. It was not uncommon for ministers to consider some areas for a service only once a quarter. This was the case in areas within the parish of Applecross or the interior of Morvern. In the Park area of Lewis in the 1830s the Lochs minister would visit three times a year. Commenting on this level of provision the parish minister of Lochbroom said in the 1790s that his parish required four clergymen, not just one, to provide Christian worship and public instruction for the people. He said that 'in their present state many of them do not hear so much as one sermon a year'.[4]

There are many accounts of the demanding routines that parish ministers had to face in order to extend religious provision to Highland communities. In the parish of Kilmorack in the 1790s, there was a missionary appointed to assist the minister. He had four different preaching stations in which he took services in succession. In the Small Isles parish, in the same period, the minister officiated at Rum once a month, at Muck once a month, at Canna once a quarter and at Eigg the rest of the time. This, of course would be weather permitting. In addition, the Small Isles minister had to attend presbytery in Skye and synod in Glenelg. These few examples provide an insight into difficulties that were quite common in the Highlands and Islands in the eighteenth and nineteenth centuries.

Religious provision in the Highlands and Islands was an issue that was regularly brought before the General Assembly in the eighteenth and nineteenth centuries. The Synods of Glenelg and Argyll contributed to the debates and the General Assembly occasionally appointed committees to consider the spiritual needs of the Highland parishes. One such committee concluded in 1760 that 'many parishes in these counties, especially in the western Highlands and Islands are so extensive as to render the charge of them utterly disproportioned to the ability of the most active ministers'. A similar exercise in 1817 provided information which was used to support an appeal to Parliament for more churches in the Highlands.[5]

Yet again in 1838, a Parliamentary Commission which investigated access to churches in Scotland focused attention on the same deficiencies. The report noted that there were seventy-four Highland parishes that were considered to be deficient in terms of opportunities for public religious worship and the means of religious instruction and pastoral superintendence. The concerns that the Commissioners of Religious Instruction identified in parishes were as follows; population size, territorial extent, obstructed church access, inconvenient parish divisions, ministers responsible for more than one church, inconvenient situation, inadequate size of parish church, condition of parish church and small stipends.[6]

Thus in the Highlands and Islands in the eighteenth and early nineteenth-century there was a need for more ministers and there was a need for smaller parishes. There was a need for new church buildings and the repair of old church buildings. Many church buildings were in a poor and ruinous condition and required attention. Much of this duty fell to heritors who, in some cases, proved quite reluctant to improve the conditions under which people worshipped and in which ministers lived with their families. The church also looked to Government for assistance with these needs.

GAELIC

❊

The Church of Scotland had a shortage of Gaelic-speaking ministers in the eighteenth-century. This added to the problems of religious provision that originated from the nature and size of parishes. In the years after 1690 there were not enough Gaelic-

TIOMNADH NUADH

A R

TIGHEARNA agus ar SLANUIGH-FHIR

IOSA CRIOSD.

'Eidir-theangaicht'
O'n Ghreugais chum Gaidhlig Albannaich.

Maille re feòlannaibh aith-ghearra chum a' chàn'ain fin a leughadh.

Air iarrtas na Cuideachd urramaich, a'ta chum eòlas CRIOSDUIDH a fgaoileadh feadh Gaidhealtachd agus eileana na h ALBA·

Clòdh-bhuailt' ann DUN-EUDAIN,

Le BALFOUR, AULD, agus SMELLIE.

M.DCC,LXVII.

Gaelic New Testament. The first New Testament in Scots Gaelic was produced in 1767,
funded by the SSPCK, translated by James Stuart, minister of Killin, and the printing
in Edinburgh was supervised by the Gaelic poet and catechist Dugald Buchanan.
(Source: National Library of Scotland)

speaking presbyterian ministers to fill the vacancies that existed in the Highlands. Although the Church of Scotland encouraged its ministers to preach regularly in English, a number of schemes were adopted to provide Gaelic-speaking ministers.

To meet the need for ministers the Synod of Argyll proposed, shortly after the Revolution Settlement, that the stipends attached to vacant churches should be used for 'educating and maintaining youths haveing ye Irish language at schools and colledges for ye work of ye ministrie within this province'. This request was granted by Parliament. The General Assembly also encouraged presbyteries to provide bursaries for the training of students with Gaelic for the ministry. In 1710 the General Assembly appointed all presbyteries in Scotland to apply a half of their bursaries to the support of Gaelic-speaking students.[7]

In addition to the financial support for the training of Gaelic-speaking ministers the Assembly adopted other policies to secure Gaelic ministers in Highland pulpits. Ministers with Gaelic were sent from the southern synods to the Highlands for a few months. If they received a call from a congregation they would be compelled to accept. In 1708 the Assembly decreed that Gaelic speakers could be settled in a Lowland congregation only if that minister had served for a year in the Highlands supplying vacancies without a call. If such a minister subsequently went to the Lowlands and a call came from a Highland parish, that minister would be obliged to return. In addition, to strengthen this further, the Assembly decided that no Gaelic-speaking minister could be removed from the Highlands without Assembly consent.

It is difficult to know the extent to which these and other measures were adhered to or how successful they were. The numbers of Gaelic-speaking ministers, however, did increase, vacancies were filled and by the 1840s there was adequate provision with about 230 ministers who regularly used Gaelic in their services.

ROMAN CATHOLICISM IN THE HIGHLANDS

❧

There was extreme concern about the presence of Roman Catholicism in the Highlands. This was fuelled by the Synods of Glenelg and Argyll who persisted in raising this issue regularly in the Assembly. A variety of solutions were suggested to counter this threat including the extension of churches and schools and the use of missionaries and catechists. However, there was anxiety about the activity of catholic priests and some areas that suffered from lack of presbyterian supervision were considered to be vulnerable to catholic encroachment.

The areas that were predominantly catholic stretch from the islands in the Outer Hebrides to Aberdeenshire. The highest percentages of catholics were found in Barra, Eigg, Canna, South Uist, Benbecula, Moidart, Arisaig, and South Morar. Other areas in which there were significant catholic communities included Knoydart, North Morar, Glengarry, Lochaber, Badenoch, Glenmoriston, Braemar, Deeside and Strathglass.

There were a few attempts to provide an accurate number for Scottish catholics. Both those initiated by the General Assembly and the Roman Catholic Church arrived at similar figures of between 11,000 and 12,000 communicants in the mid eighteenth-century. Some of the reports indicated that there had been a considerable advance of catholics in the first half of the eighteenth-century. This was of great concern to the Church of Scotland.

Catholic advances in the Highlands between 1700 and 1750 were identified in Lochaber, Glenmoriston, Glenurquhart, Laggan, Huntly, Crathie, Kilmorack, Kiltarlity, Glenroy, Glenspean, Abertarff and Fort Augustus. This advance was put down to the activity of priests in these areas. One report described travelling priests as being 'now so insolent that they come within four miles of the Garrison of Fort William'.

The Synod of Argyll noted in 1720 that in the parish of Kilmonivaig there were previously only four families that were catholic, yet 'of late, through the diligence and industries of traficking priests among them there are above four hundred persons converted'. The same synod, eight years later, expressed concern about the Parish of Ardnamurchan as it was in danger of being 'overrun with popery by the frequent recourse of priests to these bounds, these priests being known enemies to our civil constitution and fills peoples' heads with prejudices against our only sovereign King George, as well as against the truths of our holy religion'.

There was an increased focus on the needs of the Roman Catholic Church in the Highlands when in 1732 the Scottish mission was divided into two districts, Highland and Lowland. Bishop MacDonald, who came from the Loch Morar area, was consecrated Vicar Apostolic of the Highland district. At this time there were twelve priests working in the Highland district and they were all Scottish Highlanders. There were also attempts to establish a seminary in the Highlands. The aim was to train Gaelic-speaking priests for work in the Highlands or for further training abroad. A Catholic seminary was located in a number of sites such as Morar, Scalan, Moidart, Lismore and Aquhorties before the last two amalgamated with Blairs College in 1829.

There is a general agreement as to what were the catholic areas of the Highlands. In some areas of catholic population the landowners were Protestant. The maintenance of catholics in the Highlands was undoubtedly assisted by sympathetic landlords such as MacDonald of Clanranald, MacNeill of Barra and the Duke of Gordon. The Highland territory of the Duke of Gordon expanded from Glenlivet to Lochaber and within this area the catholic faith was protected and catholic schools were established. In 1728, however, the Duke of Gordon died and his wife, who was a Protestant, brought up their sons according to her tradition.

It is perhaps not surprising that the Highland Roman Catholic Church was in such a poor condition in the early nineteenth-century. Many priests did not have adequate or permanent houses. Places that were used as chapels often looked more like barns than places of worship. Although the Highlands and Islands remained a concern of the catholic church, the creation of the Western District in 1827 must have been a difficult area in which to focus on the needs of remote Highland communities. The new Western District included the north west Highlands but it also included the industrial south west of Scotland in which needs were also arising from Irish immigration, industrialisation and the growth of urban centres.

POLITICAL ANXIETIES

❋

Both episcopalianism and catholicism were perceived to be sources of Jacobitism in the eighteenth-century. Both were, therefore, considered to be a threat and their containment essential. The extension of protestant Christianity into the Highlands was, therefore, an objective which was jointly held by both church and

Father Allan MacDonald was appointed parish priest for Daliburgh, South Uist in 1884 and for Eriskay in 1893. He made an important contribution to preserving the oral traditions of the Southern Isles which remained predominantly Roman Catholic. Allan MacDonald is standing on the pathway. (Source: SLA, NMS)

state. The aim was to civilise and christianise, to eradicate popery and episcopalianism, and to encourage loyalty to crown and constitution.

It is not possible to discuss the established church's objective of extending religious provision in the Highlands without also considering the parallel objective of containing the Roman Catholic presence in the area. The various activities supported by the established church in the Highlands; schools, catechists and missionaries all shared the aim of containing the threat they perceived in catholicism and episcopalianism.

Some sections of the established church responded by recommending stronger counter measures. The Presbytery of Skye suggested payment of a premium for every catholic brought over to the protestant faith. The Presbytery of Lorn recommended the appointment of protestant factors and the settlement of protestant tenants among Roman Catholics. Similarly, the Royal Bounty Committee in 1728 suggested that 'colonies of protestants be planted in the popish parts' and that 'loyal persons be preferred for long leases'.[8] Then there was the approach adopted by the MacLean chief of Coll who, after he became a protestant, was reputed to have driven his people to church with his '*bata buidhe*' (yellow stick). Thus protestantism became popularly referred to as the religion of the yellow stick. These measures were suggested in addition to the slightly more moderate activities of missionaries and school teachers.

In 1819 the catholic threat remained a useful device. Dr John Inglis in a report to the Government said 'perhaps it will not be surprising that the popish religion is even gaining ground in some of these parishes when it is farther considered that popish priests have their residence in a variety of remote districts to whom it is scarcely possible that the labours of the parish ministers should extend oftener than once or twice a year'. The message was clear; increased resources were necessary to secure a loyal and informed population and the national Church of Scotland alone could deliver this.[9]

TERRITORIAL REORGANISATION

❈

In the early eighteenth-century many of the churches in the mid-western Highlands and Islands were contained in one extremely large administrative unit; the Synod of Argyll. This stretched from Mull of Kintyre to Ness in Lewis and contained most of the islands off the west coast. Within the Synod or Argyll some presbyteries were clearly too large. Before 1724 the Outer Hebrides, Skye and the Small Isles formed one presbytery.

In response to expressed concerns, in May 1724, the General Assembly created the Synod of Glenelg. This was made up of four presbyteries; Skye, Gairloch, Abertarff and the Long Island. These presbyteries were in turn composed of the following parishes; the Long Island - Harris, Barra, North Uist, South Uist, Stornoway, Uig, Lochs and Barvas; Gairloch - Glenelg, Kintail, Lochalsh, Lochcarron, Lochbroom, Assynt and Gairloch; Abertarff - Kilmallie, Kilmonivaig, Laggan, Abertarff and Urquhart and Glenmoriston. The Presbytery of Skye consisted of the Skye parishes; Kilmuir, Duirnish, Snizort, Bracadale, Portree, Strath, Sleat and the Small Isles parish.

From the point of view of the established church this was an area of great need and the problems that the church saw in the Highlands were at their most desperate in the Glenelg area. It was an area that required the focusing of considerable attention and resources.

The new Synod of Glenelg was concerned with improving the quality of religious provision within its area, filling vacancies and promoting loyalty. The needs that the Synod of Glenelg perceived were communicated to the Assembly in 1725. The synod's representatives listed vacant churches, large parishes, lack of schools, lack of adequate church buildings, manses and glebes and the need for more itinerant missionaries and catechists. In addition, this increased attention would also have to guard against the 'poisonous influence of popish emissaries and others disaffected to our happy establishment'.

EXTENDING PROVISION
❊

In addition to the changes associated with the creation of the Synod of Glenelg there were other parishes and presbyteries formed in the Highlands in the first half of the eighteenth-century. These adjustments which were made to the ecclesiastical map of the Highlands were for the purpose of providing a more responsive structure for the needs of the region. There were a number of further measures which were proposed in order to secure the place of the Church of Scotland in the Highlands. These measures included schools, missionaries, catechists and church extension.

Central to this period was the work of the Society in Scotland for Propagating Christian Knowledge (SSPCK) and the Royal Bounty Committee (RBC). Both shared much in common and adequately represented the mood of eighteenth-century militant protestantism. The SSPCK was granted a charter in 1709. Its aim was to establish schools, predominantly in the Highlands. These schools would promote the protestant faith and endeavour to counter catholicism in the Highlands.

Along with teaching duties, SSPCK teachers often provided religious services on the Sabbath and contributed to catechising duties in the parish. SSPCK schoolmasters were carefully selected and also had to commit themselves to the eradication of popery. One commentator, writing in 1775, said of the SSPCK schools, that Christian knowledge was increased, heathenish customs were abandoned, the numbers of papists were diminished, disaffection to the Government was lessened and the English language was more widely used.

The policy of the SSPCK has more recently been described as 'civilisation through anglicisation'[10] because it was committed to promoting English education and the wearing out of the Gaelic language. Although this was clearly SSPCK policy and the Society did alter the means by which it sought to achieve this, it is not certain if this was always adhered to in SSPCK schools. Many prominent Gaelic-speakers were SSPCK teachers and it is doubtful if they would have shared this view. Those such as Dugald Buchanan, poet; Norman MacLeod, separatist minister, Alexander MacDonald, poet, and Finlay Munro, evangelist, all taught in SSPCK schools.

The other initiative that was important for eighteenth-century Highland religion resulted from a donation of £1,000 by George I in 1725 to the General Assembly. This was 'to be employed for the reformation of the Highlands and Islands and other places where popery and ignorance abound'. It became an annual grant which was under the control of a committee of the Assembly known as the Committee of the General Assembly for the Regeneration of the Highlands and Islands of Scotland and for the Management of the King's Bounty for that End.

The Assembly charged the RBC with the responsibility to 'appoint itinerant preachers and catechists – pious, loyal to his majesty and skilled in the principles of divinity and popish controversy'. Missionary districts were to be designated within large parishes and the Royal Bounty was to be directed towards such districts. The RBC was to pay particular attention to parishes in which popery and ignorance prevailed. Most parishes of this nature were in the Synods of Argyll and Glenelg.

The Royal Bounty grant was used to provide missionary ministers and catechists for remote areas in the larger parishes. The missionaries were mostly university educated men and had salaries of between £25 to £30 per year by the mid eighteenth-century. It would be unlikely for them to have a fixed house or glebe and they would probably have to itinerate between three or four preaching stations. Often these would be in the open-air. The typical missionary minister might be trained and licensed but as yet not ordained. There was potential for tension here as the missionary might be young and enthusiastic and the parish minister might be older and more moderate in his religious outlook. Many notable Highland ministers such as John MacDonald, Ferintosh, and Finlay Cook, Reay, started their ministerial career as missionary ministers.

Even as late as 1819 there were still large parishes such as Laggan, Barvas, Lochs, Gairloch and Assynt in which the parish minister did not have the assistance of a missionary minister. Parishes that had one minister and one missionary such as Applecross, Glenelg, Lochbroom, Farr, Kilmorack, and Urquhart and Glenmoriston could have used further assistance. Missionaries had responsibility for pastoral superintendence but they were not permitted to baptise, dispense communion or have the assistance of a kirk session.

The RBC also sent out catechists who, unlike missionaries, generally had no academic training. The catechist's duty was to instruct the people in the doctrines of the Christian faith by means of teaching the people to recite set answers to set questions. They were often local men selected and approved by their kirk sessions. Divinity students were sometimes sent out as summer catechists. A catechist's annual salary would be betwen £5 and £15 per year in the mid eighteenth-century. The task of the catechist was to prepare the people for the annual catechising by the parish minister and to prepare parents for baptism. Catechists moved around yet if they decided that there was particular ignorance in certain areas then the catechist would be encouraged to remain there for longer. The quality of catechists varied greatly in terms of their education and literacy.

There was also Parliamentary interest. In 1817 a commission of the General Assembly was appointed to collect details that might be useful in support of an application to Parliament. The Convener of the committee was Dr John Inglis, minister of Old Greyfriars church in Edinburgh. The report gave a clear list of the parishes where the established church faced difficulties. It indicated that many in the Highlands could not attend church regularly and the Royal Bounty scheme of missionaries and catechists could not adequately compensate for the want of additional ministers who were established with stipends and in charge of parishes of a reasonable size.

In 1823 Parliament turned its attention to the religious needs of the Highlands. An Act was passed in July of that year and commissioners were appointed to consider the building of churches in the Highlands and Islands of Scotland. Initially the number of churches was not to exceed forty and no more than £1500 was to be spent on one site. The task of the commissioners was to select the forty sites and supervise the building of churches and manses on these sites. Eventually forty-three sites were settled on. A number of these were in some of the more problematic parishes. In some cases two churches were built in the one parish. In Kilmallie, churches were built in Ardgour and at Ballachulish. In Fortingall, churches were built at Innerwick and at Rannoch. In Kilchoan, churches were built at Strontian and at Acharacle. Some other churches built in needy areas included Cross in Ness, Plockton in Lochalsh, Poolewe in Gairloch, Stoer in Assynt, Sheildaig in Applecross, Strathy in Farr and Ullapool in Lochbroom.

These initiatives were introduced to improve and extend effective religious provision in the Highlands and Islands. Although it is difficult to measure their success they would undoubtedly have contributed to the effectiveness of the Church of Scotland in the region. However, in addition to the specific initiatives, the new position of the presbyterian Church of Scotland within the community was also significant.

Ministers in parish and parliamentary churches were established by law. They were supported by local heritors and associated with education and improvement. Parish ministers in particular had status and contacts that secured them a considerable standing within the community. This would carry influence both in terms of attracting men to go in for the ministry and in terms of developing an attachment of parishioners to the ministry of the established church. Along with the various schemes to overcome obstacles and difficulties which the church faced in the Highlands, the very fact of its social position would have carried considerable influence. The status of the Church of Scotland was enhanced as a result of the position it was given in the community and further secured by the denial of similar standing to other religious alternatives. This was of great importance in terms of developing popular adherence to the Church of Scotland in the Highlands and Islands. By the beginning of the nineteenth-century it could be said of the established church in the Highlands, that having begun as 'an alien intrusion offensive to the majority of the Gaelic people' it had become 'in a relatively short time the beloved and venerated spiritual mother'.[11]

CHAPTER 4

Mission

*'The Assembly further declare that the conduct of any minister
of the church, who exercises his pastoral functions in a vagrant manner,
preaching during his journeys from place to place, in the open-air, in other
parishes than his own, or officiating in any meeting for religious exercises without
the special invitation of the minister within whose parish it shall be held, and by
whom such meetings shall be called, is disorderly and unbecoming the
character of a member of this church.'*

THE GENERAL ASSEMBLY OF THE CHURCH OF SCOTLAND, 1818

In the late eighteenth-century and early nineteenth-century
itinerant preachers were common in the Highlands as they were
elsewhere in Scotland. Itinerant preachers, however, had a
remarkable impact in the north and west. News would be
circulated that a preacher was coming to the area and people would
gather, sometimes in their thousands. They would travel many
miles to attend. A tent would be erected to provide the preacher
with some shelter. Sometimes it might just be a canvas draped over
the branches of a tree. The tent would contain a lectern for the
preacher or it might even be the back of a chair which the preacher
would stand behind. A sermon would be delivered in Gaelic and
psalms would be sung in Gaelic. The whole event would stretch
over several hours and we are informed that neither wind, rain or
snow would deter people from attending nor induce them to leave
prematurely.

The mood of the message would vary. At times it would be
deeply disturbing and at other times it would bring great comfort.
The singing would also vary. At times it would be uplifting and at
other times the people would be so emotionally affected that they
would scarcely be able to sing. There would be weeping, groaning,
cries for mercy, shouts of relief and sometimes fainting, or as one
report phrased it 'persons who were religiously impressed not

In the early eighteenth-century open-air communions took place in both the Lowlands and Highlands of Scotland. The tradition of open-air services remained a familiar aspect of the Highland Christianity. This gathering is at Migdale in Creich. (Source: SLA, NMS)

infrequently fell'. The event would be concluded with great reluctance and the people would implore the preacher to return soon. The events described above were very common in the Highlands and Islands in this period. Accounts of such events came from Caithness and Kintyre, from Perthshire and the Hebrides and from many of the areas in between. Such events shaped the spirituality and expectations of Highlanders and were among the most culturally significant events in the Highlands at this time.

In this period there was a remarkable increase of missionary activity, producing 'nothing less than a religious revolution in the Highlands'.[1] This revolution produced a strong and enduring popular attachment to evangelical Christianity. It also introduced what might be described as a new religious culture, it established new forms and institutions, and it modified the social structure. It was a revolution of beliefs, attitudes, habits and social arrangements. This evangelical revolution arrived largely through the agency of Gaelic-speaking Highlanders. It arrived with education, Gaelic literacy and a compelling certainty. The culture that resulted carried the potential for penetrating every family and being rigorously enforced at a grass roots level.

By the early nineteenth-century we thus have a mixed group of individuals participating in Highland mission; parish ministers, school teachers, catechists and laymen. Some were ordained ministers, some were attached to mission-societies, some had no formal link to either church or mission-society. They were also drawn from both presbyterian and other protestant dissenting denominations. Some preachers covered the whole of the Highlands and Islands while others imposed a much narrower territorial limitation on their activities. There were features of this evangelical work which were not particularly new. Revivals, itinerants and open-air preaching had all been seen before in some areas. They had, however, previously been more effectively regulated by the established church and a more limited range of people had participated.

The aim of extending the Christian message through the Highlands was, of course, not new. However, the eighteenth-century commitment of the national church to extend religious provision and the later diverse evangelical impulse were quite distinct. Neither movement was wholly exclusive to the main period of its activity. In the early eighteenth-century when the established church was concerned with creating an effective presbyterian structure there were also pockets of intense evangelicalism that could be found in some areas of the Highlands such as Easter Ross. Similarly, in the later eighteenth-century and early nineteenth-century when evangelicalism was advancing inside and outside the established church there were churchmen who continued to stress the importance of establishing or maintaining a strict presbyterian structure.

Despite a measure of continuity it is possible to identify certain characteristics in each period. To an extent the emphasis of the mid eighteenth-century was more social and that of the late eighteenth century more individual. The earlier emphasis placed considerable weight on the establishment of a uniform national religion by means of the parish structure. This would secure a law-abiding, loyal, educated, presbyterian community. The new evangelicalism carried less of a political agenda; less reference to Hanoverian loyalty, anglicisation and extending the benefits of civilisation. The emphasis of the new evangelicalism was more on personal salvation; it was about the individual's response to the message of Christianity. The new evangelicals were more likely to refer to human sinfulness, the need for repentance and God's gracious offer of forgiveness and salvation. The later movement at times contained an emphasis on an effective presbyterian presence in every community but they also hoped for an increase of individual believers. The new evangelicalism could be an intensely emotional affair. Missionaries and preachers displayed a zealous attachment to their calling and those who responded to their message developed a personal spirituality that was characterised by a deep emotional commitment.

Another significant difference was the degree of parish control over the two movements. In the mid eighteenth-century, mission activities had been firmly under parish control. The new evangelicals often ignored this. A diverse collection of preachers and itinerant evangelists increasingly disregarded clerical authority and parish boundaries and considered it their duty to spread the gospel message wherever they could. This sense of duty was derived more from their understanding of the teaching of Scripture and less from a concern from the jurisdiction of a presbytery or kirk session. This created a problem for the Church of Scotland. For them the minister alone was the constituted authority who was licensed to preach in a parish. The established church thus regarded itinerants not only as a serious challenge to the position of ministers but also as a threat to public order. If such a breach of public order was permitted then society generally would be less stable. If this trend continued then Scotland might also face upheavals that would resemble the French Revolution.

Although presbyterianism lost a measure of control over religious affairs in parishes in the early nineteenth-century the dominance of its forms and structures ensured that it remained and was able to accommodate much of this mixed mission impulse. Itinerants were able to challenge a minister's right to regulate parish activities, yet they were not so successful in challenging the dominance that presbyterian structures had assumed in Highland parishes. Thus, despite the vitality and independence of itinerant preachers it was the presbyterian structures that benefited from this impulse. The creation of the Free Church further consolidated this process.

THE MISSION IMPULSE

✳

This renewed interest in Highland mission was in part stimulated by interest in world mission. In the late eighteenth-century a number of interdenominational mission societies had been formed with the aim of taking the Christian message to foreign countries. Many of the leading figures of Highland mission outside the established church shared this dual interest in foreign mission and Highland mission. James Haldane said that the 'propagation of the gospel abroad is intimately connected with familiar exertions at home'. The Highlands and Islands of Scotland were considered to be an area that desperately needed to be lifted above ignorance and superstition and to benefit from the evangelical message in much the same way as attention was focused on other more distant countries.

A variety of groups were influenced by this mission impulse and focused their energies on the Highlands and Islands. In 1796 the Relief Church appointed a home mission committee and sent ministers and probationers on preaching tours of the Highlands. Most of their work was in Argyll. Another group that had a profound effect was the Society for the Promotion of the Gospel at Home (SPGH). This society was formed by the Haldane brothers in 1798 and had as its objective the establishment of schools and Sabbath schools, the distribution of gospel tracts, the promotion of scripture reading and the preaching of the gospel. To achieve this it commissioned itinerant preachers. The SPGH trained their agents in seminaries in Edinburgh, Glasgow and Dundee before sending them out on preaching tours. They then moved through many areas of the Highlands preaching in Breadalbane, Arran, Cowal, Kintyre, Moray, Strathspey, Badenoch, Inverness, Ross, Sutherland and Skye. By the close of 1799 the SPGH had forty agents operating in Gaelic speaking areas.

The SPGH was in part financed by the sale of land belonging to the brothers James and Robert Haldane. They were also assisted by John Campbell who had an ironmonger's business in Edinburgh's Grassmarket. Campbell printed and circulated gospel tracts and later formed the Scottish Tract Society. In 1799 the Haldanes severed their links with the established church and formed a connection with Congregationalists. This lasted until 1808 when they again shifted allegiance, this time to the Baptists.

Although this last move seems to have impaired the progress of the SPGH there were a number of other societies which were formed in the early nineteenth-century that shared their objectives. These included the Northern Missionary Society (1800), the Baptist Itinerant Society (1808) and the Highland Mission Society (1819). An Edinburgh Baptist minister, Christopher Anderson, founder of the the Baptist Itinerant Society, also helped establish another extremely important evangelical society; the Edinburgh Society for the Support of Gaelic Schools, founded in 1811. This society concentrated its activities in the north west and the islands and established schools to promote literacy and the reading of the scriptures in Gaelic.

The diverse nature of this mission enterprise can be seen in a brief consideration of some of the individuals who can be considered as itinerant preachers. In the districts of Argyll, Dugald Sinclair was active in the early nineteenth-century. He commenced his itinerant activity as a layman with the Baptist Itinerant Society.

Most of his preaching was in the open-air and one preaching trip lasted six months. He was later ordained as the minister of Lochgilphead Baptist Church but continued his preaching tours after his ordination. Most of his itinerant preaching was done between 1810 and 1815, although he continued to itinerate until 1831, when he emigrated to Ontario.

Finlay Munro from Tain, Easter Ross, had been an SSPCK teacher in Latheron parish in Caithness. From about 1820 he became a travelling evangelist. As such he covered most of the Highlands and Islands. He was irregular, unattached, dressed very plainly and was described as the 'lad who went about with a Bible'. In his first trip to Lewis, Finlay Munro was landed somewhere between Tolsta and Skiggersta. The selection of this location as a starting point for his Lewis mission does not indicate a high level of planning. However, he soon encountered some people at the sheilings and preached to them. Although this would appear to be a rather haphazard start to Finlay Munro's itinerancy in Lewis, he subsequently made an extremely important contribution to evangelicalism in Lewis.

In Skye, Donald Munro is regarded as the father of evangelical religion. Munro was born in 1773, he was blind from age fourteen and later became the Portree catechist. He combined this with fiddle-playing which he gave up following his conversion to evangelical Christianity. Munro's conversion took place under the ministry of SPGH missionary John Farquharson in 1805. Munro then preached and held prayer meetings throughout Skye and focused his activities on Snizort and Kilmuir. An awakening that took place between 1812 and 1814 was attributed to Munro's activity.

In Harris, John Morrison was converted under the ministry of Dr John MacDonald in 1822. Morrison seems to have possessed remarkable abilities. He was a blacksmith and has also been described as the 'last great figure in Highland spiritual poetry'. Following his conversion, he proceeded to hold prayer meetings and preach throughout Harris. He was appointed as an SSPCK catechist in 1828 and his work led to a notable awakening in Harris in 1834. There are many other names that could be added to this list.

In the early nineteenth-century in the Highlands, itinerant preachers had to contend with a measure of hostility from parish ministers and land owners. Neil Douglas, a missionary from the Relief Church who worked in lower Argyll, encountered opposition from parish ministers. On one occasion James Haldane and John Campbell were briefly arrested in Kintyre and another SPGH missionary John Farquharson was imprisoned in Braemar in 1804. There was also an incident in which an Argyll Baptist preacher, Donald MacArthur was apprehended and impressed into naval service for several weeks in 1805. It was not only preachers that got themselves into trouble. One group of evangelical Christians found themselves in jail in Dingwall as a consequence of disrupting a communion service in the parish of Lochs in Lewis. The unorthodox approach adopted by itinerants and evangelicals was clearly offensive to those who regarded the position of the parish minister as being established by both civil and divine order.

Many ministers regarded the activities of itinerant preachers as being unwelcome in their parishes. Such ministers were in agreement with the advice of the General Assembly which had, in 1799, warned against a 'set of men whose proceedings threaten no small disorder in this country. We mean those who assuming the name of missionaries from what they call the Society for the Propagation of the Gospel at Home, as if they had some special commission from heaven'. The Assembly noted that these itinerants are going through the land, acting as teachers, and intruding themselves into parishes without invitation and establishing Sabbath schools without consulting the local presbytery. Furthermore, they were placing religious instruction in the hands of unsuitable people and those 'notoriously disaffected to the civil constitution of this country'. Although most itinerant preachers were unwelcome, this statement from the General Assembly was directed at the Haldanes and their supporters who, it was believed, constituted a more serious threat to public order.

THE BAPTIST CHURCHES
✵

Along with the SPGH another group that were seen as a challenge to the ecclesiastical and territorial arrangements of the parish system were the Baptists. Our understanding of the Baptist contribution to evangelicalism in the Highlands is largely due to the work of Profesor Donald Meek. Without his detailed reconstruction of

*John MacRae, 'MacRath Mòr'. His nickname rests on his status as a Highland preacher
and on his impressive physical presence. One story tells how as a student in Aberdeen someone
knocked a hole in his new hat. MacRae reacted violently. At the point when MacRae's knee
was on the man's chest, he was exhorted, 'Oh John! remember grace'. The victorious MacRae
apparently replied, 'but for grace the beggar would never breathe again'.*
(Source: by kind permission, Miss I Stewart, Edinburgh)

Baptist mission activity in the Highlands this could easily have
remained an undifferentiated aspect of the general evangelical
impulse that the Free Church incorporated in 1843.

The two principal areas of Baptist activity in the early
nineteenth-century were Argyll and Perthshire. The interest that
developed in Argyll resulted from the work of itinerant missionaries and local preachers such as Donald MacArthur and Dugald
Sinclair. MacArthur adopted Baptist principles in 1801. He had
previously worked as a curer and carrier of herring. He was
responsible for a Baptist congregation in Port Bannatyne, Bute,
and possibly for another in Strachur. He preached throughout
Argyll and, as mentioned previously, encountered a measure of

opposition from local landowners. 1801 was also significant for Dugald Sinclair. In this year he was baptised in Glasgow and began to preach throughout mainland Argyll and the islands.

Further interest in Baptist Highland mission was shown by Christopher Anderson from Edinburgh and George Barclay from Kilwinning. From 1805 they took an interest in establishing churches in the Highlands and in 1808 Anderson formed a society known as the Baptist Itinerant Society to promote Baptist mission in the Highlands.

The activity of these itinerant missionaries, Congregational or Baptist, often led to the creation of churches in the Highlands. In the early years of the nineteenth-century a few Baptist churches had emerged in Argyll and some Congregational churches had been established in Perthshire. The Congregational churches were largely a result of the Haldane mission work. However, in 1808, the Haldanes adopted Baptist principles. As a result some of the Congregational churches divided, producing Baptist congregations and adding to Baptist strength in the Highlands. Thereafter there were a number of locations in which both Baptist and Congregational churches existed. These included Aberfeldy, Dunkeld, Glenlyon, Grantown on Spey, Killin, Kingussie, Lawers and Tullymet.

The Baptists were further strengthened by the formation in 1827 of the Baptist Home Missionary Society for Scotland. This society was formed from a few smaller societies with the same aim and principles. From 1829 this society focused its attention on the Highlands and Islands. In 1827 it had nineteen missionaries that travelled, preached and established gatherings in the Highlands and Islands.

Most of the Baptist churches in the Highlands were formed in the first half of the nineteenth-century and along with nine congregations in Perthshire and ten in Argyll there were Baptist churches in Uig, Broadford, Fortrose, Grantown on Spey and Kingussie. There were, in addition, three Baptist congregations in Caithness in this period. Even following the formation of a church it was not uncommon for Baptist ministers to undertake long preaching tours in the summer months. By 1905 there were thirty-one Baptist churches in the Gaelic speaking areas of the Highlands. Their missionary activity, however, penetrated many more Highland communities.

Although the Baptists did not manage to establish a church in Lewis in this period, their missionary activity certainly extended to that island and caused the parish minister, Mr John Cameron, some concern. Cameron claimed that in 1825, when he arrived in Stornoway, there were seven itinerant dissenting preachers in Lewis and these were followed by another four. After a period of tolerance Cameron prohibited Baptists from having access to any meeting houses in the parish, and into these he said 'no Anabaptists shall enter or preach'. Cameron also claimed that the Uig minister, Alexander MacLeod, would not entertain dissenters and that 'by his orders the Baptists got no countenance'.

Cameron's difficulties were compounded by the encouragment which Mrs Stewart-MacKenzie, the Lewis heritor, gave to Baptists. He complained that she was 'opening a wide door for dissenters' by inviting an evangelist, who remained in Lewis under her patronage, 'to preach in the female seminary'.

The Baptists were able to gain support when there was a desire for evangelical religion and the local Church of Scotland minister might be moderate in his sympathies. Baptists were vulnerable following the establishment of the Free Church with its passionate evangelical message. Baptist strength also suffered badly from the effects of emigration. Many of their early leaders and members emigrated to Canada and America. Both Donald MacArthur and Dugald Sinclair, who had made an important contribution in Argyll, emigrated in 1811 and 1831 respectively. Much of the initial interest was from outside the Highlands but it became an initiative that took root in Highland culture and was driven by Gaelic speaking Highlanders. Indeed, one of the most important collections of Gaelic hymns was written by Peter Grant who was the Baptist minister in Grantown on Spey. This collection was published in 1815 and went through numerous reprints.

HIGHLAND MODERATES

✤

Evangelical Christianity advanced both inside and outside the established church. Outside the established church this impulse was largely contained in the Baptist and Congregational churches. As evangelicalism advanced within the established church it heightened the internal divisions between evangelicals and moderates. This division that emerged in the eighteenth-century remained within the established church until in 1843 the Disruption provided ecclesiastical alternatives for both parties. Those labelled moderates remained in the Church of Scotland while many, but certainly not all, evangelicals opted for the Free Church.

Highland moderatism is a very difficult category to define. It is possible to advance certain characteristics to describe moderates, yet it is also possible to find some ministers castigated as moderates who shared none of these characteristics. At times moderates seem to be those who had the misfortune to share their parish with more extreme evangelicals. As they fell short of exacting evangelical standards so they unavoidably fell into the moderate category. In addition, there were many ministers who would have been regarded as evangelicals but their decision not to join the Free Church would unavoidably categorise them as moderates in 1843 and later.

Evangelical rhetoric and literature made a significant contribution to a caricature of moderatism that emerged in the nineteenth-century. As evangelical writers reviewed the state of Highland religion in the late eighteenth and early nineteenth centuries there was a clear consensus on the absolute failure of the moderate ministers to meet the religious needs of the people. Moderatism was often mentioned in the same sentence as superstition, ignorance and spiritual darkness. Moderate ministers, it was claimed, did not deliver the people from this pre-evangelical amalgam of vague religious notions.

A typical example is found in an article on Alexander MacLeod, minister of Uig. With reference to moderatism the writer said 'it was perfectly compatible with the system to grant toleration to superstitions and superstitious observances which had been handed down through the dark age of popery from the still darker age of druidical idolatry'.[2] It was moderatism that was held to be responsible for this apparent state of spiritual poverty in the Highlands when 'the land was held in the deadening grip of the black frost of moderatism' or the people were suppressed by the 'soporific drowse of a benumbing moderatism'.

A term that was frequently used to characterise moderates was neglect. Many were accused of neglecting their spiritual functions and pastoral duties. Thus we find moderates referred to as 'lazy workers', 'stipend lifters', 'wolves in sheep's clothing' and 'shepherds that feed not the flock'. There were, however, moderates who were extremely diligent in their duties. In this case they would fall into this category because their religion was more moral and social rather than one that emphasised the need for personal salvation.

Moderates were frequently regarded as being more worldly-minded than spiritually-minded and showed little concern for the eternal welfare of their parishioners. Dr John Kennedy of Dingwall described the moderate minister as being the one who 'was the great cattle dealer at the market, the leading dancer at the wedding, the toast master at the farmer's dinner and if the last to slide off his chair at the drinking bout, it was because he was more seasoned than the rest'.[3] In the early nineteenth-century, all Highland ministers, to some extent, were farmers. At times their worldliness was seen in the pursuit of this vocation. Walter Ross, minister of Clyne from 1777 to 1793, was described as 'a farmer, a cattle dealer, a house keeper and a first rate sportsman and he knew how to turn these different occupations to a profit'.[4]

The itinerant missionary, Neil Douglas, said of moderate ministers, 'what his boat is to one, his farm is to another and his horse couping, droving etc is to a third; and betwixt these serious avocations the poor flock is left to the mercy of the foxes and the wolves.' James Haldane considered that ministers' farming activities would distract them from spiritual concerns. He thought that such a pursuit 'would have a very bad effect on the mind' and would foster a 'temptation to worldly mindedness'. Haldane's advice was that as 'ministers are so anxious that laymen should be prevented from interfering with what is called clerical business, they would do well to set them an example by abstaining from secular employments'.[5]

Another area of neglect that moderates were accused of was their approach to sermons. In this area they came in for much criticism. It was often said that moderates would preach borrowed sermons or even read out something from a newspaper. One account referred to a tradition in Caithness of passing round sermons for other ministers to read to their congregations. Yet again, a minister of Duthil was said to rotate two sermons, yet introduce them with a different text each week. In Lochalsh, Dr Downie translated Hugh Blair's sermons into Gaelic and delivered them to his congregation.

Other areas of neglect included their disregard for visiting parishioners and catechising. There were accounts of Highland parishes in which these practices were wilfully avoided. Moderates were also accused of being indifferent to the morals of their people and being too tolerant. Evangelicals thought moderates had little impact on the morals or religious opinions of their people. John Kennedy, minister of Dingwall, claimed that 'there were outlying districts, on the mainland and in the Western Isles, never before visited by evangelical preachers and where the people remained in a state of heathenism'.[6] In addition to the above, moderates were criticised for their opposition to evangelical preaching and revivals. It was also felt that they did not have a sufficient regard for the Sabbath and that their preference for polite society led them to support the system of patronage which forced unacceptable ministers on congregations.

Highland ministers cannot all be fitted easily into the categories of moderates and evangelicals. The range of ministerial belief and practice in the Highlands was much more diverse than the two categories of moderate and evangelical would allow. The partisan character of much church history that was written in the nineteenth-century did not help this over-simplification. Indeed, it tended to reinforce the two categories. Despite the difficulties of definition and categorisation there were clearly cases of ministerial neglect in the Highlands. Those neglecting their duties were likely to be labelled moderates.   Those who saw Christianity as a message of personal salvation rather than a moral and social message had less chance of being labelled moderates.

HIGHLAND EVANGELICALS
✣

Evangelicalism was not new in the established church. The Easter Ross area claimed to have a continuous evangelical tradition stretching back to the Covenanting period. This tradition was represented by men such as Thomas Hog of Kiltearn and John MacKillican of Alness. Although the Haldane style of evangelicalism was not welcomed by many in the established church,

John MacDonald, the Apostle of the North, was minister of Urquhart parish yet he got into trouble for preaching in other parishes. His activity as an itinerant preacher was impressive and extended as far as Ireland and St Kilda.

evangelicalism continued to make progress within the Church of Scotland. Apart from the ministers in the Easter Ross area, a number of evangelical preachers were rising to prominence in the Highlands and Islands. These included Lachlan MacKenzie, Lochcarron, Roderick MacLeod, Bracadale and Snizort, Alexander MacLeod, Uig and Rogart, John MacRae, Knockbain, and many more.

Arguably the most prominent Church of Scotland evangelical was John MacDonald who was referred to as 'the apostle of the north'. He was minister of the Edinburgh Gaelic congregation from 1807 to 1813 and Urquhart from 1813 to 1849. He went on many preaching trips and was in great demand as a Highland preacher. His evangelical trips even took him to Ireland, as well as to St Kilda on four occasions.

By 1817 MacDonald's itinerant work had increased so much

that it was the smaller part of the year he actually spent at home. In summer and autumn he was rarely to be found in his own pulpit. Kennedy said of him that 'during three months of each year he preached on an average, two sermons a day, and in no year of his life in Ross-shire did he preach fewer than three hundred sermons. He preached upwards of ten thousand times during the last thirty-six years of his life'.[7] He was immensely popular and it was not uncommon for thousands to attend his open-air meetings. These occasions would often be deeply emotional events with weeping, screaming and fainting being in evidence. In some areas such scenes had never been witnessed before and his preaching had a remarkable effect on those who came to hear him.

Given the mood of the time it was perhaps inevitable that MacDonald would get into trouble with his fellow ministers. When MacDonald was travelling it was not uncommon for him to preach in the parishes he travelled through on his way home. It was in such a situation that his activities became the focus of a General Assembly censure. On one of his travels in 1817 he preached in a dissenting chapel in Strathbogie. The local presbytery complained about this and a motion was prepared for the General Assembly in 1818.

The wording of the motion prepared on behalf of the presbyteries of Strathbogie and Aberlour stated that 'the performance of divine service, or any part of public worship or service, by members in this church in meeting houses of dissenters, is irregular and unconstitutional, and ought on no occasion to take place'. This motion also called into question the actions of a minister 'exercising his pastoral functions in a vagrant manner' and preaching 'in other parishes than his own . . . without the special invitation of the minister within whose parish it shall be held'. Strathbogie presbytery considered such activity to be 'disorderly and unbecoming the character of a member of this church'. This could only weaken the position of the parish minister and damage the interests of true religion. Ministers of the established church were, therefore, encouraged not to welcome or entertain other ministers persisting in such activity.

On one occasion MacDonald was asked by the people of Dornoch to preach in their parish. This was in 1816 and the parish minister refused to give his consent for such a service. In order to overcome this obstacle a meeting was arranged at the boundary of the parish. MacDonald was welcome to preach in the neighbouring parish of Creich. He, therefore, preached in Creich parish and the people sat and listened on the other side of the parish boundary in Dornoch.

There were two distinct sources of Highland evangelicalism in this period. One was the Easter Ross tradition and the other came from the Lowland based mission-societies. Different historians have placed different emphasis on these two sources. Kenneth MacDonald, writing at the start of this century established a strong continuity between the evangelicalism of Easter Ross in the eighteenth-century and its later spread throughout the Highlands and Islands. In the 1950s John MacInnes similarly argued that it was 'the evangelical piety of Easter Ross fortified by the revivals of the third and fourth decades, which eventually captured the whole of the northern Highlands'.

An alternative view is found in the writing of John MacKay who placed importance on the evangelicalism spreading from the Lowlands in the 1790s. MacKay himself operated as a Highland evangelist, first for the Free Church then for the United Free Church. When he referred to the visit of James Haldane and Charles Simeon to Moulin and the revival which followed he said, 'from that day the glens and the straths that radiated from Moulin began to show first the blade then the ear, till the full corn in the ear was reaped in the joyful harvest of the Moulin revival'. MacKay also described 11 January 1798, the day on which the SPGH was formed, as 'the red letter day for modern Highland evangelicalism'.[8]

More recent writers than those mentioned above have also emphasised one or the other as the predominant source of Highland evangelicalism. A related question is whether Highland evangelicalism was perceived to be predominantly an indigenous or an external development. In one sense it is possible to regard Easter Ross evangelicalism as indigenous and the Lowland mission societies as external. These judgements, however, require some qualification. It is possible to trace the Easter Ross religion to Covenanting sources which were reinforced by the Lowland revivals of the early eighteenth-century in Scotland.

On the other hand the SPGH, although inspired by English

nonconformity and the wider world mission impulse, had a number of indigenous elements. The Christian message was taken into the region by Highlanders, it was communicated in Gaelic and it produced local leaders to advance the work. This has led one historian of the Highlands, James Hunter, to suggest that these local lay evangelicals were the 'first leadership of any sort to emerge from the crofting population's own ranks'.

The question of categorising movements as external or indigenous to the Highlands is quite complex. To an extent external influences were adapted and indigenous elements were incorporated to create a unique and distinct spirituality in the Highlands. A further issue remains. Whether evangelicalism was an indigenous or an external influence it must have arrived as a violent intrusion into some families and communities. In such cases the culture they were familiar with was described as the 'old nonsense' and the changes to the social structure enabled evangelicals to step into positions of influence in Highland communities. This new prominence and the structures that followed provided evangelicals with both an increased authority and access to such communities. This enabled them to shape the habits and manners of Highlanders in the districts in which they had a dominating influence.

EVANGELICAL SUCCESS
✣

Why was this so successful? Recent scholarship has been profoundly influenced by James Hunter's book, *The Making of the Crofting Community*. In this Hunter saw the origins of evangelical Christianity in the 'social and psychological consequences of the collapse of the old order'. He observed that 'a people whose former way of life had been destroyed found in a particularly fervent brand of Christianity a place to feel at home and a way of coping with the problems inherent in the commercial world into which they had been propelled'.

The appeal of Hunter's argument is that it links religious change with social and economic upheaval. Considerable support for this view is found in the work of historians such as Eric Richards, Charles Withers and Callum Brown. The collapse of the old-kin based order, it was argued, produced a cultural vacuum and a demoralised and leaderless community. Evangelical Christianity stepped into this vacuum and offered social cohesion, psychological compensation, leaders, values and a way of coping with change.

More recently other historians have been more guarded in their judgements. Professor Macinnes has claimed that there was no connection between economic privation and local revivals. He is, however, unwilling to allow revivalism to be 'disassociated from the social restlessness occasioned by clearance and by rural congestion and deprivation within rural communities'.[9] Professor Devine has also been unwilling to explain the triumph of evangelical Christianity in terms of the material changes in Highland society. He acknowledges, however, that while the missionary effort provided the direct stimulus for the growth of evangelicalism, 'the structural changes in the society may have established the cultural context for a heightening of religious enthusiasm'.[10]

Although having a measure of appeal Hunter's argument is difficult to sustain. It involves demonstrating a certain sequence of events; the collapse of the old order, the attendant social and psychological consequences and the people fleeing, as Professor Smout has said, 'towards the compensations of an intense spiritual enthusiasm like leaves before a storm'.[11] The legitimacy of Hunter's view must depend on showing that some area of the Highlands can demonstrate this sequence of events in both a meaningful time scale and location.

An alternative approach might be to suggest, not that Highland society was a demoralised leaderless vacuum, but that it did not have the means or resources to adequately resist evangelical Christianity. Highland society lacked any firm religious notions with which to counter evangelicalism. It also lacked any focus of authority or centres of learning from which an alternative community could derive direction and consolidate resistance. Highland society was poorly equipped to resist evangelical Christianity in the early nineteenth-century.

The initial successes of the evangelicals brought about a change in the social structure of Highland society. A new group was introduced who quickly became the dominant group, dominant not in a material sense but by virtue of moral and intellectual leadership. As a result of the evangelical network of teachers, catechists and elders, the evangelicals were, in many areas, able to penetrate every family. A remarkable degree of consensus was achieved which allowed the evangelicals to assume leadership and define acceptable behaviour. The changes described above gave evangelicalism a predominant position and guaranteed the success of the Free Church in 1843 in the Highlands and Islands.

CHAPTER 5

Disruption

*'The Disruption is the great epoch in the church life of the Highlands.
Its memories furnish them with the heroic materials that Scotland as a
whole finds in the covenanting struggle.'*

John MacLeod

PRINCIPAL OF FREE CHURCH COLLEGE

In May 1843 the Church of Scotland divided. This division, known as the Disruption, resulted in the creation of the Free Church of Scotland. About 470 ministers out of a total of 1195 left the Church of Scotland for the Free Church. The Free Church was soon able to list about 800 congregations in Scotland that were connected with it and between 750,000 to 800,000 people.

Within the Highland context the Disruption was a remarkable event. John MacLeod, who was principal of Free Church College from 1927 to 1943 and was intimately connected with Highland church life said of the Disruption in the Highlands that it was 'the great epoch in the church life of the Highlands, its memories furnish them with the heroic materials that Scotland as a whole finds in the covenanting struggle'.[1] An earlier minister, Dr Mackintosh MacKay, minister of Dunoon, who lived through these events commented, 'I feel the strongest conviction that never since the first light of the Reformation dawned on the land of our fathers, has there been such a universal religious movement over the whole of the Highlands and Islands as there is at this day'.[2]

The Disruption was a major event in Highland history. It has been portrayed as a movement of intense commitment and selfless sacrifice. It contained all the qualities necessary to give birth to and sustain a new movement; qualities that would thrill, inspire and motivate and provide models for later generations to emulate and aspire to.

There are many examples which can be used to support these

*The Disruption. On 18 May 1843 the Free Church of Scotland was formed when a
significant proportion of ministers and people left the Church of Scotland.*

claims. Many ministers relinquished position and prestige for the sake of principle and many more people went with them apparently without thought for the personal loss they might incur and the hardship that might result. The images that resulted from the Highland Disruption were of ministers leaving their manses, people threatened with eviction, large crowds gathering in the open-air, landlords refusing to provide sites for churches and through this all the vast majority of the people remaining resolutely committed to the Free Church.

The Free Church minister of Lochearnhead, Mr Eric Findlater, described the Disruption year as being 'more like romance than reality'.[3] He said that he was seldom three nights in the same bed in that year and he estimated that he covered 1800 miles just in preaching in his parish and elsewhere. He preached in tents, in wooden box-shelters, in cottages, in gravel pits, in caves, on hill tops, in barns, aboard ships and sheltering beside stone walls. Mr Findlater's experience was certainly not uncommon. Many Free Church ministers shared similar experiences in the years immediately after the Disruption.

PATRONAGE

❖

A few years later, in 1847, Thomas Chalmers was being questioned by a House of Commons Select Committee. He was asked what he considered to be the distinctive principle separating the Free Church from the established church. Chalmers stated clearly that it was spiritual independence. For him this meant that 'the final jurisdiction of ecclesiastical courts in things sacred is the great principle' upon which the Free Church had gone out. This principle he claimed had 'been held in Scotland for more than two centuries'.[4] In different contexts it had been more emotively described as 'the crown rights of the redeemer' and the 'headship of Christ'. Chalmers considered that this had been violated by the civil courts in Scotland in the years before the Disruption.

If spiritual independence was the great principle then patronage was the great issue. As indicated previously there had been a growing division in the established church between moderates and evangelicals. These groups differed on a number of issues, one of which was patronage. Patronage was the system

The Marnoch congregation left the Church of Scotland when a minister they had rejected was imposed on them.

whereby large landowners, or the crown, had the right to select and present ministers to vacant parishes. Most parishes in Scotland had a patron and it was a right that was often attached to property. This had been a contentious issue in Scottish history and had already produced division in the established church. Patronage carried the potential for ignoring the wishes of parishioners and presented land owners with the opportunity of placing those they favoured in parishes, thus reinforcing their social preferences and position.

The position of patronage was undermined in 1834 when an evangelical majority in the General Assembly passed the Veto Act. This Act gave male heads of families in a parish the right to veto an unpopular presentation by a patron. Some commentators have linked the Veto Act with the democratic impulse in the country that followed the Reform Act of 1832 and also with the hope of undermining the challenge which the voluntary congregations presented. Disputes concerning patronage had, however, predated both of these.

The first difficulties with the Veto Act emerged in Auchterarder, Perthshire, where the patron's choice was vetoed. The minister who was rejected appealed to the Assembly, who upheld the congregational veto. The twice-rejected minister then took his case to the Court of Session who supported him and ruled that the Veto Act was illegal. The Assembly then appealed to the House of Lords and in 1839 the House of Lords ruled that the Veto Act was illegal. The House of Lords added that in their view the church courts were subordinate to the civil courts. There were other disputes that followed. By 1842 there were thirty-nine patronage cases going through the courts.

Another notable dispute took place in the parish of Marnoch in the Presbytery of Strathbogie in 1837. The patron's nominee was vetoed and a second minister was presented and found to be satisfactory. The first minister then appealed to the Court of Session who ruled that the second presentation should not proceed. The Strathbogie Presbytery, by a majority, decided to obey the law. Those who formed the majority were then suspended by a Commission of the General Assembly and they took their case to the civil courts. The suspended ministers appealed to the Court of Session which ruled that no other ministers should preach within the parishes of the Strathbogie ministers. For evangelicals this was outrageous and a serious offence to the church's spiritual independence. The suspended ministers next proceeded to induct the minister who had been originally rejected by congregational veto. This proved to be, not surprisingly, unacceptable to the Marnoch parishioners, who had already registered their opinion of the patron's original choice.

The Court of Session which, in most instances, was supported by the moderates, adopted the position that a patron's right of nomination was a matter of civil law and the Veto Act was an example of the church operating beyond its sphere of authority and interfering in civil affairs. The Court of Session saw the Veto Act as an infringement of the property rights of patrons. For evangelicals it was the civil authorities that were meddling in spiritual affairs. The settlement of ministers and church discipline were defined by evangelicals as spiritual issues and not open to the interference of the civil courts. By interfering, the state was directly challenging the spiritual independence of the church.

These differences were exemplified and exacerbated by the various disputes which arose during the period known as the Ten Years Conflict. The opposing positions became more deeply entrenched and ultimately irreconcilable. In response to a further interference, the General Assembly, in 1842, asserted the spiritual independence of the church. This was when the Chapel Act was declared to be incompetent by the Court of Session. The Chapel Act was passed by the General Assembly in 1834. In some areas new churches had been built where the population was expanding. These churches were not represented in the church courts and consequently ministers and elders had no vote. The Chapel Act changed this. Ministers who benefitted from this Act were mostly evangelical and this gave them an enhanced status and further secured the ascendancy of the evangelicals in the General Assembly.

Following this they declared Christ to be the only head of the church and they opposed encroachments by the civil courts on the church's own authority over its own affairs, that is its spiritual independence. It was a problem of the definition of the duties and responsibilities of the two spheres of church and state.

The civil courts held to the theory that the church was created by statute and was subordinate to the state. For the evangelicals the church was a spiritual creation that was recognised by the state but it had its own sphere of jurisdiction. This was in spiritual matters. The interference of the courts in spiritual affairs was regarded by evangelicals or non-intrusionists, as they came to be known, as an unacceptable interference with the spiritual independence of the church. The document which emerged from the 1842 Assembly, which asserted the spiritual independence of the church, was known as the 'Claim of Right'. This was rejected by the civil courts and by Government and there followed further intrusion by the courts into church affairs.

Thus the evangelicals regarded the church as being encroached upon by the Court of Session. They found neither reprieve in appeals to parliament nor satisfaction in compromise proposals. They, therefore, decided to quit the establishment and subsequently seceded in May 1843. They left St Andrew's Church in George Street in Edinburgh, which was the meeting place of the 1843 General Assembly of the Church of Scotland, and marched down to Tanfield Hall in Canonmills. There they constituted the first Assembly of the Free Church of Scotland.

THE DISRUPTION IN THE HIGHLANDS

❊

These events were closely followed in the Highlands and the prevailing evangelicalism gave the people a strong attachment to the non-intrusionists. The Free Church benefited from the evangelical activity that had taken place in the Highlands in the previous fifty years. In many ways this activity had been overtaken by events at a national level. The evangelicalism of the Highlands naturally associated with the non-intrusionist position. To do otherwise would have been to support moderatism. This would be quite unthinkable for evangelicals. It would be a betrayal of their faith and a compromise of their ecclesiastical principles. The success of the Highland Free Church was thus assured because of the evangelical nature of much of Highland Christianity at this time and the nature of the national debate. Spiritual independence and the headship of Christ over the church were themes that appealed strongly to Highland evangelical Christians as they were consistent with the undivided commitment which evangelicalism required.

The Disruption in the Highlands was thus remarkable both in scale and intensity. Accurate figures for the extent of the Disruption are very hard to locate but from a variety of sources a view can be constructed.

The attachment of Highland ministers to the Free Church varied. In some areas it was strong, in other areas there was little support. Support from the people was less varied. This ranged from strong support for the Free Church in some areas to complete adherence in other areas. This was in large part a reflection of the strength of evangelicalism.

The actions of Church of Scotland ministers in the Highland synods at the Disruption presented a rather mixed picture. In the Synod of Argyll thirty-five ministers remained with the established church and seventeen joined the Free Church. In the Synod of Ross twenty-two ministers joined the Free Church and only seven remained with the established church. In the Synod of Sutherland and Caithness nineteen joined the Free Church and ten remained with the established church and in the Synod of Glenelg twenty-six ministers stayed with the established church while fourteen decided to join the Free Church.

There were of course Highland parishes in the Synod of Moray and the Synod of Perth and Stirling. In addition some synods had vacant parishes at the time of the Disruption. However, if we consider the four Highland synods of Ross, Argyll, Glenelg and Sutherland and Caithness there were seventy-two ministers who joined the Free Church and seventy-nine who remained with the Church of Scotland. There were also nine vacancies and there were preaching stations that required missionaries.

Free Church success was, however, more obvious with people than ministers. Many areas of the far north were estimated to be well over ninety per cent for the Free Church. In Sutherland with a population of around 25,000 it was estimated that just over 200 remained with the Church of Scotland. In Lewis a number of sources suggested that from a population of 17,000 only some 450 to 500 remained with the Church of Scotland and most of them were located in the town of Stornoway. In the other Lewis parishes, Church of Scotland adherence could be counted on one hand. In the parish of Lochs, in Lewis, there was apparently only one man who stayed with the Church of Scotland. Unfortunately

Alexander MacLeod, minister of Uig, was unable to attend the convocation of Ministers in
November 1842 but wrote stating his adherence to the resolutions and his willingness to leave
the established church and relinquish the attached privileges. (Source: by kind permission,
Chalmers Collection, New College, Edinburgh)

he lived on the opposite side of the Loch from both church and minister. On Sundays the minister would look to see if this man was on the edge of the loch. The minister would then row across for his parishioner and ferry him back to church. This arrangement continued quite satisfactorily until some local boys aware of this practice dressed up a scarecrow on a day that the man did not intend to go to church.

Along with Sutherland and Lewis, other areas such as Ross and Cromarty, Harris and Inverness-shire were also estimated to be over ninety per cent for the Free Church. In the Synod of Ross the population was 46,000 and from this less than 4,000 remained Church of Scotland. In many parishes only the minister and his family remained in the Church of Scotland. In Harris, John MacRae, minister of Knockbain, estimated that '4000 of the people are conscientiously attached to the Free Church'. This accounted for the population of Harris at this time. In the Presbytery of Lochcarrron the population was over 21,000 yet of these only about 2,000 remained with the Church of Scotland. In the Presbytery of Latheron in Caithness where the population was 8,000 and there were six churches it was noted that only one man remained with the established church.

Skye varied from parish to parish but most parishes had a strong majority of people who were attached to the Free Church. Only Sleat and Strath had a Church of Scotland majority. In Snizort where the population was between 3,000 to 3,200 there were 2,500 who adhered to the Free Church. In Trumisgarry, North Uist, with a population of 1,100, there were 950 who belonged to the Free Church. This left 150 with the Church of Scotland but, it was reported that only somewhere between ten to fifty attended their services. In Coigach, Sutherland, where the population was 1,300 there were only four or five who stayed with the established church. Even in St Kilda the islands small population all opted to join the Free Church. A similar picture emerged from many other Highland communities.

PREPARATION FOR THE DISRUPTION
❈

As events moved closer to the Disruption, ministers, teachers, catechists and elders became active in explaining to their people the principles that were at stake. The habits of itinerancy and open air preaching were again employed as evangelicals campaigned on behalf of the non-intrusionist position. For this purpose ministers, including prominent church leaders from the Lowlands, moved throughout the Highlands. The main tasks, however, fell to a number of local evangelical ministers. John MacRae, minister of Knockbain, was appointed to tour the Highlands as an agent of the evangelicals. In 1842 and 1843 he travelled throughout the north west and the islands preparing the people for the Disruption. Also, John MacDonald, minister of Urquhart, devoted himself to the task of preparing the Highland congregations for the approaching Disruption. At the November Convocation, which was a gathering for evangelical ministers in 1842, MacDonald and Mr Allan, minister of Kincardine, were asked to preach throughout the north. They went up and down the east coast above Dingwall and across to Assynt and Lochinver. They encountered both large crowds and, on the west coast, appalling weather conditions. At every place they preached they collected signatures of those who supported the non-intrusionist position.

In Perthshire and Argyll, Dr MacGilvray, minister in Glasgow, travelled and preached, preparing the people for the Disruption. He also took in islands such as Arran and Islay in his preaching tours. His meetings were in the open-air and in the winter before the Disruption he said that 'more than once he had to address' the people 'with wet clothes drying on his back and his feet sunk to the ankles in snow'.

In Skye, Mr Roderick MacLeod, minister of Snizort, was similarly active before the Disruption. He held meetings which passed resolutions and encouraged the Skye people to declare themselves for non-intrusion and spiritual independence. There was also considerable lay participation in this task. In Skye and Uist, Norman MacLeod held meetings to explain matters to the people. MacLeod was converted under the ministry of John MacDonald when he was minister of the Gaelic chapel in Edinburgh. On returning to his native Skye he was employed as a teacher by the Gaelic School Society. In the months before the Disruption the increase of evangelical activity led to a religious awakening among the people in Skye.

In Harris, John Morrison, poet, teacher and blacksmith

performed a similar function and in Lewis two Uig teachers Alexander MacColl and Angus MacIver toured and appealed to the people to prepare for secession if the Government would not yield to the demands of the evangelicals. MacColl and MacIver travelled throughout the whole island. They held public meetings and asked the people to raise their hands to indicate their support for the evangelical position. In many areas the role of laymen was crucial. This pattern was repeated throughout the Highlands and Islands and as a result of such activity the people were informed where their duty lay in the imminent schism. Principal John MacLeod, of the Free Church College, said later of one area at the time of the Disruption, 'when it came, Lochaber was prepared for it'. This was true of many areas in the Highlands and it was because of the activity of both ministers and lay preachers.

By 1843 there were many evangelical ministers in the Church of Scotland. Evangelicalism was still regarded as a new movement and those who were regarded as the founding fathers of this movement moved into the Free Church. Parish ministers such as John MacRae of Knockbain, Alexander MacLeod of Uig, John MacDonald of Urquhart, Roderick MacLeod of Snizort, and many others of similar standing provided the initial leadership for the Free Church in the Highlands. Such men were both in the front of the evangelical revival and also in the front of the Disruption in the north. Curiously, however, many ministers that had displayed an unwavering attachment to the evangelical non-intrusionist position throughout the Ten Years Conflict remained with the established church at the point of Disruption.

RIVALRY AND HOSTILITY
*

In many areas the established church was clearly out of favour with the people. James Cameron Lees, who was later to become minister of St Giles in Edinburgh was Church of Scotland minister of Carnoch, Strathconan, from 1856 to 1859. Here he claimed to encounter not only empty pews but hostility from the local people. Lees also describes an unfortunate incident in which his father was involved. His father was the Church of Scotland minister of Stornoway and as such was acccompanying Mr David Watson to his induction as the parish minister of Uig shortly after the

Disruption. This party encountered some difficulties on this trip. The Church of Scotland presbytery records state that 'the Frees had combined neither to . . . allow or aid in giving the ferry to Mr Watson or any clergyman of the established church'.[5] The account which Lees provides of his father's trip is slightly different. Lees claimed that in leaving Callanish for Uig, 'when half way over they found the plug had been taken out of the boat and they narrowly escaped being drowned'.[6]

On the other side of the country the Tain Presbytery records of the Church of Scotland said that 'the members of the presbytery and their adherents in the various parishes are in the midst of a fiercely hostile population and not unfrequently exposed to insults and even personal danger'. In this area, in Resolis, there is an account of the Free Church people resisting an attempt by the established church to have a minister settled in the parish. The induction was made possible only by the arrival of a detachment of soldiers from Fort George who first fired blank cartridges then live ball and shot over the heads of the Free Church crowd. The soldiers were encouraged in this by the minister to be inducted who thereafter became known as Rev Ball-Cartridge. In this area the Church of Scotland claimed that many people had joined the Free Church 'from mere terror of the punishment they should meet with from their neighbours were they to remain in connection with the establishment'.[7]

For some Free Church people the threat was different. They faced the prospect of losing land and home as a result of their attachment to the Free Church. There were examples of this in North Uist, Skye and Harris. In Skye a number of families lost tenancies because they had collected funds for the Free Church. One of these was Donald Matheson from Portree. As a result of collecting for the Free Church sustentation fund he was given notice, by the factor, to quit his home and land. He first appealed to the factor without success. He then decided to appeal to Lord MacDonald and set off for his London address. On arriving he discovered that Lord MacDonald was in Yorkshire and he followed him there. When he got to Lord MacDonald's Yorkshire address Matheson discovered that he was out for the day and then Matheson also missed him the following morning on account of MacDonald's early return to London. Donald Matheson followed

him there and, although able to gain an interview with Lord
MacDonald, Matheson was advised that he was content with his
factor's arrangements and would not listen to Matheson's appeal.
Matheson then returned to Skye and got home two days before he
had to move out of his home.[8]

In North Uist some families lost their homes for helping to
build a temporary place of worship. John MacRae testified of this
in evidence to the Select Committee on Sites. He said that when he
'was in Harris in the Spring of 1845, threat upon threat was
circulated among the people that any person actively engaged in
the cause of the Free Church was certain to lose his croft'.[9] John
Morrison, who can be considered the leader of the Free Church in
Harris, lost his home as a result of threats such as this being carried
out. In Kilmodan parish in Cowal, Argyllshire, all the elders and
most of the people, in the village of Glendaruel, joined their
minister, Mr MacLean, in the Free Church. They were threatened
with violent removal if they went ahead with an open-air meeting
on the Sunday following the Disruption.

A DISTINCT DISRUPTION

❊

It has frequently been suggested that the Disruption of the Church
of Scotland was quite distinct in the Highlands and Hebrides.
Distinct in terms of scale, intensity and appeal. Distinctiveness in
terms of scale can be demonstrated with regard to numbers
attached to the Free Church. Distinctiveness in terms of appeal
can be discussed by consideration of social composition of the Free
Church in the Highlands. It is, however, less straightforward to
determine why the Disruption seemed to leave a deeper mark on
the Highlands.

How can we account for this distinct Highland experience?
Some historians have emphasised the difference between the rural
and the urban religious experience. Rural society has been
regarded as more religious than urban society. The picture that
they have presented is of a more simple rural environment in which
the church remained at the centre of community life. Although this
is a valid observation it remains unsatisfactory as the Highland
experience was not true of all rural communities.

Evangelical Christianity was judged to be a new feature in

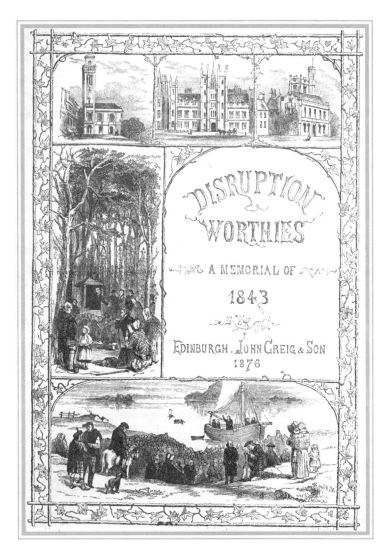

Disruption Worthies. A remarkable quantity of Highland church history was produced in the
nineteenth-century. Many regarded this period as a major and memorable turning point in
Highland history and that the memories of such people and events should not be allowed to be
forgotten. The two illustrations of outdoor meetings are clearly drawn from Highland
experience and demonstrate the importance of the Highland Free Church to
the Free Church as a whole.

Highland life. The gospel message, evangelicals believed, had only penetrated successfully into some Highland communities in the early nineteenth-century. It was seen as a new beginning and as such shaped evangelical Highlanders' identity and informed their self understanding.

When this movement was perceived to be fresh and young, the Disruption took place and the Free Church provided the institutional structure to contain this new impulse. This was an impulse characterised by passion, sacrifice, unwavering commitment and heroism. As mentioned above it contained all the qualities necessary to give birth to a new movement that would thrill, inspire and motivate. It was not just the simplicity of a rural setting that gave the Highland Disruption its intensity. It was its proximity to and acceptance of a dramatic movement that had transformed Highland communities. The Disruption was distinct in the Highlands and its intensity can be explained by its closeness to the cultural transformation that resulted from evangelicalism.

The Disruption took place at a point at which the emotional intensity of the previous decades was fed into a structure that Highland people could identify with and felt belonged to them. The Free Church was a most timely structure. It arrived at an appropriate time to represent the religious aspirations of many Highland people. It belonged to them, it represented them and it provided a way of sanctioning the social changes that evangelicalism had brought. For these reasons it was a distinct experience in the Highlands and Islands.

CHAPTER 6

The Free Church

*'We will serve you, we will enlist as soldiers or join the navy if
you wish, we will follow you as our fathers followed your fathers in the days
of old, we will stand by you to the last, but our consciences are our own
and our religious convictions we cannot surrender.'*

RESPONSE FROM COLL FREE CHURCH PEOPLE TO THE
MACLEAN CHIEF AND PROPRIETOR OF THE ISLAND

The Disruption in the Highlands brought out a much greater percentage of people than it did ministers. This meant that many new Free Church congregations were not only without a church building but also without a minister. This was, however, an area of concern which the church sought to address. One account stated that the four Highland synods of Argyll, Ross, Glenelg and Sutherland and Caithness had eighty-seven vacancies following the Disruption. This number was still greater when Highland Gaelic speaking congregations outwith these four synods and preaching stations were also included. A few months after the Disruption, the Free Church provided this larger figure. They calculated that there were 150 vacant congregations or preaching stations in the Gaelic speaking districts.

In some areas the need was greater than in others. In 1845 the Free Church estimated that from Kintyre to Assynt and including all the west coast islands there was a population of over 200,000. This population was mostly Free Church yet there were only thirteen ministers settled in this area. There were many districts of Argyll where there was an absence of Free Church ministers. In the Presbytery of Inveraray, out of eight ministers not one joined the Free Church. In Mull there were no Free Church ministers. In the Presbytery of Weem in central Perthshire only two ministers, those at Killin and Strathfillan, out of ten joined the Free Church. In Skye, after a short time, there was only one Free Church minister out of nine. In the Presbytery of Uist, which stretched from Barra to Harris, there was only one Free Church minister. In the other five parishes the ministers remained with the Church of Scotland. In Lewis four out of six ministers joined the Free Church but by the end of 1844 three had left the island. This left Robert Finlayson of Lochs as the only Free Church minister in the island of Lewis. Indeed, by 1844, in the whole of Skye, the Outer Hebrides and the Small Isles together, there were only four Free Church ministers. They were: Mr Norman MacLeod, Trumisgarry, North Uist, Mr Roderick MacLeod, Snizort, Skye, Mr John Swanson in the Small Isles along with Mr Finlayson mentioned above.

An immediate measure taken by the new church was to release John MacRae, minister of Knockbain, from his congregation and appoint him to work in the Outer Hebrides and other 'destitute parts' as a superintending pastor. MacRae, known in Gaelic as 'MacRath Mòr', was a man of uncommon strength, quick wit and arguably one of the finest Highland preachers at this time. He was very popular with Highland congregations and in great demand as a communion preacher. At the end of 1844 there were many in the Outer Hebrides who hoped to see MacRae's period as a superintending pastor extended.

In the summer of 1845, in response to the continuing need, the Free Church prepared a list of ministers who could speak Gaelic and a list of vacant churches and preaching stations. In this same year a number of Gaelic students of Divinity were licensed without having completed the full theological course. From this list eleven names were put forward and licensed after two years of study. In addition, presbyteries were asked to submit the names of young men from Gaelic-speaking areas who could be trained for the ministry. In the meantime, congregations were sustained by catechists, elders and teachers. They took services, managed the congregations, supervised the building of churches and the collection of church funds.

By 1847 the Free Church still had an urgent need for ministers in the Highlands and Islands. The General Assembly noted that there were 100 vacancies in the Highlands. Some of these could be joined together reducing the number to eighty-four. Of these eighty-four, eighty had, in the previous year, been visited by ministers on deputation work. Ninety-two ministers had made themselves available for this. Of this ninety-two, twelve ministers were set apart from their congregations for six months and eighty more were set apart for five or six weeks. In addition, there were forty-four catechists operating in the Highlands in 1847.

THE BREADALBANE

❊

Once vacancies had been identified and ministers set apart to provide for these congregations there remained the difficulty of transporting ministers to the vacant churches. Many congregations without ministers were on islands or in parts of the Highlands that were difficult to get to. A boat was proposed as a reliable solution to this problem. A Free Church report in 1845 advocated a vessel to convey ministers to and from distant and inaccessible parts of the western Highlands and Islands. A special committee was appointed for 'the arrangement of deputations to the Highlands and other labours demanded by the present exigencies of these parts, including the regulation of the *Breadalbane* yacht'. The *Breadalbane* was described as a rigged schooner of 30 tons. It was 49 feet long and 13 feet 6 inches broad with a cabin height of 6 feet. It had accommodation for six plus the captain and four of a crew. It was described as safe, fast and elegant and the General Assembly were informed that annual running costs were £247.13.7d.[1]

The task of the *Breadalbane*, named after the Earl who was a prominent Free Church supporter, was to transport ministers from island to island, including St Kilda, and to the mainland. In 1845 it carried twenty-two ministers and in the following four years it transported forty-six, forty-three, twenty-five and thirty ministers. The *Breadalbane* also transported Free Church literature such as the magazine *An Fhianuis* to various Highland and Island locations.

The *Breadalbane* came to play an important role in countering the effects of the Highland famine which began in 1846. This was as a result of widespread potato failure. In 1846 the Free Church issued a questionnaire to Highland ministers and catechists in distressed districts asking them to estimate the extent of potato failure in their area. As a result the Free Church was the first body to organise relief and direct it to those areas which were the worst

June 2. Landed Rev. Donald Clarke at Tarbert, in Harris, and sailed for Lochalsh.

3. Sailed from Lochalsh for Oban.

5. Arrived at Oban, and sailed with Rev. P. Mac-Lean, Tobermory, and Rev. Mr. M'Coll, probationer, for Aros Bay and Tobermory.

6. Returned to Oban.

8. Sailed with Rev. Norman M'Leod, Trumisgarry, Uist, and Rev. Donald Murray, Knock, Lewis, for Stornoway and Uist.

10. Landed Rev. N. M'Leod at Lochmaddy;

11. Landed Rev. D. Murray at Stornoway.

15. Sailed from Stornoway with Rev. Andrew Mackenzie, Beauly, on his way homeward; and called for Rev. D. Clarke, Aberfeldy, at Tarbert, in Harris.

16. Called at Lochmaddy for Rev. Colin M'Kenzie, Arrochar, and sailed for Lochalsh.

17. Landed Rev. Andrew M'Kenzie at Lochalsh.

18. Sailed with Rev. D. Clarke and Rev. Colin Mackenzie, from Lochalsh, bound for Oban.

22. Landed Rev. D. Clarke and Rev. C. M'Kenzie at Oban.

25. Sailed from Oban, with Rev. Alexander Mac-Innes, Tummel Bridge, for Tobermory and Ulva.

26. Landed Rev. A. M'Innes at Ulva.

27. Returned for Tobermory and Oban; at Tobermory took on board Rev. Peter M'Lean, Tobermory, Rev. A. M'Coll, probationer, and Mr. J. M'Kay, Inspector of Associations, and sailed for Glen Borodale in Loch Sunart.

28. Arrived at Oban.

July 3. Sailed for Loch-carron with Rev. P. Mac-Lean and Mr. Campbell.

6. Returned to Oban with Rev. P. M'Lean, Mr. Campbell, and Rev. H. Fraser, Ardchattan.

8. Sailed from Oban with Rev. Mr. Stewart, Blair-Atholl, for Loch Spelvie, in Mull; landed Mr. Stewart, and returned to Oban.

10. Sailed with Rev. Donald Stewart, Cromar, and Rev. J. Stark, Kilfinnan, bound for Harris, Uist, and Rasay.

11. Landed Rev. D. Stewart at Rowdale, Harris, landed Rev. D. Stark at Lochmaddy.

13. Sailed from Lochmaddy with Rev. N. M'Leod, Trumisgarry, for Stornoway, and Rev. J. Stark, for Rasay, and crossed to Loch Snizort, in Skye.

14. Landed Rev. N. M'Leod at Stornoway, and proceeded with Rev. J. Stark to Rasay.

15. Landed Rev. J. Stark at Rasay, and proceeded to Lochalsh.

18. Sailed for Stornoway to convey Rev. D. Murray, Knock, to Uist. Not prepared to go.

21. Sailed from Stornoway with Rev. Alexander M'Leod, Rogart (on his way homeward), for Loch Inver, and Rev. R. Finlayson, Lochs, Lewis, bound for Lochalsh.

22. Landed Rev. A. M'Leod at Loch Inver, and proceeded for Lochalsh.

23. Made Island of Rona. Heavy gale, and detained by storm at Rona.

28. Landed Rev. R. Finlayson at Lochalsh.

29. Sailed for Loch Boisdale, South Uist, to take Rev. Roderick M'Leod, Snizort, to St. Kilda.

August 3. Took on board Rev. Roderick M'Leod and Mr. M'Lennan at Loch Boisdale, and sailed for St. Kilda.

5. Arrived at St. Kilda.

7. Sailed from St. Kilda with Rev. Roderick Mac-Leod and Mr. M'Lennan.

9. Arrived at Harris; landed Rev. R. M'Leod on Island of Bernera.

10. Landed Mr. M'Lennan at Lochmaddy, and proceeded for Rowdale, Harris, to take on board Rev. D. Stewart, Cromar, and Rev. Roderick M'Leod, on their way homeward.

11. Landed, Rev. Roderick MacLeod and Rev. D. Stewart, at Loch Snizort, in Skye; and proceeded to Stornoway, to take on board Rev. N. M'Leod, Trumisgarry, homeward, and Rev. D. Murray, Knock, for Uist.

12. Called at Tarbert, in Harris, for Rev. J. Fraser, Kiltarlity, serving there, who would not leave till Monday following. Arrived at Stornoway.

13. Left Stornoway, and landed Rev. N. M'Leod and Rev. D. Murray at Lochmaddy, and sailed for Lochalsh, to take on board ministers from Ross-shire. Arrived at Lochalsh (13th), and received letters. Ross-shire ministers not to be forward till 19th instant.

15. Sailed from Lochalsh, for Harris.

17. Took on board Rev. J. Fraser, Kiltarlity, at Tarbert, Harris, for home.

19. Landed Rev. J. Fraser, at Janetown, Lochcarron. Took on board Rev. C. R. Matheson, Kilmuir-Easter, and Rev. H. M'Leod, Logie-Easter, and sailed for Uist.

20. Arrived at Lochmaddy, Uist, and landed Rev. C. R. Matheson and Rev. H. M'Leod.

21. Sailed for Rowdale and Tarbert, in Harris, with Rev. Messrs. Matheson and M'Leod.

24. Sailed, with Rev. Messrs. Matheson and Mac-Leod, bound for Stornoway.

25. Arrived at Stornoway, and landed Rev. C. R. Matheson, and sailed with Rev. H. M'Leod for Lochcarron, on his way homeward (26th).

27. Landed, Rev. H. M'Leod, at Janetown, Lochcarron; and sailed, bound for Oban.

29. Arrived at Oban.

September 1. Took on board Rev. H. Fraser, Ardchattan, Dr. Aldcorn, and several young men, students.

2. Arrived at Campbellton.

4. Sailed from Campbellton, bound for Rothesay, for stores, &c., taking on board, homeward, from synod meeting, Rev. A. Cameron, Kilchoman, Islay; Rev. H. Fraser, Ardchattan; Rev. Dr. Mackay, Dunoon; Rev. J. Mackenzie, Lochgilphead, and Rev. J. Campbell, Tarbert, with several students, homeward from synod; calm.

5. Arrived near Tarbert; put ministers for westward on board steamer; made Kyles of Bute.

7. Arrived at Rothesay.

9. Sailed from Rothesay, bound for S. Uist, to call at Iona, Tobermory, and Tyree, by instructions. Weather calm and foggy.

17. Arrived at Lochmaddy; proceeded to Rowdale, Harris. Took on board three Rev. D. Murray; proceeded for Stornoway.

18. Landed Rev. D. Murray at Stornoway, and waited for Rev. D. M'Rae, Cross, till 21st.

24. Delayed at Stornoway till now, waiting for the Rev. D. M'Rae, and he not having come forward, sailed for Oban for further orders.

26. Came to Oban at noon.

27. Dr. Aldcorn and Dr. Campbell having come off requesting the schooner to proceed with them direct to Easdale on a medical visit to the Rev. Peter M'Bride, suddenly taken ill there, sailed immediately for Easdale. Landed Dr. Aldcorn and Dr. Campbell. Came to anchor at Easdale; and at 2 P.M. returned to Oban with Dr. Campbell.

30. No further orders. At 3 P.M. sailed for Loch Alin in Morven, to carry back the Rev. J. M'Kenzie and Mr. Auld of Edinburgh, gone there on the business of the Church. Anchored at Loch Alin at 9 P.M. the following day.

Following the Disruption many Highland and Island Free Church congregations did not have a minister. The yacht, Breadalbane was used for the purpose of transporting ministers to vacant congregations throughout the Highlands and Islands. This is an extract from its log-book for June, July and August, 1846.

affected. Funds were raised from Free Church congregations and supplies were provided. Within a very short time in 1846 the Free Church had raised £15,000 for famine relief. The Free Church assistance was invaluable. The Free Church boat was active at a critical period and along with transporting ministers and literature the *Breadalbane* collected information and transported supplies.

By 1853 there had been considerable improvement in the movement of steamers and commercial shipping on the north west coast. It was decided that the Free Church did not now need its own boat and it was sold. In its time it had been regarded as a source of encouragement and as an important symbol which demonstrated that the Free Church people would not be neglected by their church.

THE REFUSAL OF SITES

❋

In 1843, as we have seen, about 470 ministers and 800 congregations came out of the Church of Scotland. In the years after the Disruption, most of these congregations needed somewhere to hold services, and a wide range of temporary church accommodation was employed. A cottage was used in Berriedale, Caithness, a masonic lodge in Muthil, a malt barn in Fort Augustus, a distillery in Campbeltown, a barn in Creich and a storehouse in Resolis. Many congregations met in the open-air, tents were widely used as were temporary wooden structures. In Applecross and Shieldaig the congregations met on beaches and only the preacher had a tent for protection.

Many congregations, by various means, had obtained sites for new churches by 1847. There were a number of places throughout the Highlands and Islands where sites were initially refused but within the first year or two some arrangement had been arrived at between landlord and congregation. For example the Duke of Sutherland refused to grant sites in 1843 but had acquiesced by 1844. His reasons for initially refusing were stated by James Loch in a letter to Golspie elders in October 1843. In this Loch said that the Duke 'believes there is no difference in doctrine between those who have left the establishment and those who have adhered to it'.[2]

By 1847, in Scotland as a whole, 725 churches had either been built or were in the process of being built. The sites refused in 1847 did not exceed thirty-five. The total number of members and adherents of the Free Church was somewhere between 750,000 and 800,000, yet site refusal was judged only to affect 16,000. By 1847, there were still some outstanding cases where landlords had not offered sites for churches or manses. In areas such as Duthil, Grantown, North Uist, Harris, Strontian, Coigach, Lochbroom, Skye.and Mull it was a more protracted problem. At the General Assembly in 1845 a committee had been set up to focus on the difficulties created by landlords refusing sites for churches and manses and in 1847 the House of Commons set up a committee of enquiry.

Those who joined the Free Church often had to step into an uncertain future. For ministers it meant moving out of their manse, and finding alternative accommodation. Mr John Swanson, who was minister of the Small Isles, had to move his family to Skye while he spent much of his time in a floating manse, a boat known as the *Betsy*. Swanson could hold his services in a Gaelic school in Eigg. He was, however, unable to obtain a site for a manse. He, therefore, had to resort to living in his boat when he visited his parish. In Eigg there were only about six people that did not join the Free Church yet the proprietor said he did not want to give the minister a site for a manse as this would encourage religious strife.

For some ministers, leaving the manse for so uncertain a future was a painful experience. Mr Findlater, minister of Durness, described his parting from the manse which he had occupied for thirty-one years in such terms: 'My feelings and those of my family on leaving the manse after a residence of thirty-one years I cannot describe'. His wife was born in the manse, two of their children died there and with the other six they left 'all hitherto unprovided for to sojourn among strangers'.[3]

Some ministers had to cope with very poor accommodation. Mr Thomas Davidson, minister of Kilmallie, at one point, kept his family in a hut that was only twelve feet square. An attempt was made to keep out the wind and the rain by blankets. Mr Davidson also had to change address five times in the same number of months. Davidson's wife died shortly after this episode. Another unfortunate example was that of the MacKenzies of Tongue; father and son. Their family had occupied the manse for nearly 100 years. The elder MacKenzie was aged seventy-five and his son had hoped to follow him as minister of Tongue. Their families were sent away to Thurso while father and son rented some poor accommodation within the parish. Within a short space of time both were dead. Meanwhile in Lewis both Duncan Matheson and Robert Finlayson moved their families to Stornoway and travelled to their congregations in Knock and Lochs. In Trumisgarry, North Uist, Norman MacLeod had built his own manse, at his own expense and now found himself locked out of it. The accommodation to which MacLeod and his family next moved was not only inferior to that which he had constructed but was twenty miles away.

CHURCH SITES

✤

In some areas such difficulties were resolved within a year or two after the Disruption. In other areas, however, the proprietors proved more intractable. The most famous example of site refusal in the Highlands, and Free Church determination was probably that of Strontian. The land owner of much of Ardnamurchan was Sir James Riddell. There had been letters exchanged between the General Assembly committee dealing with sites and Riddell. This was without any success. The same committee placed a contract for a floating iron church with a Port Glasgow shipyard. This was finished in June 1846 at a cost of £1,400, towed to Loch Sunart and moored 150 yards offshore.

This boat was welcomed by the local congregation after they had held services on the hillside for three years. On Sundays small boats took members of the congregation out to the floating church. The church held between 600 to 700 people and it was reported that it sank one inch for every 100 people. The floating church had benches inside, a pulpit and a vestry. Light entered through skylights and it had a large blue flag with the inscription *An Eaglais Shaor* (The Free Church) marked on it. At a later date Riddell allowed the floating church to be moored closer to the shore. It remained in use throughout the ministry of John MacQueen, 1853-67, and it was not until 1873 that a new church was completed on land for this Free Church congregation.

There was only one floating church but it was an important symbol of the Free Church's determination to overcome the problems of site refusal and make provision for its distant congregations. It was also important in evoking the qualities that were

A number of Free Church congregations were refused sites for churches after the Disruption.
The congregation at Duthil, Inverness-shire, met in a forest for some years.

ascribed to the Disruption generation; commitment, faithfulness and sacrifice.

Further south the Free Church people of Torosay, Mull were also denied a site on which to build a church. They therefore met in a gravel pit within high water mark. A canvas tent was erected but often it was not big enough for the people who attended. Sometimes 500 to 600 would turn up at the gravel pit. At times of high tide the sea would encroach on the area where meetings were held and the congregation would be obliged to move. There is an account of one particular communion Sabbath in which a large crowd was assembled and the tide came in. The report noted that 'the tide had crawled up unperceived and there sat the congregation and not one left his seat and there stood the preacher, all ankle deep in the tide which had thus stealthily crept up to them while they were solemnly engaged in the most sacred rite of the church'. In Mull there were no ministers who joined the Free Church, however, by the end of 1848 it was estimated that three quarters of the Mull population of 10,000 belonged to the Free Church.

In Skye, site difficulties were experienced in areas that were owned by Lord MacDonald. Before the Disruption, Roderick MacLeod had supervised the building of a church in Uig in Skye. Some funds had come from the Church Extension Committee and others had come from money collected privately by MacLeod. Lord MacDonald, the proprietor, had also been asked for support but had not provided anything. The Uig church was built on land belonging to a Skye tenant. Despite this background, in March 1844, the church was shut by Lord MacDonald and was then used every second Sunday by the established church. In Snizort, where the greater percentage of people belonged to the Free Church, they had been denied access to a site. Their services were held in the open-air. There was a form of shelter for the minister but not for the people who had to endure wind, rain and snow. After one severe snow shower, Mr Roderick MacLeod observed that 'when the shower was over, I could hardly distinguish them from the ground except by their faces'.[4]

Lord MacDonald also owned land in North Uist and the congregation there had similar difficulties. In North Uist the Free Church people had erected a shelter of sorts from turf and stone.

The materials that were used for this structure were removed by the factor, and crofters who had helped construct it were ejected from their homes and some were fined. In addition to Snizort and North Uist, Lord MacDonald also refused sites in Portree, Kilmuir, Sleat, Stenscholl and Uig. On the mainland some congregations also had difficulties with sites. In Duthil, the Free Church congregation met in a forest near Carrbridge while in Kilmallie the Free Church was offered a piece of unsuitable marshy ground. Even in distant St Kilda both church and manse were shut to the Free Church people until 1857 despite their complete adherence to the Free Church.

When the parliamentary committee on sites reported in 1847 it noted that large numbers of Her Majesty's subjects had been 'deprived of the means of religious worship by the refusal of certain proprietors' to grant them sites for churches. The report concluded with the 'hope that every just ground of complaint may speedily be removed, by the voluntary act of those whose property gives them the means of redressing a grievance and of thereby conciliating the good will of a large body of their countrymen'.[5] As a result of this select committee's enquiries a bill was introduced to prompt landowners to grant sites. The bill did not succeed but it was part of a successful campaign to put pressure on landowners to grant sites. By 1850 the battle for sites was virtually over. In 1854 the General Assembly committee which had responsibility for these matters was wound up as there were now 'no outstanding cases before the church' of site refusal.

The question of sites for churches was of great symbolic significance. It was a minority of congregations that suffered. Yet it helped to portray the Free Church as a church characterised by unwavering commitment and selfless sacrifice. These events carried more importance for the Free Church than their numerical significance. They were stirring and inspirational, and reinforced a certain image of the Free Church.

Dr Thomas Guthrie of Edinburgh described a visit to the two MacKenzies, mentioned above, before they died. Guthrie said he would never forget to his dying day the scene he witnessed in the manse in Tongue and he described the two MacKenzies, father and son, as 'martyrs for those great principles'. Dr Begg, another leading Edinburgh Free Church minister, after attending an open-air meeting shortly after the Disruption, asked 'I question, if the world, at this moment can match such scenes as these'. Lord Cockburn wrote in his diary that, 'These are the men to make churches. These are the men to whom some wretched lairds think themselves superior'. It was clearly not just a propaganda success. Sacrifices were made and an unshakeable faith was in evidence in many places. John MacRae said that 'every time that they assemble in the open-air, every shower of rain, every blast of wind, every flake of snow, on these occasions, not to speak of the injury done to health, reminds these poor people of the injustice they suffer for conscience sake'.[6] Thus a minority experience was adopted as the prevailing ethos of the Highland Free Church.

CLEARANCE AND CLASS

✻

The Disruption in the Highlands has been described as more class conflict than ecclesiastical dispute. This view has been sustained by a number of historians, in some cases more by assertion than investigation. This is mainly based on James Hunter's *The Making of the Crofting Community*. It has proved to be an extremely valuable book for the study of Highland church history and has led to a number of new approaches being adopted. Hunter described the Disruption as following clear class lines. On one side of this schism was the Free Church and the small tenantry while on the other side was the established church, factors and proprietors.

In order to sustain the argument that the Disruption was more class conflict than ecclesiastical dispute, it is necessary to demonstrate that material considerations both defined and to an extent motivated the social groups that parted in 1843. Both of these tasks present a considerable challenge. Free Church loyalty in the Highlands crossed class lines at a number of points, and the one element held in common was religious preference. The social groups that parted at the Disruption were groups that could be defined by religious preference, thus making the Disruption more of a religious divide than class conflict. This might present difficulties for some social historians who would contend that the only significant social groups are those which can be defined in economic terms.

The class conflict model requires evidence which demonstrates

EAGLAIS SHAOR NA H-ALBA.

AN CEATHRAMH ÀIREAMH,] MIOS DEIREANNACH AN EARRAICH. MDCCCXLV.

MINEACHADH A' PHROTEST.

AN ROIMH-RADH.

Tha roimh-radh a' Phrotest, a' cur an céill air mhodh àraid nan aobhar fa leth, troimh nach robh e 'n a ni comasach dhoibh-san a chuir an ainmean ris, suidhe mar bhuill an Ard-Sheanaidh, no fuireach ni 's faide 'n an luchd-dreuchd 's an Eaglais Shuidhichte. Ach is e an gearan àraid a chi sibh iad a' dèanamh, nach robh e an comas an Ard-Sheanaidh coinneachadh no suidhe 's an t-saorsa sin a bhuineas do Eaglais Chriosd, no na dleasdanasan sin a choimhlionadh a tha mar fhiachaibh air an Eaglais, agus 'n an gnothuch dhi, mar a sochair agus a còir, bhi 'g an coimhlionadh do Chriosd, mar a h-Ughdair, a Ceann, agus a Tighearn; agus d' a phobull-sa, mar bhuill a chuirp.

A nis, feudaidh cuid do ar luchd-leughaidh bhi gun làn-shoilleireachd aca 'n am beachd féin, cionnus chaidh an t-saorsa so àicheadh do 'n Eaglais; no ciod e a thàinig eadar i agus i bhi a' gnàthachadh na saorsa sin. Oidhir-pichidh sinn so a mhìneachadh. Ach roimh dhuibh so a leughadh, dh' iarradh sinn gu 'n leughadh sibh a ris am Protest féin, o thois-each, sìos gu ruig, far am bheil e ag ràdh—" 'S a' cheud àit." Leughaibh air bhur socair e, agus gus am bi na tha an earrann sin a' cur an céill agaibh 'n ur cuimhne gu soilleir, réidh. Feumaidh an gnothuch so foighidinn, agus dol 'n a cheann le suidheachadh inntinn, a' cur roimhibh gu 'n tuig sibh e. Tha cuid, agus mur faic, 's mur tog iad an ni a chuirear rompa, leis a' cheud amharc a iad air, nach saothraich ni 's fhaide ris,—cha luidh an inn-tinn ris; agus mar so tha meadhonan an eòlais, ann an tomhas mòr air an call leo, gun bhuannachd 's am bith fhaotainn uatha. Cha mheudaich sinn ann an eòlas, gun saothair. Ach os ceann gach ni, 's e tha feumail dhuinn,

a Chàirdean, gu 'n cuireadh sinn an Tighearn romhainn, anns gach cùis; gu 'n sireadh sinn naithe féin an teagasg agus an t-eòlas a bhiodh do rireadh a chum ar leas spioradail agus siorruidh. Is e Focal na firinn stéidh agus bunait gach eolais spioradail agus slàinteil. Cha 'n eil ni a 's priseile dhuinn mar mheadh-on, na bhi a' meudachadh ann an eòlas an fhocail. Agus gu h-àraid 's an là an diugh,—tha cor ar n-Eaglais féin,—tha, agus cor gach Eaglais air talamh 'g ar gairm air mhodh àraid, gu 'n dlùthaicheadh sinn ni 's mò agus ni 's mò ri focal Dhé mar aon riaghailt ar creidimh agus ar cleachdaimh. Oir feudaidh sinn gu firinneach a ràdh, " A mhuinntir ionmhuinn, na creidibh gach uile spiorad, ach dearbhaibh na spioradan, an ann o Dhia a tha iad: do bhrigh gu 'm bheil mòran do fhàidh-ibh bréige air dol a mach do 'n t-saoghal." I. Eoin. iv. 1. Gheibhear a ghnàth, mar tha an Spiorad a' cur an céill 's an earrann do 'n sgriobtur a dh' ainmich sinn an dràsd—gheibh-ear an fhìrinn, agus luchd-leanmhuinn na fir-inn, a' glòrachadh Chriosd, 'g a thaisbeanadh, 'g a aithneachadh, agus a' toirt urraim dha. Is e obair shònruichte an Spioraid ann an an-amaibh a phobuill, bhi a' nochdadh Chriosd dhoibh, gus an glòraichear leo e. Agus is i so obair urramach na fìor Eaglais, fuidh threòrachadh an Spioraid, bhi a' cur a chliù-san an céill. Tha sinne, a chàirdean, ann an earrannaibh iomallach na talmhainn. Tha mòran a' dol air aghaidh 's an là an diugh, air nach 'eil sinn a' cluinntinn ach beag iom-raidh. Ach tha oibre freasdail Dhé 'n ar là, a' nochdadh, mar gu 'm bitheadh amanna deuchainn, trioblaid, dearbhaidh, agus feud-aidh e bhi—geur-leanmhuinn—a' tarruing am fagus oirnn. Ach eadar gu 'm bheil no nach 'eil,—agus is ann an làmhaibh an Tigh-earn tha a' chùis,—is e an t-aon ni feumail aig gach àm, bhi a' meudachadh ann an eòlas Chriosd. Is diomhain do rireadh gach meadh-

---

An Fhianuis. *Magazines such as this kept congregations informed of Free Church develop-ments. The image on the top-right is meant to be the* Breadalbane *which transported ministers and Free Church literature such as* An Fhianuis *to remote areas.*

a correlation between the Free Church and the crofting population on the one hand and between the established church and factors and landowners on the other. Such evidence can be found, but it is by no means uniform throughout the Highlands and Islands. There are examples of landowners who supported the Free Church and of established church ministers who were alienated from their proprietors. Support for the Free Church was provided by major landowners such as the Marquis of Breadalbane, the Duke of Argyll, Cluny of MacPherson and James Matheson. In Mr Alexander Beith's book, *A Highland Tour*, he describes Mr Walter Campbell, nephew of the Duke of Argyll and proprietor of most of Islay, and his factor, as Free Church supporters. There was also support from a number of lesser landowners and tacksmen. Indeed, in some Highland areas the antipathy felt by landlowners to the Free Church was somewhat short-lived. There were landowners who came to an early acceptance of the Free Church and in some cases attended its services.

There is considerable evidence which suggests that the poorer people found a home in the Free Church. Throughout the Highlands and Islands it was the crofting population that largely determined the character of the Free Church. This is, however, more a recognition of the nature of the Highland population than of the nature of the Disruption and does not indicate that the Disruption was necessarily a class conflict.

Indeed, an analysis crucially centred on 'class conflict' also hints at the motivation behind the Disruption. This raises the question of the Free Church's attitude towards landlords. There has also been some disagreement in this area. Professor Withers, has stated that evangelicalism was 'essentially a reaction against the landlords and against the established church',[7] whereas Professor Macinnes has argued that the 'Free Church was not inherently opposed to landlordism'.[8]

In the 1840s John MacRae was asked, 'Do you think that the circumstances of sites being granted for Free Churches in the island of Lewis has done anything to diminish the attachment of the people to the Queen and to the authorities in the land?' MacRae responded by saying that he thought 'it had an effect very much to the contrary'. He was then asked 'has it done anything to diminish the attachment of the people to the resident landlord'. MacRae claimed that this had 'increased their attachment to him'. Still on this theme MacRae was asked about the effects of Free Church teaching and whether it has 'been to encourage the people to good order, to respect for their superiors, and to obedience to the laws'. To this MacRae answered 'yes'. The same committee also questioned Thomas Chalmers on Free Church teaching. He responded by stating that 'all the doctrines and all the doings of the Free Church are on the side of social order and the well being of society'.[9] To an extent opposition to patronage denied the rights of a landlord. However, it did not follow that Free Church people opposed landlords as a class. The Disruption, it could be said, was a specific challenge to landlords from people who generally respected their rights.

A related issue is that of the clearances and again there is no clear correlation between the Free Church and anti-landlord views and established church and the pro-landlord position. In some sources there remains the view that the unpopularity of the established church was in part derived from doing little while landlords pursued eviction policies and that evangelicals were more likely to be opposed to landlords. There are, however, too many examples which do not conform to this model to sustain it. Some evangelicals seem to have been somewhat ambivalent concerning landlord eviction policies, but then led their people into the Free Church. On the other hand some who remained in the established church had a strong record of opposing landlord removals.

While significant numbers of people were being cleared from Uig in Lewis the evangelical minister, Mr Alexander MacLeod, who entered the Free Church, said that his people were 'contented with their circumstances and situation in life'. Ministers such as MacKenzie of Farr, Findlater of Durness and MacKay of Clyne have been accused of some complicity with landlord policies; yet they entered the Free Church and took their people with them. MacKenzie and Findlater were both initially denied sites and had to hold their services in the open-air and in tents. On the other hand MacRae of Barvas, often represented his parishioners grievances to the proprietors. However, he remained Church of Scotland and his people deserted him. He was described as the 'poor man's lawyer' as he frequently attended court to plead on behalf of his people. The popularity of ministers, it would seem,

depended more on the content of a minister's preaching and less so
on their attitude to landlord policies.

THE FREE CHURCH AND HISTORY

❊

The evangelicalism of the nineteenth-century generated a
remarkable amount of historical writing about the church in the
Highlands. To a great extent this resulted from the importance
attached to the events in the first half of the nineteenth-century.
The introduction of evangelical Christianity to the north west was
regarded as a major and memorable turning point in Highland
history. It was a new beginning and a break with the past. One
minister, Malcolm MacPhail of Kilmartin, writing at the end of the
nineteenth-century, said 'things thus came down the centuries
almost unchanged until the year 1822'.[10] Another anonymous
writer claimed in the 1820s that as far as he could ascertain 'the
first time these doctrines, called the doctrines of grace, were
preached in Skye is not farther back than 1805'.[11] In many
Highland communities they were able to identify the point at which
evangelical Christianity was introduced, the preacher who first
brought the message and those who initially responded.

The early decades of the nineteenth-century were regarded
almost as a golden age of evangelicalism. Those who held this view
believed that the memories of such times should not be allowed to
be forgotten. It was crucial that the people and the events of these
glorious times should live on within the memory of the Highland
church. This determination produced an unusual quantity of
writing in church history. Articles on evangelical history were
serialised in the Highland press and many accounts of notable men
and ministers were prepared. Examples of these include, *Disruption
Worthies of the Highlands, The Men of the Lews, The Men of Skye,
Ministers and Men of the Far North* and there are many other similar
accounts.

In this view of history the participants were regarded as
exemplary characters and the principles pursued were to serve as a
standard for future generations and to encourage greater piety.
The accounts of evangelical history that emerged from the Free
Church were intended to reaffirm a particular set of values, beliefs
and priorities. One Free Church minister, John Noble from Lairg,

Two images of the floating church of Loch Sunart. Following the Disruption the Free Church
was denied a site in Ardnamurchan. The solution was a floating church. It held about 700
people and apparently sank one inch in the water for every 100 people on board.
(Source: by kind permission, Free Church College, Edinburgh)

wrote in the front of an account of Highland church history that 'desirable religious results also may be achieved by calling the attention of the present generation to a period so notable as the one embraced in the present publication'.[12] There were many other examples of evangelical writers who confessed to similar motives for writing. MacCowan, who wrote about Skye, said his main desire was to 'perpetuate the memories of the worthy fathers of Skye, and that the example of their lives may serve as a stimulus to many'.[13] It was a highly selective view of history that at times is more homily than history. Most accounts rely heavily on memory, and have a vested interest in the survival and propagation of evangelical Christianity.

In the nineteenth-century it was predominantly those who regarded themselves as second-generation evangelicals that committed these things to writing. These evangelicals, as a result of friendships and family connections, had a living link with the origins of evangelicalism in the north west. This gave them access to the recent past by means of accounts circulating in the churches. Such accounts were elicited from the common memory of the evangelical community. Many writers confessed their debt to old church members as they pieced together their versions of Highland church history.

One elderly church member from Lewis, from whom Principal John MacLeod obtained many stories, was described as 'a veritable repository of evangelical tradition, a living contact with the saints of earlier generations'.[14] Other writers confessed to making use of eye witnesses and of older men and women as they constructed their accounts of Highland evangelicalism. These writers wrote because the details of what they considered to be the most important development in recent Highland history was contained within the memory of the evangelical community. The importance of these events demanded that they must not be forgotten and this required their details to be recorded.

Ministers who constructed these accounts deeply treasured their own recollections of what they believed to be a glorious era of Christianity in the Highlands. Norman MacFarlane was one writer whose pleasure was obvious at having contact with some of the great figures of the evangelical past. When he heard John MacRae preach in 1870, 'it was a never to be forgotten experience' and he considered it 'the greatest public utterance' he had ever heard. Similarly, when he heard Alexander MacLeod, Uig and Rogart, preach, he considered that he was uniquely privileged to be able to 'rest his eyes on the apostle of the Lews and to hear a voice that carried life and grace to multitudes of men and women'.[15]

In contrast, the Church of Scotland failed to make any significant response of this kind. In the Highlands they were a defeated group who were cast adrift as evangelicalism advanced from within the Free Church. The established church could not point to any new beginnings, few notable 'saints' and no vital memories that should be cherished and written down for the edification of future generations. It is possible to locate, for example, as many as eight short biographies which applaud the life and work of Robert Finlayson and six for John MacRae. However, there was no equivalent literary effort on behalf of Highland Church of Scotland ministers.

A certain perspective of Free Church history emerged in the years after 1843. This is evident in the accounts that were produced in the nineteenth-century. This perspective drew heavily on distinct events and exceptional individuals. Neither men nor events, however, were uniform or typical throughout the Highlands. Many Free Church congregations in the Highlands had secured sites within a short space of time. Yet the image of the Free Church as a suffering and sacrificial community remained. In the decades following the Disruption, the Free Church established and expanded its ecclesiastical structure but also in this period it established a distinctive identity derived from its history. The structure that was established remained dominant in Highland communities for the remainder of the nineteenth-century. The identity that was established was utilised to inspire those who followed to reproduce the qualities of their predecesors. Thus the dominance of the Highland Free Church was secured as later generations sought to emulate the qualities of those who had given shape to both the structure and identity of the Free Church.

CHAPTER 7
Education

'The establishment of charity schools hath wrought a happy change in
many places: ignorance hath been in a great measure dispelled; the English
language hath made considerable progress; the arts of civilisation have been
in some degree introduced; and thousands have been educated in the
principles of loyalty and the protestant religion.'

STATEMENT FROM THE DIRECTORS OF THE SSPCK

Highland education was far from neutral. Education in the Highlands in the eighteenth and nineteenth centuries was not simply the process of acquiring knowledge and understanding. Education was a means to securing other objectives. These changed, reflecting social and religious changes in the Highlands, and depended on what groups were in the ascendant. Education was many things in the Highlands over this period. It was a means of containing Jacobitism and catholicism, it was a strategy for removing Gaelic, it was a technique for spreading presbyterianism and Hanoverian loyalty, it was an aspect of the struggle against moderatism, it was a facet of evangelical mission and much more. By means of education, powerful interests imposed their agendas on Highland culture and Highland society.

The aim of the Scottish church from the Reformation was that every parish in Scotland should have, along with a church and a minister, a school and a teacher. In 1616 the Scottish Privy Council had ordained that a school should be planted in every parish. This was reinforced in legislation throughout the seventeenth-century. The Synod of Argyll and the Isles was established in 1639 and it soon began to give some consideration to the provision of parish schools in the Highlands. Following the Revolution Settlement there was generally a renewed emphasis on schooling and in Argyll, after 1690, the Synod began to re-direct the stipends from vacant churches towards the establishment of Highland schools.

A further Act for the settling of schools was passed by the Scottish Parliament in 1696 and this again underlined the policy of having a school in every parish. This Act placed the responsibility for the house, the school and the salary of the schoolmaster, which was not to be under 100 merks nor above 200 merks, with the heritors. The schoolmaster was jointly appointed by the heritor and the minister and the school would be supervised by the presbytery and by the parish minister. The parish schoolmaster would usually be a university trained man. He would often be a probationer minister who was waiting for his first parish.

The existence of legislation, however, did not mean that the Act was universally applied in every parish. Despite the Act of 1696, school provision in the Highlands has often been described as deficient. There is, however, some debate about the extent to which Highland parishes ignored or implemented the Act of 1696. The view that Highland heritors were avoiding their obligation to provide parish schools can find some support from SSPCK and Church of Scotland sources. The SSPCK often complained that presbyteries were not enforcing the Act of 1696 but were relying on charity schools. This was supported by Drs Hyndman and Dick who, on behalf of the Church of Scotland, conducted a mission of enquiry into the Highlands in 1760. They visited fifty-two parishes and noted that only twenty-three had legal parochial schools. In addition, the Walker Commission, which reported to the General Assembly in 1765, also identified the same problems. These sources concluded that there had been slow progress in erecting parish schools in the Highlands.

A number of more recent historians have also supported this assessment. They have argued that the evasion of the Act for settling schools was widespread in the Highlands in the eighteenth-century. Professor Charles Withers has suggested that in the Highlands the main problem was simply that the 1696 Act had had little effect.[1] Other historians have suggested that schools were few and far between in the Highlands and that 175 parishes in the Highlands did not have a legally provided school. This claim is derived from a 1755 SSPCK survey which said that there were 'no parochial schools in 175 parishes where society schools are erected'.[2]

This has been competently challenged by the work of Donald Withrington. The view that is widely held is that the parish schools in the Highlands were scarce and consequently education in the Highlands depended almost entirely, where it existed at all, on agencies such as the SSPCK. Withrington contends that the SSPCK evidence is seriously misleading and that there is reliable evidence which 'runs strongly counter to these views'. He further describes the arguments based on SSPCK evidence as a 'crippling misrepresentation of Highland schooling' and proceeds to argue that it is wrong to assume 'that little or nothing could have been achieved from within and that everything must have depended more rather than less, on the activities of outside agencies such as the SSPCK or the Gaelic societies'.[3]

One basis of this disagreement seems to proceed from the definition of what constituted a parish school. The SSPCK appear to have defined a parochial school as one in which a schoolmaster was paid at least the minimum stipend by heritors, required in the 1696 Act. Many schools that fell short of this standard were quite simply not counted by the SSPCK or by Drs Hyndman and Dick. They, therefore, misrepresented the state of Highland schooling in their surveys. It is quite incorrect, Withrington argues, to claim that there were 175 parishes in the Highlands that were devoid of education. In the first place the SSPCK operated in many areas outwith the highlands. Therefore, when the SSPCK spoke of parishes without a parish school it should not be seen as a percentage of Highland parishes.

In addition, in some extensive parishes the stipend from the heritors would be split between two or more schools on two or more sites within the one parish. By the SSPCK definition none of these schools would qualify as a school receiving the minimum stipend. In some places a number of parishes would combine all their available funds in order to establish one well supported school. This happened in South Uist, North Uist and Harris. These parishes combined their stipends and erected one 'good' school. Hyndman and Dick noted that there was a parish school in North Uist but none in Harris or in South Uist even though they had a joint arrangement.

This kind of arrangement was also in place in Skye between Kilmuir, Snizort and Portree and also between Bracadale and Duirinish. In these arrangements, although one legal parochial school would be serving two or three parishes, only the parish with the school would be counted by the SSPCK as having any educational provision. For the other contributing parishes, 'no parish school' would be entered and the joint arrangement was not recognised. Withrington, therefore, suggests that the extent of Highland education was much wider than SSPCK surveys indicated.

Along with parish schools there was also a range of schools that were established by alternative means in the eighteenth-century. There were schools, in addition to those required by law, that were supported by donations or endowments made by individual estate owners or by the wills of substantial tenants. There were also many schools in which groups of local families made arrangements for their own children, with their teachers entirely dependent on fees for their incomes. In 1755 the parish of Blair Atholl had seven schools. These consisted of a parish school, an SSPCK school, two schools provided by the commissioners of the forfeited estates and three schools whose teachers had 'no substance but what they got from parents of their scholars'.

There is indeed considerable evidence to support the claim that there was a wider range of schooling in Highland parishes than was formally acknowledged by the SSPCK. The SSPCK returns themselves show that in a Kintyre parish there were five schools maintained by the heritors from a common fund considerably larger than the minimum required by law. Similarly, in a parish in Arran, there were four parochial schools, and in the presbytery of Aberlour it is reported that every parish had a parish school even though few managed the minimum legal salary of 100 merks.

As a result of his re-assessment of the extent of Highland schooling, Donald Withrington has calculated from SSPCK records alone that over seventy-three per cent of Highland parishes had schools that were supported by landlords and tenants. It is, however, clear that some of these did not meet the narrow SSPCK definition. If information on schools from other sources is included, it is possible for the figure to increase to about 84 per cent of parishes in the Highlands having schools. Many of these parishes would, of course, have had more than one school; parish, charity and privately funded.

Towards the end of the eighteenth-century the *Old Statistical Account* provides an insight into school provision in the Highlands. This source indicates that in Sutherland and Caithness all the parishes had parochial schools. Similarly, in Ross and Cromarty and in Inverness-shire most of the parishes certainly had schools of some kind. In Latheron, Caithness, for example, in 1790s there was a parish school plus two SSPCK schools and three other schools which were supported by local people in distant parts of the parish. Wick had one parochial school and five other schools, Kilmallie had the same, Kilmonivaig had one parochial and two SSPCK schools and Kilmorack had one parochial and one SSPCK.

If there is an absence of consensus about the extent of the provision of parish schooling there are some clear descriptions of the poor state of some schools in the Highlands. It is easy to find, in the eighteenth-century, frequent complaints about the condition of Highland parish schools and sometimes of the limited salaries that came with the appointments. Donald Sage, described a school in the west end of the parish of Resolis in which the teacher in the parish was 'an old man, and the school, like himself was for years verging on decrepitude. The people, dissatisfied with his mode of teaching, withdrew their children one after another from his school until the attendance was at last at a nullity'.[4] This account also demonstrates that at least there was another school available for them to attend.

It was not uncommon for parish schools to be described as being in a very poor condition, inadequately housed and with little income from fees because of the tenants' poverty which barely offered a living above subsistence level. The *Old Statistical Account* contains many descriptions of such schools. Even in the 1790s some teachers barely received £6 per annum. They would supplement this, however, with other duties such as precentor and session clerk. This would provide a small increase to their salaries.

Parish schoolmasters in rural areas would teach reading, writing and arithmetic and sometimes Latin. In more prosperous and populous areas; book-keeping, geography and French could also have been included. One parish teacher at Dornoch was described as an excellent classical scholar. He was, however, a merciless disciplinarian, inflicting punishment for the slightest offence. In one incident he apparently seized a boy by the neck, 'threw him on his face on a form and with the knotted end of a rope, so beat him that the boy fainted and in that state was carried home, where for many weeks he lay in bed dangerously ill'.[5]

❖

The Society in Scotland for Propagating Christian Knowledge received its charter in 1709. The aim of the Society was to establish schools, mainly in the Highlands. SSPCK schools were mostly located in the east and central Highlands yet there were some in the north west and the islands. The schools increased in number from five in 1711 to 229 in 1795. The Society, as its name suggests, was essentially religious. Its aim was to civilise and christianise the Highlands by means of extending presbyterianism and opposing catholicism. The Society expected its teachers to sign a formula renouncing catholicism. The formula stated, 'I, ... , schoolmaster in the parish of . . . . , do sincerely from my heart profess and declare before God, who searcheth the heart, that I deny, disown and abhor these tenets and doctrines of the papal romish church'. There then followed a list of Roman Catholic doctrines and principles that were considered offensive and required to be renounced.

SSPCK teachers were selected by a central committee, they were interviewed in Edinburgh and were given a course of instruction by an SSPCK teacher. They were expected to be persons of 'loyalty, prudence, gravity, competent knowledge and literature'. Along with reading, writing and arithmetic, SSPCK schools would teach scripture and catechise their scholars. The teachers conducted worship on Sundays in remote areas if the parish church was too distant.

It was intended that no SSPCK school should be erected where a parish school had not been legally settled, although this was not always adhered to. This was so that heritors would not use the existence of a charity school as their reason for not establishing a parish school. In Glenmoriston and Glenurquhart the failure of the heritors to provide the means of education which the law required of them (narrowly interpreted as this may have been) led the Society in 1770 to threaten to withdraw their charity teacher unless a 'legal' parochial schoolmaster was appointed. The threat had the desired effect and a parish school was opened.

When the SSPCK commenced in 1709 it was committed to the removal of the Gaelic language. The learning and teaching in the

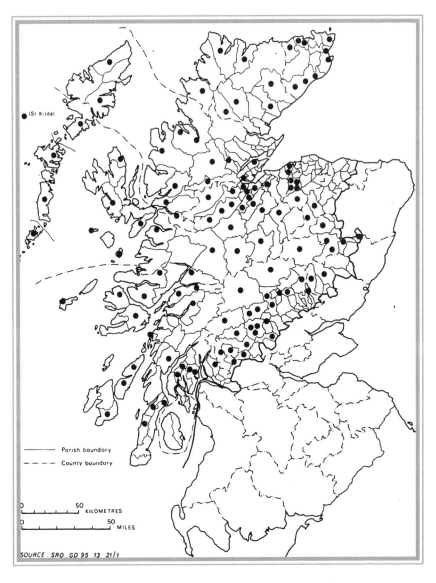

(St Kilda)

Parish boundary
County boundary

0   50
           KILOMETRES
0   50
           MILES

SOURCE : SRO. GD 95 13 21/1

*Map showing the location of SSPCK schools in the
Scottish Highlands and Islands in 1755. This map demonstrates the SSPCK
preference for the eastern and southern Highlands.
(Source: by kind permission, CWJ Withers:* Gaelic Scotland, *p 129)*

schools was all to be in English, irrespective of the language of the local community in which the school was established. The absurdity of this policy became apparent in many areas where Gaelic was almost exclusively spoken and the teachers' efforts made little impression. Even in St Kilda, in 1710, the SSPCK catechist and teacher, Alexander Buchanan, was instructed to 'be diligent not only to teach them English but also to write'.[6] After some time it became clear that Buchanan's efforts met with little success. He was, however, still prohibited from teaching the islanders Gaelic reading or to instruct them in their native language.

Although it is possible to account for the Society's antipathy towards Gaelic, their position was not without its flaws. Gaelic, by association, was lined up with a number of things that the Society held in contempt. These included Jacobitism, catholicism, episcopalianism and superstition. The association of Gaelic with the above and its consequent opposition involved a degree of wilful blindness as Gaelic was the language of many loyal Highland protestants at this time. However, English was linked with loyalty, civilisation and true religion and was, therefore, firmly set within the SSPCK's agenda for the Highlands. In this the Society was more hostile to Gaelic than the General Assembly at the time.

The SSPCK soon discovered that English education in Gaelic communities produced scholars that could read, but without much understanding. Rote learning without comprehension characterised this educational system in which English was the only language of conversation permitted and where Gaelic was initially excluded from the schools. The aim of teaching SSPCK scholars to read the English Bible would be fruitless as long as scholars could not understand what they were reading.

There would appear to be a number of breaches by SSPCK teachers of this policy. On several occasions the SSPCK committee had to write to teachers who appear to have been teaching Gaelic reading and to order them to stop. In 1713 William MacKay, SSPCK teacher in Durness, Sutherland asked if he could pray and sing with pupils in Gaelic. In 1720, James Robertson, minister of Balquidder, had told the SSPCK committee that his parishioners were keen that scholars should be taught to read Gaelic psalms for the good of their families. On this the SSPCK remained inflexible saying that SSPCK schoolmasters were not to teach Latin or Irish, but only English in their schools. Similarly, James Murray, the SSPCK teacher in Blair Atholl informed the SSPCK directors in 1719 that his pupils were taught to read the Gaelic psalms once they had mastered English reading. Murray was told by the SSPCK directors to give no encouragement whatsoever to the teaching of Gaelic reading.

In 1720, suspecting that considerable Gaelic was being used in schools and that some teachers were having difficulties with SSPCK policy, the Society wrote to teachers and ministers saying that English alone was to be taught. There was some SSPCK dissent with regard to the Society's Gaelic policy. Teachers and ministers pointed out in 1721 that scholars did not understand a thing from what they read. A petition from some Highland clergymen followed, claiming that the aim of the Society was being frustrated by its refusal to allow the teaching of Gaelic reading. It was suggested that a scheme of simultaneous translation should be adopted in the Society's schools allowing the Bible and the Catechism to be translated into Gaelic.

In 1723 the general committee of the SSPCK responded and said that Gaelic translation could be used but only when the catechism could be read in English. All conversation in schools was still to be in English. The SSPCK aim, however, was still the removal of Gaelic and putting English in its place. The general committee of the SSPCK sent out letters to all teachers instructing them that Gaelic could now be used in translation, for purposes of comprehension, only after the pupils could read the catechism in English. The SSPCK had conceded that there was little point in teaching English if they did not understand it.

In order to further assist this strategy the SSPCK agreed, in 1725, to provide a Gaelic-English vocabulary. This was produced by the poet and Ardnamurchan teacher, Alexander MacDonald in 1739 and printed in Edinburgh in 1741. MacDonald soon parted company with the SSPCK by converting to the catholic faith and actively supporting the Jacobite cause. The vocabulary was introduced in order to aid students in their study of English. In 1754 the SSPCK proposed to print a New Testament in which one page would be in Gaelic and the facing page in English, again for purposes of English comprehension.

The SSPCK, despite this adjustment of policy, still adopted a hard line on language. In 1750 the SSPCK directors said that scholars should be informed that either in the school-house or when playing about the doors they should not speak Gaelic 'on pain of being chastised and that the schoolmasters appoint censors to note down and report to the schoolmaster such as transgress this rule'.[7] In Urquhart parish school in the 1790s the teacher enforced this policy by handing a roughly carved piece of wood to one boy. This was passed on to the first pupil who spoke in Gaelic and so on to the next. At the end of the day the child possessing the piece of wood was disciplined as were the previous possessors.[8]

Despite the concessions made by the SSPCK, many scholars still could not understand English with much ease. This led to a further change. From 1766 SSPCK schoolmasters were permitted to read both Gaelic and English as this was the 'most effectual method to make them read, speak and understand the English language'. Gaelic was used to translate what English was read and learnt but Gaelic as a medium of instruction was still proscribed as was conversation in Gaelic around the school. This was to ensure greater comprehension of English and was to provoke a greater desire to learn English.[9]

In 1766 the SSPCK stated that 'the propagation of the English language appears to be the most effectual method of diffusing through those countries the advantages of religion and civil society'. SSPCK also established working schools for trades and crafts in the 1730s and towards the end of the eighteenth-century spinning schools. Again in these schools the emphasis was on English. The SSPCK were clearly of the opinion that the progress of civilisation in the Highlands depended on the English language.

In 1825, the SSPCK adjusted its approach again. They agreed to the use of Gaelic as the prime educational medium. They provided instruction in Gaelic reading first and held out an English education as a premium for those who showed themselves to be competent in Gaelic. There were clearly changes in SSPCK policy in the 1720s, 1760s and 1820s yet despite the differing approaches the consistent policy was to remove Gaelic and replace it with English. The SSPCK educational policy in the Highlands has thus justly been described as 'a potent form of anglicisation'.[10]

The SSPCK had much in common with the forfeited estates

schools. Both considered anglicisation necessary for progress and civilisation in the Highlands. These were schools that were established in estates in the Highlands that were forfeited following the Jacobite episode of 1745. After 1715, fifty estates were forfeited to the Crown and sold for a considerable sum of money (£411,682). After 1745, however, the Crown retained the estates that were forfeited and commissioners were appointed to administer them for the benefit of the Highland people.

The commissioners for the forfeited estates first met in 1755. They gave consideration to a variety of measures. These included the division of parishes, building of new churches, roads, bridges and also the need for more schools. The remit of the Commission had included the instruction to 'erect publick schools on the said estates or in other parts of the Highlands or Islands of Scotland for instructing young persons in reading and writing the English language'. At this point, in nine of the annexed parishes there were said to be no legal schools and in other parishes the schools were said for various reasons not to be functioning to a satisfactory standard.

The Commission saw a strong link between English and education. The educational strategy of the Commission was thus geared to eradicate Gaelic and put English in its place. Only this would produce progress and civilisation as Gaelic was associated with economic backwardness. From 1763 to 1784 the Forfeited Estates Commission spent over £4,000 on schools and salaries. By 1784 the Commission had 24 schools which, at this point, were handed over to the SSPCK.

EDINBURGH SOCIETY FOR
THE SUPPORT OF GAELIC SCHOOLS

❃

The Edinburgh Society for the Support of Gaelic Schools operated with a different set of priorities to the SSPCK and did not share the agenda of eighteenth-century militant protestantism. ESSGS was more concerned with extending evangelical spirituality than producing loyal citizens. It was the product of the new evangelicalism and was itself an evangelical educational mission. Its object was to teach people to read the scriptures in their mother tongue. It was yet another expression of the active evangelical faith of the

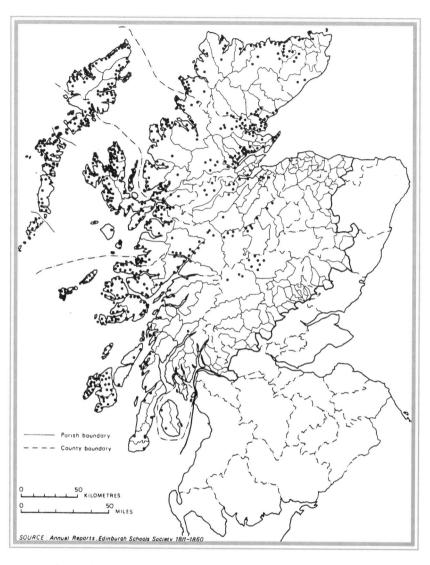

SOURCE : Annual Reports , Edinburgh Schools Society 1811–1860

This map shows the sites at which Gaelic Schools were located, 1811-1860.
The dots do not indicate the continuous existence of a school but
the sites of schools at any one time in the period given.
(Source: CWJ Withers: Gaelic Scotland, *p 150)*

Legend:
——— Parish boundary
- - - County boundary

0   50 KILOMETRES

0   50 MILES

early nineteenth-century which found expression in a wide variety of societies such as mission-societies, Bible-societies, anti-slavery societies, tract-societies and others.

Although the ESSGS shared the evangelical ambivalence concerning Gaelic culture it regarded language as neutral, and Gaelic simply as a vehicle for communicating a message. The ESSGS was, therefore, content to employ Gaelic to achieve their first priority, namely the spread of their message. The Society has been credited with making a significant contribution to literacy, and especially to Gaelic literacy, in the Highlands.

The first meeting of this Society was held towards the end of 1810 in the Royal Exchange Coffee House in Edinburgh. A committee of twenty-four was appointed and they were commissioned to gather information and write a report on the state of education in the Highlands and Islands and to suggest the best means of addressing these needs. By 15 January 1811 their report was in print. It claimed that few Gaelic-speakers in the Highlands and Islands could read and write in their own language. The committee suggested the establishment of circulating schools which would teach the reading and writing of the Gaelic language. These schools would be settled in a community for about a year to eighteen months and then move on. The Society would provide the teachers, and local communities would provide accommodation for the teachers and a school house. Another notable innovation was that instruction would be free.

Christopher Anderson and Alexander MacLaurin were prominent in the formation of this Society. Anderson was an Edinburgh Baptist minister who had already displayed an interest in Highland mission. He had conducted evangelical tours in the Highlands and it was while engaged in one of these that his biographer said he 'first conceived the idea of forming a society for promoting the cause of education in the Highlands'.[11] In the formation of this Society Anderson's contact with the Welsh model of circulating schools provided the source of inspiration. This approach was also adopted by others such as Alexander MacLaurin, a retired Edinburgh postmaster who was from Perthshire, had previously been an SSPCK teacher, and was also acquainted with the the Welsh circulating schools.

The Gaelic school classes were generally held during the day, although it was quite common for classes to be held in the evening too. The Society looked to communities to provide accommodation but 'if the inhabitants are unable to pay for the school room or to provide suitable accommodations that expense shall be defrayed by the Society'. The Society also stated that 'every teacher upon going out, shall be furnished with books, and those parents who can afford the expense, shall purchase them, while the schoolmaster shall possess a discretionary power to give books to any who may be unable to pay the reduced price for them'.

In some remote areas the schoolmaster also assisted with religious duties such as reading the scriptures to the people on the Sabbath and conducting prayer meetings. Teachers were, however, informed that they should not be 'preachers nor public exhorters of any denomination whatsoever'.[12] A number of ESSGS teachers were associated with local revivals in the Highlands and Islands. As a result, there were occasions when teachers disobeyed the Society's rule not to preach. This rule was not strictly enforced and became a problem only if relations with the parish minister deteriorated. In one such instance, John MacLeod, who was the Gaelic teacher in Galson, Lewis, was dismissed by the Society for preaching. He did, however, continue as a teacher in Lewis, where he was supported locally. Another Lewis teacher, Angus MacIver, ran into difficulties with the Stornoway minister but found favour with the Uig minister, Alexander MacLeod.

ESSGS schools were very popular and frequent letters were sent to the Society headquarters requesting a school. Following the establishment of the ESSGS in 1811, similar societies were set up in Glasgow in 1812, Dundee in 1817 and Inverness in 1818. In 1811 there were three ESSGS schools and by 1826 this had increased to eighty-five schools. The Glasgow Gaelic Society had forty-eight schools in 1824 and the Inverness Society had sixty-five schools in 1824. By 1861, the Edinburgh Society estimated that it had taught 110,360 people and distributed 118,884 elementary books and Bible extracts and 82,346 Bibles and New Testaments. In this time it had opened schools in 687 locations. The greatest number of pupils it taught in any one year was 8,387 in 1830. Between 1812 and 1860 the average pupils attending ESSGS schools were 3,335.[13]

The Edinburgh Society schools also attracted a higher percentage of girls. In some places girls made up fifty per cent of the scholars and in some schools there was a still higher percentage. By comparison in SSPCK schools in 1797 there were 4,266 boys and 1,601 girls and for General Assembly Schools in 1829 there were 4,405 boys and 2,034 girls. ESSGS also admitted adults to their schools, both to classes during the day and in the evening.

The ESSGS was credited with having had a profound effect on the moral habits and conduct of Highland communities. In answering questions before the Sites Committee in 1847, John MacRae, minister of Knockbain, when asked to account for the improvement of morals and habits of the Highlanders, answered, 'I would ascribe a good deal of it to the Gaelic School Society and to the teachers employed by that Society by whose means the people learned to read the scriptures in their own language'.[14] Similarly, in 1837, an anonymous correspondent wrote claiming that the Gaelic schools 'have done more good in spreading knowledge and in warming the hearts of the common people to the true religion, than all the other means they have enjoyed for a century'.[15]

The Society was also credited with making copies of the scriptures widely available and encouraging the habit of reading the Bible. One report said of Ard of Coigach that 'in this populous township of a distance of twelve miles from the parish church and in some measure detached from the world, where one year ago, except in the house of the principal tenant, a single Bible was not to be found, now there is not a house in which a portion of the Word of God is not read and his worship performed twice a day'.

The Church of Scotland also contributed to Gaelic literacy by the establishment of General Assemby schools throughout the Highlands. They were set up by the education committee of the General Assembly of the Church of Scotland to promote the reading of the Gaelic Bible. The education committee was formed in 1824 and within two years the Rev Dr George Baird, Principal of Edinburgh University had collected £7,000 and had set up thirty-five schools in remote Highland areas. Similar to ESSGS, the Assembly schools taught Gaelic reading first. The Bible was again the principal text used but they also taught a range of other subjects and some taught English. These schools numbered eighty-one in 1838 and by 1865 there were 200 General Assembly schools throughout the Highlands and Islands.

Following the Disruption in 1843 the ESSGS directors appealed for 'great caution and circumspection in the present time in reference to ecclesiastical controversies'. Teachers were advised to apply themselves to the important duties of teaching 'least by any undue interference in other matters, you may impair your own usefulness and injure the Society in the estimation of the public'.[16] Despite the urging of the ESSGS directors, most of its teachers joined the Free Church in 1843 and out of sixty ESSGS teachers only two remained with the Church of Scotland. By 1846 most directors had moved in the direction of the Free Church. Indeed the ESSGS received some support from the Free Church and ESSGS reports were published in Free Church journals.

THE FREE CHURCH
❋

At its formation in 1843 the Free Church also demonstrated a keen interest in education. The Free Church educational interests were at first based on the need to provide for those teachers who were forced out of their existing posts as a result of Free Church attachments. In October 1843, in the Glasgow Assembly, it was reported that eighty parochial schoolmasters, fifty-seven Assembly school teachers, twenty-seven SSPCK teachers and 196 teachers from private schools had resigned or had been expelled from their positions as a result of Free Church sympathies.

The Free Church educational scheme received a boost from the need to provide for these dispossessed teachers but this was not the only reason. Many in the Free Church wanted in any case to provide a Free Church national scheme of education in Scotland. As a result of both impulses, depositions and Free Church ambitions, by 1847 there were about 500 schools in Scotland affiliated to or directly supported by the Free Church education committee. By 1850 this was over 640, at a time when Scotland had about 950 parishes. The 1851 census noted 719 schools which claimed a Free Church connection. This amounted to 13.7 per cent of Scottish schools which were teaching 17.1 per cent of all Scottish pupils.

The fund raising for Free Church schools was led by Mr MacDonald, minister of Blairgowrie. In 1843 he proposed to raise

£50,000 to build 500 schools. By 1844 this sum had been collected and this total soon reached £60,000. Between 1843 and 1869 the Free Church had spent £600,000 on education and had erected school buildings at a cost of £220,000.[17]

Education in the Highlands was the particular focus of a Free Church initiative led by Dr Mackintosh MacKay of Dunoon. He proposed that the training of students should be carried out in connection with a scheme for the education and religious improvement of the remote areas of the Highlands and Islands. At the General Assembly of 1850, MacKay proposed that schools should be established in remote areas of the Highlands and Islands, and he appealed for assistance to the ladies of Edinburgh and Glasgow. In November 1850, the Edinburgh Ladies Association was formed and by April 1851 they had opened five schools in Harris. Glasgow followed in similar fashion.

MacKay was convinced that high levels of illiteracy still existed in remote areas of the north, The schools that were to be established in these localities would be taught from April to autumn by Highland students and then they would return to college to pursue their studies. In most cases it was Gaelic that was the language to be used in the school. They also studied the Bible, catechism, English, and where appropriate, teachers could also teach Latin, Greek and mathematics. The schools were free.

They were also a source of religious improvement and of mission. In the *Annals of the Free Church* it said of the Ladies Association schools 'invaluable as all this was, the educational work was only a means to a higher end, the religious improvement of these localities and the bringing forward of Gaelic speaking young men for the work of the ministry, strictly speaking the schools were missionary schools'. In addition to teaching duties the teachers in these Free Church schools were encouraged to preach and visit families. By 1859, 3,000 pupils were being taught by the Ladies Association schools and between the years 1850 to 1882 the Edinburgh Ladies Associaion sent out 307 students as teachers to remote communities. The majority of these schools were in the Outer Hebrides, Skye and the north west. They aimed to settle schools in some of the more remote places such as Mingalay, Scarp, Heisker, Berneray and Rona.

Until the Education Act of 1872, a great diversity of schooling could be found in the Highlands. These included parish schools, charity schools, Gaelic schools, ladies schools, Assembly schools, forfeited estate schools, spinning schools, bounty schools, working schools and adventure or private schools. In most of these the church carried considerable influence and religious texts featured prominently in the lessons.

GAELIC

❀

The fate of Gaelic depended on where it fitted into the larger priorities of the time. The educational endeavours of the eighteenth-century were not well disposed towards the Gaelic language. Instead, they regarded it as an obstacle to progress and an element that tied the Highlands to an undesirable past of priests, chiefs and Jacobites.

A crucial change came in the later eighteenth-century and then, more emphatically, in the early nineteenth-century with the Gaelic Society and its auxilliaries. Gaelic was valued by the evangelicals as the most suitable means by which the people could learn to read the Bible. This secured their more important objective of getting the gospel message to the many communities in the Highlands and Islands. Gaelic literacy was, therefore, regarded as the key to the evangelisation of the Highlands.

A strong link was forged between Gaelic and the gospel. The language was the means of extending the gospel and the gospel became the means of securing a measure of Gaelic literacy. As Gaelic was the language of the evangelical impulse in the Highlands, so it was also the language of the Church in the Highlands. In particular, the Free Church provided the institutional form that contained much of the evangelical impulse that was judged to have transformed the Highlands. It was of vital importance that this impulse was very largely transmitted through the medium of Gaelic.

The evangelical message was communicated by means of Gaelic and the evangelical faith was expressed through Gaelic. Thus Gaelic and evangelicalism were inextricably bound together and Gaelic became a fundamental element of the identity of the church in the Highlands. Evidence of this relationship has remained to present times. Gaelic benefitted from the dominant position which the churches occcupied in Highland society. This added a welcome element of prestige for the language and provided Gaelic with one of the few institutional means of resisting the increasing use and domination of English. At the same time Gaelic contributed to the distinctiveness of the church in the Highlands. This distinctiveness provided the Free Church in particular with its own Highland identity and thus enabled it to resist the changes which the Lowland leadership of the Free Church promoted in the late nineteenth-century.

CHAPTER 8

Spirituality

*'In every period of history – even at this day – the Christianity of the
Highlands was and is characterised by peculiarities of its own; and to have
its history fairly before us would require that it should be written separately.'*

Thomas McLauchlan

MINISTER OF ST COLUMBA'S FREE CHURCH, EDINBURGH

The subject of Highland spirituality covers a diverse range of issues
and the following pages will consider both the forms that were used
to express belief and the attitudes that flowed from belief. The focus
will be on the main presbyterian tradition in the Highlands. This was
by no means the only tradition. It was, however, the predominant
tradition and as such shaped the spirituality of the region.

The faith and worship of the Highland church was individual
and collective, devotional and propositional. The Highland church
required members and adherents to attend worship on the
Sabbath, to respect the teaching of Scripture, to understand the
doctrines of the Christian faith, to observe the Sabbath, to practise
family worship, to attend communion, to present young children
for baptism, to respond accurately to questions of the catechism
and to cultivate a life of personal righteousness and Christian
devotion. Much of the above was, of course, shared with other
groups of Christians in the rest of the country but the particular
language and culture of the Highlands and Islands ensured the
development of a distinct and unique spirituality.

The aim of personal righteousness, at times, introduced a
tension into believers' lives with regard to the place they should
give to social and recreational activities. As evangelical piety
demanded priority to be given to Christian duties, such activities as
sport and music could be regarded as a diversion that could lead
the believer astray from a godly life. Their piety thus involved a
certain ambivalence about the wider culture of the Highlands.

BELIEF

❋

The faith of the Highland presbyterian church was based on the teaching of the Bible and was further defined by the documents produced by the Westminster Assembly of 1643 to 1648. These documents set out in a systematic manner what the Assembly considered was prescribed by or deducible from Scripture. In doctrine, worship and church government, Scottish presbyterianism followed the principles contained in the Westminster documents. These documents included the Westminster Confession of Faith, the Larger and Shorter Catechisms, the Directory of Public Worship, the Form of Church Government and a version of the metrical psalms. In the Revolution Settlement the importance of the Westminster documents was acknowledged and in 1693 they were approved by the Scottish Parliament.

One of the most effective ways of communicating the teaching of the Christian faith was by means of the parish catechist. The catechist would direct questions from the catechism at children, young people and adults and expect them to produce the corresponding answer. It was common for this activity to commence with children aged about seven. The parish catechist would work with individuals, families and larger groups. Although catechising was principally the duty of the parish catechist, ministers and school teachers would also participate in this duty. Catechists were generally local men, selected by the kirk session, yet many were paid by the Royal Bounty Fund. This system enabled the church to define acceptable behaviour and belief and thus extend its influence throughout the community.

Another means of communicating a clear understanding of the teaching of the Christian faith was by means of the sermon. Arguably, this was the principal focus of public worship and the principal duty of the minister. It was expected that preaching would focus on the Bible and would be for the purpose of exhorting, encouraging and educating. There had been a concern expressed by evangelical ministers that some moderates had been somewhat remiss in attending to this duty. However, whatever deficiencies in preaching they claimed were evident in moderates were rectified as evangelicals came to establish their presence in the Highlands and Islands. It is perhaps curious that a tradition that put such a strong emphasis on the teaching of the Bible should have to wait until 1801 before the scriptures obtained an adequate translation in Gaelic. This was in marked contrast to the Welsh translation which was available in 1588 and the Irish Gaelic translation of the New Testament which was available in 1602 and the full Bible in 1685.

Although there was a considerable delay in translating the Bible into Gaelic, there was some translation work which was of benefit to the Highland church. In 1653 the Synod of Argyll had translated the shorter catechism into Gaelic and in 1659 they produced a translation of the first fifty metrical psalms. The translation of all the psalms was completed by 1694, again by the Synod of Argyll. In 1675 it had produced a Gaelic confession of faith which included both the larger and shorter catechisms. The Synod had also commenced translating the Bible into Gaelic in 1657 but the imminent political changes and the subsequent changes within the church halted progress on this project. Many of those appointed for the work of translation were ejected from their churches after the Restoration.

The delay in an adequate translation of the Bible into Gaelic can be explained by a number of factors. In the first place the work of translation would have been hindered by the antipathy of Lowland Scots to Gaelic in both Government and in church circles. Gaelic was frequently regarded as barbaric and backward. Also, as a result of the widespread illiteracy in the Highlands, pressure for a Gaelic Bible would have been limited. It is unlikely that there would have been much popular demand for a Gaelic Bible.

For those who could read and write, and possessed a measure of education, the Irish translation in Classical Gaelic would have been adequate. Classical Gaelic was a common literary language that was distinct from the spoken forms of Scots and Irish Gaelic and this translation of the Bible was printed in a Gaelic script that was more common in Ireland.

It was quite common for Highland ministers to use an English Bible, yet when they read to the people, they would translate into Gaelic and preach in Gaelic. Both ministers and people were content with such extemporaneous translations. In addition, as mentioned above, the political and ecclesiastical turmoil and conflict of the seventeenth-century in Scotland hindered translation work. In the eighteenth-century, however, there was a gradual reduction in ecclesiastical conflict. There was also an increase in the number of schools and preaching stations in the Highlands. These factors would have made the situation more favourable for the demand for a Gaelic Bible to increase.

In 1688 Robert Kirk, episcopalian minister in Aberfoyle, began converting the Irish translation from the classical Gaelic script into the Roman script. This was completed in 1690 and 2,000 copies were printed in London. In the mid eighteenth-century the SSPCK also took an interest. They commissioned Mr James Stuart, minister of Killin, to produce a translation of the New Testament. Stuart was born in 1700 and was minister of Killin from 1739 to 1789. This translation was published in Edinburgh in 1767 with Dugald Buchanan, poet and SSPCK teacher, supervising the printing. Ten thousand copies of the New Testament were produced in Scots Gaelic. Stuart translated from the Greek but also compared with English, Irish and with Kirk's Bible.

In 1783 work began on the translation of the Old Testament. This was accomplished by John Stuart, son of James Stuart of Killin and with some assistance from John Smith, minister of Campbeltown. John Stuart was born in 1743 and was minister successively at Arrochar, at Weem and at Luss. Following Stuart's work on the Old Testament the full Bible was available in Gaelic in 1801. This translation of the Bible was revised in 1813 and recognised by the General Assembly of the Church of Scotland in 1816. These translations were much closer to the Gaelic spoken in Scotland and both the Old Testament and the New Testament were produced in sufficient numbers. There were, however, regional difficulties that remained. As the Gaelic used in the translations was predominantly that of Perthshire and Argyll, it presented some difficulties to some areas such as Ross-shire and some congregations remained content with their ministers extemporary translations.

WORSHIP

✼

Public worship was not limited to any particular time or place. However, public worship on the Sabbath was the most important gathering of the week. The basis for this was found in the fourth commandment and this was further emphasised by the catechism

The highpoint of public worship was the communion season. As crowds were so large, services had to be held in the open-air, even in poor weather. This service was at Ferintosh in 1873. (Source: SLA, NMS)

which stated that 'worldly employments and recreations as are lawful on other days' should cease on the Sabbath and that the whole day should be spent 'in the public and private exercises of God's worship.' With the re-establishment of presbyterianism after 1689 there was a renewed emphasis on Sabbath observance in the Highlands and Islands, yet in some areas it took a long time for the habit to be established. The main Sabbath breaches that the Church had to contend with were sport, work, and drinking. Even as late as 1750 the minister of Laggan could commence his Sunday service only when shinty was finished, and in Lochcarron, Aeneas Sage had to compete with sportsmen in order to win their respect. Sage promised one sportsman a pound of snuff for every time he brought his family to church on the Sabbath.

Kirk sessions were concerned that some people worked on the Sabbath and in 1810 Lochcarron Presbytery proposed withdrawing baptism and communion from those who went fishing on the Sabbath. When Alexander MacLeod was appointed minister of Uig in 1824 he encountered on his first Sabbath the 'lively marketing which went on at the church door. One man was selling whisky from a jar and another was busy disposing of his stock of tobacco'. Many of the evangelical ministers of this period favoured a strict code of Sabbath observance. There is one story told of Alexander MacLeod which claims that in 1843 he made 'some poor fishermen who had been cast on shore in his parish and who, on Sunday, had ventured to bake bread for themselves, to stand before the congregation and receive public rebuke for Sabbath breaking'. MacLeod evidently did not consider the excuse of 'mercy or necessity' was applicable in this instance.

The high point of public worship was to be found in the observance of the sacrament of communion. In the Highlands and Islands communion was held in a parish about once a year. People would come from neighbouring parishes and visiting preachers would also attend. This would result, at times, in large gatherings. The meetings were commonly held over several days; they would be in the open-air and visitors would stay with church members. The preachers would address the people from a small tent or a small wooden pulpit. When moderatism was in the ascendant this was not always an exclusively spiritual occassion. There might be stalls with sweets, fruit and whisky tents. In some areas in the

eighteenth-century communion services had been badly neglected
with parishes going for several years without a communion service.

Communions lasting a few days, were common throughout
Scotland in the early eighteenth-century. Although this practice
was to be discontinued in the Lowlands it remained a distinctive
feature of Highland presbyterianism. The communion season
consisted of Thursday, the fast day. Friday was the day of self
examination and the fellowship meeting. Saturday was the day of
preparation at which tokens would be distributed. The Sabbath
was the day of communion and the Monday was a day of thanks-
giving. Accounts of these solemn gatherings have been provided
by both visiting observers and local participants. The picture that
emerges is one of deeply moving occasions at which the central
event of the Christian faith was celebrated. The crowds attending
could number from 1,000 to 10,000. People frequently travelled
great distances to attend.

One such observer, Lord Teignmouth, described a Skye
Communion in Sleat in the early nineteenth-century. He described
the tables as made of long planks of wood about two feet in
breadth. These rested on clods of earth, were about a foot off the
ground and were covered by a white cloth. At a certain point in the
service the ministers took their places at the head of the tables and
gave a short message, distinct from the sermon, before the bread
and the wine was passed round. When this was done, the ministers
would address each table again and those at each table would then
rise to make way for others who would again be spoken to and
served by the ministers.

Although vast crowds attended, only a small percentage took
communion. This was because people were encouraged to examine
themselves morally and spiritually. The outcome of this intro-
spection would indicate whether individuals judged themselves to
be fit to take communion or not. Ministers were also concerned
about the character of those whom they admitted to the sacrament,
and emphasised the high moral standards required of those who
would take communion. This process was referred to as 'fencing
the table' and was for the purpose of denying privilege to those who
were unworthy. At times ministers applied such rigorous standards
that many felt excluded. In one account, Duncan Matheson,
minister of Gairloch, and himself no liberal, described MacLeod of

Uig as demanding such high standards of those taking communion that all those attending, ministers included, felt excluded from taking communion.

The high standards expected of communicants spread with the evangelicalism of the nineteenth-century. In time these came to be a characteristic of Highland spirituality and as such contributed to the distinction between Highland and Lowland religion. Before the evangelical awakenings, admission to the sacraments was less strict. In Uig, Alexander MacLeod complained that 'all and sundry' were admitted and upon arriving in Uig in 1824 he managed first to postpone communion and then reduce the communicant list from over 800 to six. When Roderick MacLeod arrived in Bracadale in 1823 there were 150 communicants on the roll. In approaching his first communion he reduced this to under ten by saying only 'God-fearing consistent Christians' could participate. Even by 1840 there were only twenty communicants in Bracadale.

At such services and on the Sabbath, psalms were sung in public worship and not hymns. In Gaelic psalm singing, which has elsewhere been described as a 'great tumult of heterophony', a precentor would be used to sing a line and then the congregation would repeat it or join in as appropriate. William Laidlaw, a friend of Sir Walter Scott, who attended a large gathering at Ferintosh said of the singing, 'I can compare the singing to nothing earthly, except it be imagining what would be the effect of a gigantic aeolian harp with hundreds of strings'. Laidlaw estimated that there were over 9,500 in attendance. Although it was only psalms that were sung in the Highland church services, verse played an extremely important part in Gaelic culture and similarly in Highland religious life.

The creation of verse within the Highland Church was a widespread activity. Poems and songs dealt with issues of Christian doctrine and devotion. Spiritual poets also produced elegies to godly individuals and explored contentious issues in verse. Within this form there were some such as Dugald Buchanan, Peter Grant and John Morrison who excelled. While these poets were highly regarded this, however, should not convey the impression that this activity was only for a few. The spiritual poets enabled people to sing about their faith. These hymns became very popular, not for church worship but for smaller gatherings in homes and for private use. Such poems and hymns were also a means of instruction in the Christian message as they were sung, recited and memorised.

Principal Donald MacLean of the Free Church College said of the spiritual bards that they 'wielded a great influence, and were the auxilliaries of the church in disseminating evangelical doctrine and in formulating the religious views of the community'.[1] Their poems gained wide circulation in the Highlands and Islands and their hymns helped shape the religious life of the people.

REVIVAL
❊

The religion of this period was, at times, an intensely emotional affair. Communities in the Highlands and Islands developed a remarkable attachment to certain preachers and responded similarly to the message they brought. It was, therefore, not uncommon for the collective response of Highland communities to be deeply emotional and at times this resulted in what have been described as revivals of religion.

Revivals of religion happened throughout the period of this study. These were usually intense, emotional periods of religious awakening which involved people becoming acutely aware of the own unworthiness and sinful condition and of the forgiveness and consolation that was contained in the Christian message.

There are accounts of revival which date from the 1720s in Easter Ross. There were also impressive gatherings and revivals in Cambuslang and Kilsyth in the Lowlands in the early 1740s. A number of Highland visitors attended these gatherings and hoped to reproduce this vitality in their own congregations. Vast crowds attended the Lowland gatherings and communion would often be the focal point. The formation of praying societies and fellowship meetings often resulted from the revivals in both the Highlands and the Lowlands.

In the Highlands in the 1740s, there were accounts of revivals of religion in Nigg, Rosskeen, Rosemarkie, Golspie and Rogart. Later in the eighteenth-century, in the 1770s and 80s, there were religious awakenings at Tongue, Ardclach, Moy and Strathspey. Revivals inspired by a different source also entered the Highlands in the 1790s and early nineteenth-century. These resulted from the

Dr John Kennedy, minister of Dingwall Free Church, was a strong supporter of Highland spirituality and it was said of him that he was contemplating a Caledonian church. He said, 'I believe the Lord has a remnant in our land . . . that will separate, and I think the separating party will be found especially in the districts lying north west of the Caledonian canal'.
(Source: by kind permission, Free Presbyterian Archive, Inverness)

work of the Haldanes and their agents, yet in some revivals in this period, for example in Perthshire, there was also presbyterian involvement. There was revival at Moulin, in Arran, in Skye, in Breadalbane and in Lewis. Many other areas in the Highlands were similarly affected and revival became a feature of nineteenth-century evangelical Christianity throughout the Highlands and Islands.

By the late nineteenth-century a number of tensions had emerged in the Free Church. To an extent divisions were emerging between the Highland and Lowland sections of the Free Church. One of the factors which produced division was revival. In 1873 and 1874 the American evangelist Dwight L Moody arrived in Scotland and conducted lively enthusiastic meetings which included appealing hymn tunes and emotive preaching which offered instant conversion.

John Kennedy, Free Church minister of Dingwall, was prominent in opposing this revivalism. Kennedy produced a rather unflattering picture of the typical Moody revival convert whom he described as a 'molluscuous, flabby creature without pith or symmetry, breathing freely only in the heated air of meetings, craving to be pampered with vapid sentiment, and so puffed up by foolish flattery as to be in a state of chronic flatulency, requiring relief in frequent bursts of hymn singing, in spouting addresses as void of scripture truth as of common sense and in belching flippant questions.'[2]

The sudden conversions offered by the Moody mission caused Kennedy some concern. He was troubled by the Moody converts' confidence in their salvation and their over-familiarity with spiritual things. The approach of the Moody mission undermined Calvinism for Kennedy as it made conversion more dependent on human management than on divine sovereignty. The Calvinist emphasis on divine sovereignty meant that salvation was not for the believer to select but for God to impart. Thus believers should never rush to presume on their eternal destination. This uncertainty, combined with the essential belief in sinfulness of the human condition, tended towards a more serious approach to religion.

The Moody mission urged people to accept that they were saved on the basis of assent to a few propositions and then to be confident in the assurance of their salvation. For Kennedy, however, the salvation offered by Moody was too instantaneous, assurance should be a separate matter and came much later than faith. Kennedy considered that faith should be confirmed by a consistently godly life before the believer could claim the assurance of salvation.

More recently there has been in some quarters of the Highland church a desire to make the religious outbursts respectable and to ignore the physical aspects of revivals. In 1953, Murdoch Campbell, Free Church minister of Resolis, spoke of revival with the 'absence of undesirable emotional excesses' and again complimented revivals in which 'nothing could be seen or heard calculated to distract either preacher or people'.[3] Examples from the nineteenth-century, however, refuse to comply with this preference.

In a description of the Skye revival of 1843 there is a reference in which it was said of the minister that 'the cries of the people were such that his voice was drowned and he had to stop speaking'. In the same revival the minister commented that 'hundreds fell down as if they were dead. This usually commences with violent shaking and crying out, with clapping of hands'.[4] From many parts of the Highlands there are accounts of revivals in which there were prostrations, shouting and weeping. Outward physical manifestations frequently accompanied revivals. In Lewis, 1822 was referred to as *Bliadhna an Aomaidh*, the year of the swooning or collapsing because of the prevalence of this phenomenon at meetings.

CHURCH ORGANISATION
❧

Admission to the church was secured by the sacrament of baptism. This was generally administered to young children by the parish minister. In some parishes in the nineteenth-century evangelicals who lacked respect for a moderate parish minister would take their children to an evangelical minister in a neighbouring parish for baptism. This was, however, considered a breach of ecclesiastical order yet it was supported by some evangelical ministers. On the other hand parents who were refused baptism by evangelical ministers would also go to neighbouring parishes to obtain baptism for their children. When MacLeod of Uig refused baptism to 'unworthy' parents they travelled to Harris where the minister was happy to oblige.

In the nineteenth-century some ministers began to take a closer look at who they should admit for baptism. Tensions in this area are mostly associated with Roderick MacLeod of Bracadale and Snizort. There were other ministers who adopted similar practices of looking for exemplary conduct in parents and expecting parents to answer questions from scripture before ministers would agree to baptise their children. In Bracadale, Roderick MacLeod refused baptism to a number of parents on the grounds that 'they were deficient in religious knowledge and irregular in their attendance on religious ordinances'. MacLeod wanted to apply the same

The Free Church of Scotland

MONTHLY RECORD

PUBLISHED BY T. NELSON & SONS,   EDINBURGH AND LONDON.

No. 8.—New Series.]   MARCH 2, 1863.   [Price One Penny

PORTRAIT OF THE REV. RODERICK MACLEOD.

Roderick MacLeod, 1794-1868. He was known as Maighstir Ruaraidh. He was more at home in Gaelic than English. On a number of occasions he was described as the 'Bishop of Skye' and it was claimed he single-handedly held Skye for the Disruption. He was censured by his presbytery in the 1820s and nominated Moderator of the General Assembly of the Free Church in 1863.

rigorous standards for baptism as was common for communion among evangelicals.

An appeal against this went to the Skye Presbytery and it was claimed that in a period of two and a half years there were fifty unbaptised children and only seven baptised in MacLeod's parish. The Skye Presbytery made an unsuccessful appeal to MacLeod to baptise these children and then suspended him. These events occupied the church courts in the 1820s and the matter went as far as the General Assembly where MacLeod was eventually cleared and his presbytery's suspension lifted. There was, however, considerable support for MacLeod from his parishioners. Following his suspension his supporters blocked access to the church with stones and less than twenty turned up to listen to his replacement.

Although standards for admission to baptism were raised, generally less was expected of the applicant for baptism than the candidate for communion. John Kennedy said that as baptism is 'the door of admission into the visible church, a larger exercise of charity is required in dealing with applicants for that sacrament than is called for in administering the other'. In the Free Church in the nineteenth-century it was stated that 'applicants for baptism should be admitted on an uncontradicted profession of faith'.[5] With applicants for communion, however, an accredited profession of faith was required to justify their admission to the Lord's table.

The sacrament of baptism provided accesss to the church. Those who attended church were either categorised as members or adherents and the business of the church was managed by the kirk session. This was composed of elected elders and the parish minister. Beyond the kirk session there were another three levels of church courts at which elected elders were expected to participate at every level.

THE MEN

❖

Presbyterianism encouraged strong lay participation. A distinctive aspect of Highland lay participation was the role assigned to 'the men' in the Highland church. The men were a recognised group of evangelical laymen; almost a spiritual elite or a spiritual aristocracy. The men performed important leadership functions, they were recognised for their godliness and knowledge of scripture and exemplified a standard for the church to imitate and aspire to. Some of the men also adopted a distinct appearance. They would often have their hair long, with coloured handkerchiefs on their heads and they would wear a long blue cloaks. Some writers have said that there has been too much emphasis placed on the men within the context of Highland presbyterianism. Whether true or not this aspect of Highland presbyterianism was undoubtedly important. In addition, it is from within the Highland tradition of evangelical presbyterianism that the role of the men has been emphasised and their memory cherished.

Most sources trace the men back to Thomas Hog, minister of Kiltearn from 1654 to 1661 and then again from 1690 to 1692. Hog, as a student in Aberdeen, attended fellowship meetings and praying societies. He imported these structures back to Kiltearn and provided evangelical laymen with the opportunity to exercise a measure of spiritual leadership in the community. Similarly, in the Easter Ross revivals of the eighteenth-century, the men found a sphere of usefulness in prayer meetings and fellowship meetings.

There was always a tension between ministers and men, with each providing a check to the other and each presuming they had a degree more control over the other. John Kennedy, of Dingwall, suggested it was within the power of the minister to bring men forward or not. On the other hand the men would only give support to ministers they thought measured up to their evangelical standards. Kennedy said 'when a godly Highland minister discerned a promise of usefulness in a man who seemed to have been truly converted unto God; he brought him forward into a more public position by calling him first to pray and then to speak to the question at the ordinary congregational meetings'.[6] Dependent on the individual's performance it was up to the minister then to include that individual among the Friday speakers on communion occasions.

There were some earlier attempts to restrict the influence of the men. In 1737 the Synod of Caithness and Sutherland prohibited the public fellowship meetings which were held on the Friday before the communion. This was an attempt to limit the activity of the men and deny them the opportunity to exercise a public ministry. The Synod considered such meetings as 'irregular and disorderly and tends to propagate the animosities of the people in these bounds against their ministers'. In addition, an incident at Halmadary, Strathnaver, in which, at a fellowship meeting, there was an attempt to offer a human sacrifice around 1740 must have reinforced the ministers' desire to control the fellowship meetings.

At the meeting at Halmadary, a large raven appeared at the house where the meeting was taking place. The worshippers believed it to be an evil spirit and this fear convinced them that they had to offer a human sacrifice in order to break the spell. The 'spell' was broken two days later by neighbours taking the roof off the house while one man had the sense to protect the child that had been selected for sacrifice.

In 1758, however, a Commission of the Assembly set aside the 1737 Act of the Synod of Caithness and Sutherland which had abolished the fellowship meetings. Thus the advocates of the fellowship meeting triumphed, and towards the end of the eighteenth-century such meetings were held more often. The fellowship meetings provided the principal forum for the men to exercise a public ministry. These would involve prayer, praise and scripture reading. The minister would extend an invitation for someone to put a question relating to a passage of scripture. The minister would comment on it and then call on a number of men to speak to the question. Then the minister would conclude. The Friday communion meeting would follow a similar pattern and the men would speak to the question from their spiritual experience. Although such meetings originated in Easter Ross, they were introduced into the north west by Lachlan MacKenzie, into Skye about 1810 and into Lewis in the 1820s.

SEPARATISM

❋

In some areas the tension between men and ministers became so marked that it resulted in a division within the congregation. Those who left the parish church have been categorised by John MacInnes, in an excellent study of the seventeenth-century church in the Highlands, as either seceders or separatists. For MacInnes the seceders remained members of the established church. They might not accept their own minister and so went to another parish minister for baptism, communion and Sunday services. They would attend the church of the nearest evangelical. Separatists, however, were described as going a step further, setting up rival services and taking people away from the parish church.

Separatists remained presbyterian in sentiment but did not form into structures with other separatists. They also did not call ministers but depended on the ministry of laymen. As a result of this lack of a formal structure and organisation there were few records kept by separatists. John MacLeod, minister, historian and Free Church College Principal, said this movement was 'one of the most obscure connected with the life of the northern Highlands, and it is one that is on the border line of folk lore'.[7]

A number of sources support the view that Highland separatism had its origins in Kildonan in a dispute over a communion service in 1797. For Principal MacLeod, separatism 'could not rightly be appreciated or understood otherwise than by looking at it in the light of the local problems with which our fathers were confronted'.[8] The dispute arose when Mr Sage, the parish minister, wanted to hold a small communion just for Kildonan folk. His elders were opposed to this and wanted their communion to follow the normal pattern with visiting ministers and visitors from neighbouring parishes. Mr Sage announced the communion date only a week beforehand. This did not allow much time for visitors to attend. A large number gathered yet Sage still wanted to hold the communion services in the church. With many attending from neighbouring parishes the elders withdrew to a near hillside and held their own meetings.

Separatists could be found in a number of areas in the Highlands; in the parishes of Assynt, Kildonan, Reay, Strathnaver, Latheron, Rosskeen, Fodderty, Kilmorack, Croy, Glenurquhart, Moy, Daviot and Duthil. Their leaders were often strong individuals who had been catechists or elders.

Separatism was essentially a protest against anything that was considered unsatisfactory either in church doctrine or practice. The criticism of the Separatists was not only directed at moderate ministers as many evangelical ministers were also criticised by them. They also commented on issues affecting the national church. For example the evangelical leaders of the established church were denounced for their lack of opposition to the Roman Catholic Emancipation Act of 1829. Chalmers in particular came in for criticism from Highland separatist leaders for the support which he gave to the Emancipation Act. Separatists considered that Chalmers and his allies had sacrificed the protestant character of the British constitution and that the church should have offered more resistance to catholic emancipation.

The period of separatism is roughly from the 1790s to the 1860s. The *Annals of the Free Church* estimated that at the time of the Disruption there were only ten parishes in which separatists had a secure footing. This source also claimed that the Disruption did more than anything to restrict the influence and growth of separatism. Some of the separatist criticism of the established church was contained in verse form and a number of elegies praising the qualities of separatist leaders were produced by their fellow separatists. Principal John MacLeod reckoned that the separatist tradition came to an end round about 1875 in Latheron, Caithness.

Although many separatist leaders such as Alexander Gair of Latheron, Peter Stewart of Duthil, and Joseph MacKay of Reay, appear to have been remarkable individuals, among separatists the achievement of Norman MacLeod merits additional comment. MacLeod was born in Stoer, Assynt in 1780. He led a separatist community for over fifty years and all aspects of community life were governed by him. This community travelled thousands of miles. It was held together by MacLeod in three continents until eventually, as a Gaelic speaking presbyterian community that had been created out of the religious tensions in the Scottish Highlands, they settled finally in New Zealand.

In 1806 MacLeod had developed an interest in religion and commenced a period of study Aberdeen University. This was followed by a period of theological study in Edinburgh University. MacLeod became deeply dissatisfied with much that he saw in the established church in Edinburgh and did not complete his divinity training. He moved north and taught at an SSPCK school in Ullapool. Here relations between MacLeod and the local minister, Dr Thomas Ross, were somewhat strained. MacLeod refused to attend his services and would not have his child baptised by Ross. MacLeod also began to organise separate services.

In 1817, MacLeod and followers decided to set out for Nova Scotia. About 150 went with him. In 1820 they moved to St Anne's Bay in Cape Breton. By 1840 there were about 1,200 attending his church. Some had followed from Lewis and Harris and from Ross and Sutherland. MacLeod remained minister and also exercised a great degree of control over every aspect of community life.

Letters from MacLeod's son in Australia led him to consider another move. This time, aged seventy, he supervised the building of two ships to take his community to the southern hemisphere. They set out in 1851. When they arrived in Adelaide they found that it had been gripped by the discovery of gold. This situation was not conducive to the community that MacLeod hoped to establish and so they moved on to New Zealand. They settled in Waipu in North Island. In 1854, about 800 followed and their church in Canada was passed to the Free Church. MacLeod died in 1866 in New Zealand at the age of 86. A memorial stone in St Anne's noted that as 'clergyman, schoolmaster and magistrate he moulded the character of this community for a generation'.

THE CHURCH AND HIGHLAND CULTURE
❊

In 1902, George MacKay, Free Presbyterian minister of Stornoway, apparently turned up at a wedding celebration on the west side of Lewis. The festivities were in a barn. MacKay was unable to locate the entrance so he climbed the barn wall and made a hole in the thatched roof. He saw that the entrance to the barn was by way of the house. He then entered and pulled the melodeon from the musician and sat with it on his knee defying anybody to remove it. This story demonstrated a commonly held view of the presbyterian response to Highland culture and recreation. George MacKay was certainly not alone in this type of response but neither was he typical.

The above story supports a commonly held notion of a hostile church which contributed to the demise of an indigenous culture and consistently opposed song, story, music, poetry, and sport. The record of the churches in the Highlands was, however, mixed. Within the church some played bagpipes while others destroyed them. Some renounced poetry while others used it as a medium to express their faith. Some preached against dancing while others reported seeing dancing in a minister's house. The Highland church contains examples of both support for and condemnation of

Throughout the Highlands and Islands many outdoor sites became recognised locations for religious gatherings. Perhaps the most famous was the Burn at Ferintosh

(Source: SLA, NMS)

Highland culture. Yet, the predominant image is of the presbyterian church being in opposition to culture. This image has been
re-inforced by a wide range of sources.

William MacKay who wrote about Urquhart and
Glenmoriston in 1893 took the view that the Highlands had a rich
cultural life that was progressively undermined as the presbyterian
and evangelical church extended its control in Highland
communities. MacKay said of evangelicalism that 'it had to a great
extent destroyed the songs and tales which were the wonderfully
pure intellectual pastime of our fathers; it has suppressed innocent
customs and recreation whose origin was to be found in remote
antiquity . . . it has with its iron hand crushed merriment and good
fellowship out of the souls of the people and in their place planted
an unhealthy gloominess and dread of the future'.[9]

Similarly, Alexander Nicolson writing about Skye in the 1930s,
left the strong impression that the evangelical revivals were the
principal cause of the decay of secular culture in Skye. Nicolson
claimed that the preachers of the new evangelicalism 'waged war
persistently against such popular recreations as secular music, the
ancient tales and the traditional barderie, with the result that much
of the native culture, developed during the course of the ages, has
been irretrievably lost'. Nicolson cited the example of Donald
Munro, the blind catechist, who apparently asked Skye people to
demonstrate their renunciation of all forms of worldly pleasures by
bringing their musical instruments to the head of Loch Snizort on
an appointed day for a public conflagration. Nicolson informs us
that a 'veritable mountain of fiddles and bagpipes was there
accumulated and consigned to the flames'.[10]

Criticism also came from James Cameron Lees, (1834-1913)
who was a Church of Scotland minister. Lees commenced his
ministry in the Highlands and was later minister of St Giles
Cathedral in Edinburgh. Lees identified the problem as being the
control of the men whom he said 'represented the power of
fanaticism'. Lees informs us that 'singing songs or playing the fiddle
were classed with heinous sins and punished by exclusion from
religious ordinances'. He regretted that a 'race which loves music
burnt its bagpipes and a people full of the love of song silenced
their singing'. As a young Church of Scotland minister he had
suffered in a Highland parish that was strongly Free Church and

many years later still said, 'I find it very difficult . . to forgive those who caused me so much suffering in Strathconan'.[11]

There is of course evidence which can be cited to support the assessment of MacKay, Nicolson, Lees and others. Donald Munro, the blind catechist, put away his fiddle following his conversion and Archibald Crawford, who was an important evangelical leader in Argyll, had been an impressive poet but following his conversion he never composed another verse. In Duthil, Donald MacLean tells the story of a piper and fiddler, Duncan Cameron, who, following his dramatic conversion, destroyed his instruments. Lees also recounts the story that was passed on to him by the Lewis factor Mr John Munro MacKenzie. MacKenzie had been visiting a certain village and after certain matters had been settled 'some of the old men said, Oh, these matters are but slight, but there is another matter that is calling down the wrath of heaven upon us. There is a man here who plays the fiddle'.[12] On this occasion, Lees informs us, the factor paid the fiddler to play while the villagers were paying their rent.

The art form that probably suffered least from cultural ambivalence was poetry. Verse was still a form that was used in the Highland church. There are, however, those who rejected an ability to produce secular verse. Probably the most notable was Archibald Crawford, mentioned above, who was born in 1815 and was producing verse from age eight years old onwards. By age twenty-two he had a volume of Gaelic poetry ready for publication but was converted at this point at a revival in the Cowal area. His volume of poetry was destroyed along with all other compositions and thereafter he never composed verse. Some of the sayings that have been attributed to him, however, display a remarkable ability with language. Most of Crawford's activity was in Cowal and Argyll, yet he also preached throughout the Highlands, and Islands before retiring to Argyll. He died in 1903 having moved from the Free Church into the Free Presbyterian Church in 1893.

Donald MacFarlane, minister of Raasay, and one of the leaders of the Free Presbyterian Church had some difficulty reconciling his faith with Gaelic culture. Of the national Mod, MacFarlane said, 'there are many objectionable things in connection with it, such as vain songs and dancing, which must have a deleterious effect upon the moral and religious character of those connected with it'. Of

those who were leaders and organisers in this annual festival of
Gaelic culture, MacFarlane took the view that 'Satan is using them
as instruments to keep the rising generation in his net'.[13]

Some evangelical ministers expected converts to forsake the
recreational interests that had been part of their lives before their
conversion. Roderick MacLeod of Skye spoke of 'sinful men and
women who dared to dance at weddings, sing human songs and
even play on seductive bagpipes'.[14] MacLeod considered them to
be eating and drinking damnation on themselves. Also Duncan
Matheson, who moved to Gairloch Free Church in 1844, despised
the fairy lore which he found in the district. He attempted to break
up a public dance wielding a big stick and managed to smash a
black healing stone that he had taken into the pulpit one Sunday.

The *New Statistical Account* also provides evidence of this
development in Highland communities. Alexander MacLeod, Uig,
observed that in Lewis 'the people have hardly any public games or
amusements of any kind'. Similarly, the Lochs minister, Robert
Finlayson, wrote that the 'games prevalent here were jumping,
putting the stone, the shinty or club, but these are now gone out of
use'. The mainland offers similar evidence, thus the minister of
Duirinish added that 'balls and dancing parties have been given up
throughout the parish. Indeed, all public gatherings, whether for
shinty playing or throwing the putting stone, for drinking or
dancing, for marriages or funerals have been discontinued'.
Archibald Clerk, minister of Inverness, reported that it had been
'customary for neighbours to visit each others' houses nightly and
to while away part of the long winter evenings in reciting tales and
traditions, singing songs, or playing some musical instrument'.
However, he added that 'now all this is completely gone'.

REVISION

❊

To an extent the older and harsh views of Nicolson, Lees and
MacKay have undergone a measure of revision. Later writers have
pointed out that there were other social forces which worked to
undermine the indigenous culture of the Highlands and that
evangelical presbyterianism was not a monolithic scourge of Gaelic
culture. Two of Nicolson's nephews, Calum and Sorley MacLean,
contributed significantly to this revision.

In 1959, Calum MacLean, in his book *The Highlands*, said that 'much has been said and written about the part that evangelical Calvinism played in the destruction of Gaelic folk tales, folk music, beliefs and customs . . . but the fact remains that at most it can only be one of several contributory factors. It is by no means the most important factor, and it can now be doubted if it is an important factor at all'. Other causes that have been identified by other writers include clearance, famine, emigration, education, and the English language. These factors disrupted the social structure and habits of the people and accorded prestige to one culture at the expense of another. As Gaelic culture suffered so also did the art-forms and recreations which were associated with it.

In support of his revision of the detrimental effects of presbyterianism on Highland culture, Calum MacLean has cited examples of the survival of traditions in areas that were firmly presbyterian. MacLean notes that as many examples of traditional songs could be recorded in the 1940s in presbyterian Raasay with a population of under 300 as from the predominantly catholic islands of Barra and Eriskay with a population of about 2,500. MacLean makes a similar comparison between Harris and Benbecula in which he says Harris, with a Free Church and Free Presbyterian background, contained many more examples of the survival of Gaelic tradition.

Sorley MacLean has also shared in this revision. He said, 'that Raasay went completely Free Church in 1843 and ninety per cent Free Presbyterian in 1893 certainly diminished song tradition and also most other really old traditions in the island. But now I realise when it is too late that I myself exaggerated the evangelical suppression of traditions in Raasay, thinking that the Free Church and Free Presbyterian churches had destroyed traditions that had really gone underground'. In support of this Sorley MacLean cites his grandmother, who died in 1910. She was evidently 'a fine singer and tradition bearer, especially of songs, although she was a devout Free Presbyterian'.[15]

A number of writers have contributed to the revision of the detrimental effects of evangelicalism on Highland culture by listing examples of Highland ministers who sustained the culture of the parish and have noted the prevalence of music and verse among the clergy. There are many examples of this. Mr Murdoch

MacDonald, minister of Durness, was a piper and his sons Joseph and Patrick, also a minister, published a study of piping and a collection of Gaelic songs respectively. Others who made a contribution include Dr John MacDonald of Ferintosh who wrote verse and collected traditional songs and poems. MacDonald also had considerable ability on fiddle and bagpipes and one nineteenth-century writer said 'I used to see as merry dancing in Dr MacDonald's house as anywhere, when many folks thought it was a sin to dance'.

The list of ministers who helped preserve the culture of the parish can be shown to represent different periods, different regions and different ecclesiastical backgrounds. If such a list were produced it would contain representatives from the eighteenth and nineteenth centuries. It would contain protestants and catholics and within the presbyterian tradition it would contain evangelicals and moderates.

The churches can not be held solely responsible for undermining the culture of the Highlands. It has been argued that there were other erosive forces operating. In addition, the churches did not consistently oppose Highland culture. There were many ministers and members who were supportive of the culture of the parish and significant elements of Highland culture could still be located in areas with strong presbyterian support.

Highland culture had, however, suffered in terms of status, prestige and leadership. These elements were increasingly in the possession of the evangelical, presbyterian church. It is unlikely that this situation would be reversed by ministers collecting poems and stories from their parishioners. In many Highland communities the church remained in possession of the dominant social structure and the dominant ideology. As a result of this subordinate position, Gaelic culture suffered a loss of confidence and adopted an underground role. If the church disapproved it is easy to understand why Gaelic culture went underground and why ministers were of the opinion that such practices had entirely gone out of use.

There are thus points that can be made to moderate the indictment against the church in this area. Yet many cultural expressions received cruel treatment from the church. The presbyterian church in the Highlands experienced great difficulty in separating Gaelic culture from pre-Christian superstition. Songs and stories were thus rejected as they prohibited the people from cutting their links with the past. In this, some ministers did not discriminate between witchcraft, belief in fairies, folk tale or fiddle tune. Such beliefs and practices were held by some to have no place in the Christian community. Both catholicism and moderatism were criticised by evangelicals for their lack of effort in rooting out superstitious belief and practice in the parish.

The links with superstitious ideas undoubtedly disadvantaged Gaelic culture in its acceptance by the church. In addition, the distinction between the sacred and the secular also shaped attitudes in the church. Worldly pursuits and secular activities were regarded, by some, as a distraction from the pre-eminent imperatives of the Christain life.

SUPERNATURAL

✻

There are many accounts by ministers of the survival of primitive rituals in their parishes. There are examples mentioned by ministers of bulls being sacrificed, ale being offered to the sea, healing stones built into houses, spells cast on cattle to withhold their milk and wax figures made and destroyed. When Donald MacQueen was appointed minister at Kilmuir in 1740, the belief in witchcraft was very common in so much that he had many prosecutions before his session. In 1791 a Gairloch tacksman, Kenneth MacKenzie, who had been put forward as Lochcarron catechist, was rejected because it was reported that he was using magical practices. Similar stories were still being told by ministers well into the nineteenth-century.

The presbyterian churches in the Highlands were committed to the eradication of all forms of magic and superstition in the parish. There was, however, a measure of uncertainty about some supernatural events, such as second sight, visions and miracles. The ability to foretell future events has been both shunned and applauded by the Highland church. It had been excluded as an unacceptable aspect of a superstitious society and welcomed as a spiritual gift. There are many accounts of ministers and church members foretelling deaths, predicting what text a minister would preach from, having foreknowledge of people in trouble and of

Finlay Munro's footprints. In 1827, while preaching near Invermoriston, Finlay Munro said that as proof that his words were true his footprints would remain visible. (Source: by kind permission, Knox Press, Free Church of Scotland, Edinburgh)

visitors whose arrival was imminent.

Mr Lachlan MacKenzie, minister of Lochcarron, was one to whom this ability was attributed. He once announced 'there are five young men present here today that shall be in eternity before this day, six weeks, and none of them above twenty-eight years of age'. This came true. John Kennedy, minister of Dingwall, provided a Christian rationale for second sight by describing it as 'the secret of the Lord' In 1827, the itinerant evangelist, Finlay Munro's prediction of the future had surprisingly long term effects. On this occasion he was preaching at Torgyle near Invermoriston. He was interrupted by several catholics from Glengarry. Finlay Munro said, as proof that his words were true, his footprints would remain visible. This was said in 1827 and his footprints have remained visible for most of this century.

There are a number of miraculous events which feature in

Highland church history. One of the most unusual took place by
the River Spey when a woman left instructions that her remains
should be laid with her husband's in the churchyard at Dalarossie,
on the other side of the River Spey. When the funeral party
reached the river, the waters parted and they crossed on dry land.
A large slate slab was erected at the point of crossing as a memorial
to the miraculous crossing of the Spey. The stone was close to Boat
of Garten but was later broken up by an opposing church faction.

The protestant churches in the Highlands had an ambivalent
attitude towards supernatural events. In a number of forms, supernatural events were accommodated within the church and
attributed to divine intervention. If, however, supernatural events
were associated with catholicism or some vestige of a pre-Christian
past they would be shunned along with the beliefs with which they
were linked.

A DISTINCTIVE SPIRITUALITY

❖

The predominant spirituality of the Highland church in the
nineteenth-century was given form and substance by the
Westminster documents and emotional intensity by the evangelical
impulse. The first provided the structure within which faith should
be practiced and the second provided the insistence that all other
pursuits, cultural or otherwise, should be subordinate to Christian
commitment.

The appeal of these factors was enhanced by the cultural
importance assigned to evangelical presbyterianism. It was
regarded as a defining transformation in Highland society that had
to be reinforced at every opportunity. In addition, the social
changes that evangelicalism brought about presented the church
with a greater degree of social control, enabling it to define the
spirituality of the Highlands and Islands. Thus the cultural conserv-
atism that has been identified in Highland spirituality can be traced
to these social factors.

Although the combination of presbyterianism and evangelicalism was perhaps not unique to the Highlands and Islands of
Scotland, its relationship to Highland society was quite distinctive.
This received further emphasis from the language through which it
was expressed and the culture within which it was set.

CHAPTER 9

Land

Land
❖
157

*'It may be that the clergy's silent acquiescence and even occasional
open support for the landlord has been exaggerated, but it is probably true
that not one in ten of the Highland clergymen supported the crofters in any
tangible way . . . some of them actively supported the clearances, preaching
to the people that their sufferings were God's judgement on them for their sins
and that resistance to constituted authority was sacrilege . . . a church that
considered the world a vale of tears, earthly affairs of little account, and
original sin one of the two central themes in human life could advise only
submission and resignation and an escape to religion.'*

Sorley MacLean

A persistent image in Highland church history is of the minister
who had more in common with landlords than people and in times
of clearance offered little or no support to the people. From this
perspective the church emphasised the rights of property,
encouraged the people to set their hopes on a spiritual homeland
and to regard their troubles as a result of their own sinfulness.
There were undoubtedly ministers who represented this position
but to assert that this was true of all ministers would be misleading.

It is not easy to obtain a clear understanding of the role of the
clergy in Highland land issues. There is contrasting evidence. In
some cases ministers were critical of evicting landlords and in other
cases such activity had their support. Not only is there the
difficulty of contrasting evidence but there is also the difficulty of
dealing with the widely held notion that the church failed to
respond to these questions. The extent to which this accurately
represented the Highland church is an elusive question.

A clearer picture might emerge if a wider survey of ministerial
attitudes were possible. Even if such evidence was available it
would be further complicated by the probability that what
ministers were prepared to commit to print might be very different

from what they confided to their parishioners. Indeed, this whole question of the church and land places an inordinate emphasis on the views and actions of relatively few ministers.

Some of the most damning accusations came from Donald MacLeod who was, at one point, a stonemason and Strathnaver resident. As such he was both a victim of and a witness to the Sutherland clearances and provided a bitter account of these events in *Gloomy Memories*. This book also served as a response to Harriet Beecher Stowe's *Sunny Memories of Foreign Lands*. She had previously visited the far north as a guest of the Duchess of Sutherland and had commented favourably on the land improvement policies and the benevolence of the proprietors. MacLeod's account was included initially in publications edited by Alexander MacKenzie. His publications included the *Celtic Magazine* and the *Scottish Highlander* and in 1883 a book entitled *The History of the Highland Clearances*. This contained a wide range of information on the clearances from a variety of sources.

Donald MacLeod accused the clergy of 'exhorting the people to quiet submission, helping to stifle their cries, telling them that all their sufferings came from the hand of God, and was a just punishment for their sins' and indeed that ministers told the people that the clearances were a 'merciful interposition of providence to bring them to their repentance rather than to send them all to hell, as they so richly deserve'. He added that the clergy were 'continually preaching submission, declaring these proceedings were fore-ordained of God and denouncing the vengeance of heaven and eternal damnation on those who should presume to make the least resistance'.[1]

Although MacLeod argued that the clergy employed their Calvinist theology to defend the clearances, he also saw a material motivation. He pointed out that 'beside getting their hill pasturage enclosed, their tillage lands were extended, new manses and offices were built for them and roads made specifically for their accom-modation and every arrangement made for their advantage'.[2] MacLeod saw little deviation in the views of the Sutherland clergy as they were all, except Mr Sage, 'consenting parties to the expulsion of the inhabitants'. Both MacLeod and MacKenzie were important in shaping opinion on the role of the clergy during the clearances. Their accounts contributed to the view that in the earlier clearances the church utterly failed the people.

It is possible to find examples of both opposition and complicity within the nineteenth-century church. Yet the strongest message that comes across from both nineteenth-century comment-ators and present day historians is that the church generally offered little support to the people. This has been variously attributed to evangelical spirituality which placed more hope in a future world; to a form of Calvinist theology which accepted present adversity as the immutable will of God or to the social and economic affiliations of some of the clergy.

Not only has the church been criticised for failing in its duty but it has also been suggested that the church had a profound effect on Highland character. There is, however, a measure of disagreement over this. In connection with this question it can be asked if the church rendered the people helplessly passive, undermined resistance by elevating spiritual goals and then further demoralised a down trodden people by imposing an additional burden of guilt? Alternatively, did the church in the Highlands provide a marginalised and apparently powerless culture with self confidence, organisational abilities and leadership that enabled them to resist?

On this point historians are not in complete agreement. There is, however, probably more support for the view that Highland evangelicalism produced a passive population. Professor Macinnes, for one, has portrayed evangelicalism as not being concerned with the material world but offering a reward in the next world and as such was a 'barrier to crofting radicalism'. He has described evangelicalism as producing a 'politically regressive passivity'.[3]

Similarly Professor Devine has commented that 'the evangelical gospel was not a theology of social justice but a faith designed to promote personal spiritual growth and commitment. It offered solace and the certainty of punishment for the oppressor, not by man but by God and so deflected opposition to the other side of the grave'. Devine, however, does not see this as 'an overt conspiracy of co-operation with the political and social estab-lishment but because of its evangelical commitment to the spiritual values of Christian awakening, conversion and salvation'.[4]

A number of other writers have emphasised the spiritual side of evangelicalism and suggested that this undermined ministers' involvement with the concerns of this world. Thus evangelicalism has been perceived as producing an acquiescent attitude and the evangelical clergy of encouraging this attitude among the evicted. From this perspective the church in the Highlands and Islands does not emerge with a good image and a number of criticisms have been directed at ministers. They have been criticised for supporting landlord policy and their property rights. They have been criticised for not condemning the cruelty and injustice of landlord policy. They have been criticised for telling their people that their suffering was a result of their sin. Ministers have also been criticised for offering no alternative for emigration, for failing to support their people in their difficulties and for condemning resistance by the people.

John MacInnes, minister of Halkirk, writing in 1951, identified this mood in the Gaelic spiritual poets. He said in the poets 'we find the profound spiritual experiences which during the last two centuries moulded the character of the people and enabled them to meet . . . stern and difficult circumstances with courage and hope'.[5] Perhaps the best example which represents this mood is Dugald Buchanan's poem *An Gaisgeach*. In this poem, Buchanan compares the classical military heroes of the past and comments that the true hero is someone who gains control of their inner life; someone who subdues his or her passions. This would have certainly given Christians the ability to face their difficulties with hope but it might not give them an ethic to attack and ameliorate these difficulties. In the face of eviction and social oppression, this feature of Highland spirituality has often attracted criticism. This is, however, only one mood and other commentators have seen Highland spirituality as being a more complex phenomenon that directly or indirectly provided Highlanders with confidence and with an ethic of social justice which enabled them to resist their oppressors.

RESISTANCE

❊

There are a range of opinions on this topic, from those who would contend that there was a direct link between Christian faith and resistance to those who would concede that the Christian faith provided a number of qualities which, in a different context, enabled Highland people to respond to the challenges which they would meet in this life. There are some historians who regard evangelicalisn as profoundly passive yet acknowledge that it also indirectly empowered Highland communities. Professor Macinnes has noted that the revival meetings and associated debates generated a self-confidence and organisational ability which can be held to have equipped the crofter spiritually, morally and intellectually for a political struggle.

James Hunter has identified a positive side to the evangelical contribution in its link with land reform. He has claimed that 'it was through the medium of a profoundly evangelical faith that crofters first developed a forward looking critique of the situation created in the Highlands by the actions of the region's landowning and, therefore, ruling class'. For Hunter the Disruption 'and the revivals which preceded it were largely instrumental in welding a disparate collection of small tenants into a community capable of acting collectively and possessing a distinctive character and outlook'.[6]

Hunter, therefore, sees a link between evangelicalism and land reform. Evangelicalism, he would contend, gave crofters the ability to criticise and resist their landlords, There is also similar support for this view in the work of Eric Richards. Richards has argued that 'after the Disruption there is little doubt that the Free Church ministers seized hold of social leadership and eventually helped the crofting community to organise itself against the landlords and sheepfarmers'.[7]

In Richards' writing it is claimed that it was revivalism that 'provided a bond which eventually created sufficient cohesion to permit the crofters to challenge the landlords. In this argument there is a connecting rod between the early religious movements, the Disruption of 1843 and the Land Leagues of the 1880s'.[8] A distinct community was created by evangelicalism and from this, leadership, confidence and resistance emerged. Neither Hunter nor Richards, however, would argue that it was necessarily ministers that led in the land agitation. Indeed, by the 1880s, Hunter considered most Free Church ministers to be on the side of the landlords.

Another historian who pointed to the indirect benefits was Victor Durkacz. He has argued that evangelicalism 'restored self-confidence to the demoralised poor of the Highlands'. The evangelicals were responsible for generating the 'organisational abilities which eventually found expression in political action'. Durkacz, however, cautions that for every instance where it can be shown that evangelicals were critical of landlords 'ten examples can be cited to demonstrate that evangelicalism was politically quietist'.[9] Some support for this is found in I M M MacPhail's study of the 'Crofters' War' in the 1880s. Although MacPhail mentions a number of instances in which Free Church ministers became involved in land agitation he also suggests that their emphasis on spiritual concerns undermined a more thorough engagement with crofters' grievances.[10]

The above commentators would argue for an indirect link between Highland evangelicalism and later political activity. Professor Meek has suggested that there is also a more direct link between evangelicalism and social action. At no point, however, does he contend that this would be true of all Highland Christians who were evangelical. In his view the Bible offered a framework for condemning oppression, and he argues that 'it is no exaggeration to claim that the Bible was a key document in the success of the movement for crofters' rights'. In his research Professor Meek has brought to the fore many ministers and laymen who used the Bible in this way and were thus sympathetic to land agitation. Yet he also supports the view that Highland communities benefited indirectly from the experience gained in times of revival. He has argued that 'when the Highland land agitation began to emerge in the 1870s, it owed much to a new confidence which had been engendered by the preceding revivals'.[11]

The picture that emerges is that evangelicalism emphasised spiritual goals and this often undermined a thoroughgoing engagement with social oppression. However, it has also been claimed that a number of qualities that resulted from evangelicalism were of indirect benefit to Highland communities in resisting oppression. In addition, evidence can be found of some whose Christian faith provided them with an ethic to resist oppression.

CLEARANCE 1790s TO 1830s

❊

The response of the church to land issues will be considered under three headings; clearance, 1790s to1830s, famine, 1840s and 1850s and land agitation, 1880s. The linking of these themes to these years should not be seen as an exclusive relationship as there was a much greater measure of continuity and overlap than such headings would indicate. They are, however, a useful way of looking at the church's response to these matters.

The clearances were certainly not limited to the late eighteenth and early nineteenth centuries. This was, however, a period in which Highland society experienced an unprecedented level of social upheaval as a result of clearance. The clearances of this period were produced by the introduction of large-scale sheep farming. Even without moving people from their homes this weakened the basis of the Highland economy by limiting room for cattle and crops. In many areas landlords began clearing their estates in order to make way for sheep. Their preference for this policy flowed from the increased rental return which they could obtain from sheep farms. In the early nineteenth-century the most infamous clearances took place in Sutherland. There were, however, many other areas that experienced similar upheaval.

In the earlier period there were some examples of Church of Scotland ministers who spoke out strongly against landlord eviction policies. Lachlan MacKenzie is probably the most well known of this period. He was minister of Lochcarron and died in 1819. He delivered a series of sermons against the appropriators of land in Highland society. He spoke against the the custom of depopulating parishes for the purpose of making room for sheepwalks. His series of sermons was based on Isiaiah 5:8 which says 'Woe unto them that join house to house, that lay field to field, till there be no place that they may be placed alone in the midst of the earth'.

The missionary minister of Harris, Mr Alexander MacLeod, found himself in trouble for challenging both factor and landlord. The conflict arose when the Harris proprietor was planning to convert a large area into a sheep farm. In order to do this a number of families were to be moved from their land. MacLeod protested against this proposal. and on this occasion was able to protect the people from eviction. In 1811 eviction was again being considered. MacLeod again appealed on behalf of the people, he approached the factor and wrote to the proprietor who was proposing to move forty families. MacLeod complained about the factor; a libel suit followed and MacLeod had to defend himself before his employer; the Royal Bounty Committee. In his defence he said 'the clergyman is the servant of that God who delights in justice . . . in my local situation, apparent instances of injustice, if not cruelty, have made me speak and write against some proceedings, which in time past exposed me, and now also, to the whim and caprice of a young squire, and the malicious rancour of his designing factor'.[12]

Mr Roderick MacRae, parish minister of Applecross wrote in the 1790s in the *Old Statistical Account*, that 'the oppression of the landholders is a general complaint in the Highlands . . . another circumstance which is unfriendly to population is the engrossing of farms for sheep walks. Whoever would wish to see the population of this country flourishing should do all in their power to put a stop to the sheep traffic, and to introduce manufacturers among the people'.

Mr Roderick MacLeod, parish minister of Snizort, also offered some critical comments in the *New Statistical Account*. MacLeod regarded the tacksmen as a hindrance to progress and commented that 'people are discontented with their situation; and if their complaints are not more loudly heard, one great reason is, that the system of farming has placed them in such absolute dependence on the tacksman, as to preclude any hope of amelioration'.

In this period we are forcibly confronted with comments about the failure of the established church and yet we have the above commments of MacKenzie, MacRae, R MacLeod and A MacLeod. In addition there are examples of ministers employing strong language to describe the clearances. David Carment, minister of Rosskeen, wrote in 1838 of the clearances as 'a serious evil'. It was said of John MacDonald, minister of Helmsdale, that 'neither in youth nor in his maturer years could he regard the clearing of such a population in any other light than as a sin against heaven'. Eric Findlater, minister of Lochearnhead, published a sermon in which he preached against landlord eviction policies and said that God's judgement was awaiting landlords. There are other ministers and church elders that could be added to this list.

Even the role of David MacKenzie, minister of Farr, is by no means clear. MacKenzie was accused by Donald MacLeod of colluding with the proprietors, as having read the eviction notices to his people in Sutherland in 1818 and 1819 and urging them to accept their fate as part of the immutable will of God. MacKenzie is accused of abandoning his people and providing a justification for the landlords policies. Yet in *Disruption Worthies*, published in the 1870s, it says of MacKenzie and the Strathnaver clearances, 'Mr MacKenzie was applied to for his concurrence so as to give, it is supposed, a show of expediency to the measure, but this he absolutely refused to do'. In addition, Eric Richards describes a letter to James Loch from MacKenzie as 'probably the most comprehensive rejection of the assumptions of the Sutherland policy uttered during these years'.[13]

Another minister who left a mixed record on land issues was Mr Finlay MacRae, Church of Scotland minister of North Uist from 1818 till his death in 1858. There are some traditions which suggest that MacRae gave his support to eviction policies. Yet there are also accounts that link MacRae to the eviction disturbances in Sollas in 1849, when the people refused to move in accordance with Lord MacDonald's order. In the disturbances and arrests that followed, MacRae apparently intervened, appealed on behalf of the people and put up bail for those arrested.

In Sutherland, Donald MacLeod identified only one minister that supported the people. His assessment was supported by John Prebble who said that 'with few noble exceptions the ministers chose the side of the landlords'. At this stage in the Highlands there were over 200 parish ministers plus missionary ministers. In the absence of accurate information on their opinions the evidence of a handful is hardly adequate evidence to overturn the established consensus. However, there is enough evidence to suggest that the model of the minister who abandoned his people for dogma or material gain was not to be found in every parish.

FAMINE 1840s AND 1850s

*

The land issues in this period were complicated by the potato famine which devastated areas of the Highlands in 1846 and beyond. The solution suggested by many was that the land could not sustain the people; further clearance was required and emigration would alone ease the problem. The most reliable and informative writing on this subject has been produced by Professor Devine.

In 1846, in the immediate aftermath of the onset of famine, the

*Thomas McLauchlan, minister of St Columba's Free Church, Edinburgh.
His biographer said of him that he 'objected to the pitiless extrusion of Highland families
from their holdings and casting them poor and helpless on the world. To that,
nothing could reconcile him as long as he lived'.*

Free Church conducted a detailed survey into the importance of the potato in the Highland diet. Forty-four areas were selected in the Highlands and Islands. The results showed the potato was one-half to three-quarters of the food consumption in thirty-four per cent of the areas surveyed, four-fifths of the food consumption in thirty-two per cent of the areas surveyed and in some areas the potato formed as much as eleven-twelfths of the food consumption. Of the thirteen areas most dependent on the potato, nine were in the Islands.

In 1846 the Free Church also conducted a survey of the extent of potato failure in the crofting areas. In this, seventy-six per cent of ministers in the crofting areas said their area had experienced entire failure of the potato crop. The Free Church, therefore, estimated that in 1846, as many as 200,000 people were destitute

and a further 200,000 would soon be facing a similar plight. The
Free Church was the first body to respond to the Highland famine.
It collected funds and information and began to distribute relief
throughout the region. When Government responded to the
famine the Free Church then handed over its relief organisation to
the parliamentary agencies.[14]

This famine resulted in high levels of emigration between the
years 1846 to 1857. In some areas of the Highlands there was a
level of coercion involved in this emigration. A number of sources
of opinion took the view that the Highlands were overpopulated
and could not support its population. Thus, the emigration of a
significant proportion of the Highland population was desirable.
There was, however, some resistance to this view from within the
Free Church.

In the first few years of the potato famine the Free Church had
been concerned with relief and in gathering information. With the
preparation and publication of *The Report to the Board of Supervision* by
Sir John McNeill on the Highlands and Islands in 1851 there was
an opportunity for the Free Church to provide a more analytical
response to the problems. The McNeill Report followed on from
the Poor Law Act of 1845 and focused on poverty.

This Report urged emigration as a remedy to the destitution in
the Highlands, and that funds should be made available for this.
Many Highland churchmen were not surprised at this. They did
not expect McNeill to be impartial as he was considered to be too
close to landed interests.

Indeed, many in the Free Church had no confidence in the
McNeill committee from the outset. Mackintosh MacKay, James
Begg and Thomas McLauchlan protested against the emigration
solution. They called for a wider enquiry that would also consider
landlord policies. The Free Church Destitution Committee
contended that Highland overcrowding was not the problem but
landlord land policy was, and McNeill's Report was not addressing
this.

On 29 January 1851, James Begg wrote to the *Witness*,
arguing that the McNeill committee was operating on the basis of
a number of unfounded notions which must be exposed and
abandoned. In the first place, 'the notion that the Highlands are
overpopulated'. Begg argued that the Highlands could support

twice the present number but not if good land is being put under sheep and deer and the people are driven to the fringes'. Begg argued that the destitution of the Highlands was caused by the clearance system 'by which the people are huddled together in corners where patches of ground are given them of the very worst description of soil' and by 'depriving them of their hill pasture for the purpose of its being added to large sheep farms or deer forests'.

At the point when the McNeill committee was set up the Free Church Assembly's Committee on Highland Destitution sent James Begg and Mackintosh MacKay to London to protest against the emigration solution and to appeal for a wider enquiry. The Free Church Presbytery of Edinburgh also sent a petition to Sir George Gray, Secretary of State for the Home Department. They wanted an enquiry into the causes of destitution and added that 'meantime your petitioners are anxious that the Government shall not hastily listen to any representations on the subject of alleged overpopulation or the supposed necessity of emigration'. One member of the Edinburgh Presbytery, Thomas McLauchlan, said of emigration that 'he suspected that, were the parties who in a great measure produced this misery and were now crying for emigration, to emigrate themselves, the country would not suffer much by the loss'.[15]

Following the publication of the McNeill Report the messages coming from Free Church sources remained the same. An editorial in the *Witness* on 26 July 1851 said 'we object to this proposal for various reasons' and added that the McNeil Report paid no attention to the people; 'their hunger, their unjust and cruel treatment, the iniquity of the system under which they have suffered is not so much as hinted at; but the simple landlord's remedy alone – carry them off.'

In addition, the Free Church Destitution Committee felt 'called upon to express their strong objection to the measures now prepared', and petitioned both Houses of Parliament against the Bill resulting from the McNeill Report. 'That this committee feel assured that no amount of emigrating either voluntary or compulsory will confer the slightest benefit upon the general population of this interesting portion of the empire unless some remedial measures be adopted to strike at the causes of the evil and not to palliate their effects'.[16] When Mackintosh MacKay was asked about the necessity of emigration he said that there was 'no necessity whatsoever; the very idea is monstrous'.

The Free Church was looking for a wider analysis that included land management and would introduce a new land arrangement. They were also looking for considerable Government funding, the restoration of pasture land to the crofting townships and a reversal of the landlords enthusiasm for sheep and deer. This, some identified as the root problem. Despite Free Church opposition there were, of course ministers, Free Church and Church of Scotland, who could see no alternative to emigration and some went on record for the McNeill Committee as saying this.

LAND AGITATION IN THE 1880s

❋

There had been a measure of resistance to landlord policies from the 1790s onward. The 1880s, however, saw a greater degree of agitation, more effective organisation, more media attention and increased external interest. There was a notable protest in Bernera, Lewis, in 1874 and in Skye from 1882, protests increased. In Skye the people took the initiative by refusing rent payments and re-occupying grazing lands. In other instances, sheep farms were occupied, fences were torn down and land was reclaimed. This began what is now referred to as the Crofters' War and initiated a wider campaign for crofters' rights.

Associations were formed to pursue the aims of fair rent, security of tenure and the redistribution of land. The principal body was the Highland Land Law Reform Association. This was established in 1883 and its aim was to 'unite Highlanders and their friends at home and abroad in endeavouring by constitutional means to obtain for the Highland people the right to live on their native soil under equitable conditions'. Additional support was provided by crofter candidates who stood for Parliament in the election of 1885. A Royal Commission was appointed to look into these matters and took its name from its chairman, Lord Napier. The Napier Commission questioned a number of people at different points throughout the Highlands and Islands and reported in 1884. It is regarded as a limited but significant victory for crofters' rights. This resulted in the Crofters' Holdings (Scotland) Act of 1886 which provided security of tenure as long

*Donald MacCallum was censured by the Presbytery of Skye and accused of stirring up
the poor against the rich and making the illiterate dissatisfied with their condition. An older
member of presbytery said, 'we remember how in the days of youth the fire burned in
our hearts also as we read of the wrongs inflicted on the poor. The empty glens with the
hearth-stones open to the heavens proclaim man's inhumanity to man, but we had to
learn the lessons of patience. The wrongs of a century cannot be righted in a day.'*

as rents were paid, while crofts could be bequeathed to relatives
and limitations were placed on the rights of landlords.

In this period the evangelical church is still generally regarded
by many commentators as emphasising spiritual goals and disreg-
arding material conditions. The church, therefore, is generally
perceived as an extremely reluctant supporter of land agitation in
this period. There is a difficulty here in that despite the above
image most of the leaders of the Free Church from the Highlands
identified themselves as supporters of the land agitation. Men such
as Murdoch MacAskill of Dingwall, James MacCulloch, of
Glasgow, Thomas McLauchlan of Edinburgh, Donald John
Martin of Oban, Gustavus Aird of Creich, Mackintosh MacKay of

Tarbert, John Kennedy of Dingwall, Angus Galbraith of Lochalsh, John MacMillan of Ullapool and many others in the Free Church offered strong support for land agitation.

Murdoch MacAskill, who succeeded John Kennedy as minister of Dingwall Free Church supported land reform and agitation. He shared a platform with the American land reformer, Henry George, and worked with Munro Ferguson, the Ross candidate for Parliament, who was a supporter of land reform. MacAskill was known to have favoured land raids and considered land reform to be a task for Government. Earlier when MacAskill was minister at Greenock Free Church, he remained interested and in touch with Highland land issues and was familiar with crofter difficulties.

MacAskill gave evidence before the Napier Commission in 1883. Before this he had sent schedules to almost every parish in the Highlands to obtain information on the condition of crofters. His biographer said that when he moved from Greenock to Dingwall the land agitation was at its height and 'he threw himself with characteristic energy into the campaign'. At a later point he intervened on behalf of the Park Raiders. In 1887 a conference of Highland ministers, chaired by Dr Gustavus Aird, met at Dingwall to discuss land issues. At this conference MacAskill played a prominent part in urging upon the Government the necessity of further land reform.

Thomas McLauchlan, who was minister of St Columba's Free Church in Edinburgh and had previously been at Moy and Stratherrick, spoke out strongly and consistently against deer forests and sheep farms. He condemned the depopulation of the countryside and refused to consider emigration as a solution. Along with other ministerial colleagues, McLauchlan wanted more land for crofters, manufacturing introduced and Government financial aid. He thought a few harbours built throughout the Highlands would be better use of Government funds 'than slaughtering Afghans and Zulus'.

In the many articles which he wrote for newspapers on the Highland land issue, he demonstrated a wide knowledge of the many clearances that had occurred since the 1780s. He refused to believe that the land was overpopulated and the people indolent. His biographer said that McLauchlan objected to the 'pitiless extrusion of Highland families from their holdings, and casting them poor and helpless on the world. To that nothing could reconcile him as long as he lived'.[17]

Other Free Church ministers shared these views. In Ullapool, John MacMillan protested against eviction, wrote to Highland newspapers and addressed public meetings in Inverness and elsewhere. Donald John Martin, minister of Oban and before that Stornoway, was critical of the clearances and called for larger crofts, fair rents and security of tenure. This was not a position adopted exclusively by younger ministers. Dr Aird had been minister of Creich since 1843. He supported land reform, criticised landlords and gave his support to land raids such as the Park Deer Raid. Dr Kennedy, minister of Dingwall, is another that can be added to the list of ministers who regarded landlord eviction policies as unacceptable. Kennedy described how the owners of the soil began to act as if they were also 'owners of the people, and, disposed to regard them as the vilest part of their estate. They treated them without respect to the requirements of righteousness or to the dictates of mercy . . . families by hundreds were driven across the sea, or were gathered, as the sweepings of the hillsides, into wretched hamlets on the shore. By wholesale evictions wastes were formed for the red deer that the gentry of the nineteenth-century might indulge in the sports of the savages of three centuries before'.[18]

There was also considerable activity in the courts of the Free Church in the 1880s in connection with the land issue. Questions relating to land were debated by the Free Church General Assembly and on a few occasions the Assembly was asked by the subordinate church courts to petition Parliament for a reform of the land laws.

The Church of Scotland was more reserved in its response to land questions in the 1880s. It was, however, a Church of Scotland minister who was regarded as the foremost land campaigner among the clergy. Donald MacCallum was minister at Arisaig, Waternish, Tiree and Lochs. He was in great demand as a speaker on Highland land issues. On one occassion he was arrested and jailed in Portree. He was also censured by his presbytery for stirring up the poor against the rich and making the 'illiterate' dissatisfied with their condition. In 1889 MacCallum moved to Lochs. He had a small congregation, a comfortable income and a large glebe. It was the large glebe that attracted the attention of cottars from Crossbost and Leurbost. In 1893 a land raid took place on MacCallum's glebe by landless people in Lochs.

Within the Church of Scotland, MacCallum had support from a few fellow ministers in the Highlands and Islands. Among these were his brother Malcolm, minister of Strontian, and also Angus MacIver, minister of Uig in Lewis. His father, also Angus MacIver, had been a teacher and catechist in Lewis and had shared similar views on land in the Highlands.

There would appear to have been more direct church involvement with land issues in the 1880s, principally from the Free Church. Evidence for this can be found in the biographies of ministers, in articles in Highland newspapers, in evidence to the Napier Commission and in the records of church courts. Many of the ministers that spoke out on these issues were leaders in the Free Church and had a significant effect in shaping opinion in that church in the nineteenth-century. Even Alexander MacKenzie, who was a prominent critic of the church, commented favourably on the stand taken by the Free Church in the 1880s. He said that their position 'though taken somewhat tardily, ought to secure for that church the gratitude of the Highland race whatever section of the Christian church they belong to'.

Free Church elders and church members also demanded land reform. It was not uncommon for land raids to begin and end with prayer and some elders spoke publicly on land reform and provided valuable information for the Napier Commission. In Skye, Free Church involvement in land issues led one tacksman to describe the Free Church as the 'fenians we have in Skye'.

MIGRATION
❋

In the course of the eighteenth-century sizeable Highland communities developed in Scotland's cities. They had developed for a number of reasons; temporary or permanent work, clearance, famine and army service. There was certainly a measure of upheaval in the Highlands in this period and employment opportunities were limited. This encouraged some people to move. To an extent the crofting areas depended on the income that seasonal migrants would return with, either from farming in the Lowlands

Edinburgh Gaelic Church, c 1870. Gaelic churches existed in Scotland's cities to cater for the spiritual needs of Highlanders living and working in the Lowlands. (Source: EPL)

or fishing on the east coast. These factors led to the creation of Gaelic-speaking communities in Edinburgh, Glasgow, Greenock, Aberdeen, Perth and Dundee.

The first minister who looked after the needs of Highlanders in Edinburgh was Neil MacVicar. He was appointed to the West Kirk in 1707 and once a month he held a Gaelic service. In the summer MacVicar held open-air services in Gaelic in the Lauriston area above the Grassmarket. In 1710 the General Assembly of the Church of Scotland officially recognised this and asked MacVicar to include the needs of Highlanders in his duties. He was to baptise, catechise and preach to Gaelic Highlanders in Edinburgh. MacVicar continued to do so until 1747 and was noted for his courage in expressing in prayer the thinly veiled hope that Prince Charles Edward Stuart's days on earth would not be unnecessarily prolonged. He prayed asking that 'this young person who has come among us seeking an earthly crown, do thou, in thy merciful favour, grant him a heavenly one'. This was while the Jacobite army was in charge of the city.

With MacVicar's death in 1747 there was a gap in Gaelic religious provision. Services were later held in the Relief Church in South College Street. In the mid 1760s when Dugald Buchanan was in Edinburgh overseeing the publication of the Gaelic New Testament, he regularly preached to Highlanders in Gaelic. In 1766 a group of Edinburgh businessmen, who were concerned about the needs of Highlanders in Edinburgh, began to collect funds to provide a separate ministry for them.

The SSPCK was approached for assistance and in 1769 a Gaelic chapel was built in Castle Wynd. The Gaelic chapel had no official standing in the church's organisation and as such it had no kirk session or eldership or access to church courts. The first minister was Joseph Robertson MacGregor who had formerly been an SSPCK teacher in Perthshire. MacGregor died in 1801 and was followed by James McLauchlan who subsequently moved, in 1809, to Moy in Inverness-shire. McLauchlan was followed by John MacDonald who was later to be known as 'the apostle of the north'. While in Edinburgh, MacDonald's itinerant tendency was obvious as he preached in Glasgow, Perth, Stirling, Dundee, Port Glasgow and Greenock. MacDonald left Edinburgh in 1813. A new Gaelic chapel was completed in North College

Street in 1812 and the last service was in Castle Wynd in 1815. There was also a catholic Highland chapel in Edinburgh from 1780. This was located in Blackfriars Wynd which was just off the High Street. This was for Gaelic speakers and the first priest was Robert Menzies from Perthshire.

Gaelic religious provision commenced in Glasgow in much the same way as it did in Edinburgh. Mr Neil Gillies, who was minister of the Tron Kirk, was a Gaelic speaker and ministered to Glasgow's Gaelic community from 1690 till his death in 1701. This was in addition to his other duties. In response to the increasing numbers of Gaelic-speaking Highlanders in Glasgow the Ramshorn church extended a call to Mr John MacLaurin, minister of Luss. The Dumbarton Presbytery was reluctant to release MacLaurin and based this on the General Assembly's ruling that Gaelic-speaking Highland ministers should not be settled in the Lowlands. In response the Ramshorn congregation argued that there were more Gaelic speakers in Glasgow than in Luss. The Commission of the Assembly agreed and MacLaurin was free to accept the call to Glasgow. He was advised to pay special attention to the Glasgow Highlanders and to administer the sacraments, catechise and preach to them. He applied himself to these tasks between the years 1721 and 1754.

From this beginning there was an increase in both Highlanders and Gaelic congregations in Glasgow. By 1800 Glasgow had three Gaelic congregations and this doubled within a relatively short space of time. The increase of congregations was in response to the rise in Gaelic speakers in Glasgow and also as a result of divisions in existing congregations. In addition to the presbyterian congregations there was also provision for the catholic Highlanders in Glasgow. In 1791 Father Alexander MacDonald from Glenurquhart was settled in Glasgow. He made use of temporary accommodation at first but by 1797 a chapel was opened. There was also religious provision for Gaelic speakers in other Scottish towns at this time. In Aberdeen, Perth, Greenock and Dundee, between the years 1788 and 1793, provision was made for the spiritual needs of Gaelic speakers. The presence of Gaelic-speaking communities in Lowland cities in the eighteenth and nineteenth centuries and their need for religious provision was related, in part, to land difficulties experienced within the Highlands.

For as long as the clearances are regarded as an tragic feature of Highland history, questions will be asked about the role of the clergy. It is an area that has a number of difficulties. There is an absence of information, which hinders a clear statement of the performance of the clergy. In addition, there is no agreed standard of what the churches had to do to escape the charge of having failed the people. It is an area in which an overdue emphasis is placed on the clergy. When comments are made about the church providing leadership in Highland communities it is not just ministers that are being referred to; elders, deacons, catechists, teachers, missionaries and the men are included. Sadly, there is only a small glimpse available of their involvement in land issues. This is unfortunate as the lay leadership of the church in the Highlands would undoubtedly be more familiar with the insecurity attached to eviction and possibly more sympathetic to the distress of those evicted. If a wider picture of the contribution of this group were available it is arguable that it could alter significantly the image of the church in relation to land issues.

One clear example is the Lewis Bard, Murdo MacLeod, who was a lay preacher as well as being a poet and hymn-writer. In one of his poems, *Fàsachadh na Dùthcha*, he described the plight of evicted families and, with reference to scripture, outlined what their oppressors deserved. Donald MacCallum said of Murdo MacLeod that 'in imparting courage to the sufferers and in strengthening the hands of their deliverers in the time of the crofters' agitation, no one did more than Murdo MacLeod'.

Thus, there remain difficulties in evaluating the role of the church in the Highlands in this period. Despite some useful evidence, it is difficult to measure the extent and effectiveness of the church's contribution to the land struggle. It is easy enough to identify a wide range of opinions on land agitation in the Highland church. It is not quite so easy to argue that one particular response was more representative. The balance of scholarship would, however, regard the church as avoiding serious engagement in these issues and adopting a more passive role. Most commentators emphasised the pre-eminence of spiritual concerns and the reluctance of the church to engage in material concerns. However, in the light of the available evidence it is reasonable to revise the view that Highland evangelicalism was politically passive and devoid of involvement in land issues and this world's material concerns. A common image of a Highland minister; friendly with landlords, having only spiritual concerns, linking suffering with sin and producing a passive population needs to be revised. Such an image, although having its representatives, cannot claim to have monopolised the church in the Highlands in the nineteenth-century.

CHAPTER 10

Secession

'I saw this bastard child being formed in the womb of the Free Church when Drs Dods and Bruce were appointed professors, but as the constitution was not changed I did not leave the church, but now this bastard child is born in the Declaratory Act, whatever others will do, I am done with the Declaratory Act church forever.'

Archibald Crawford

FREE CHURCH ELDER, ARGYLL. 1893

The Free Presbyterian Church was formed by Free Church dissidents in 1893. The immediate cause was the Free Church Declaratory Act. Those who left the Free Church considered the Declaratory Act to have altered the beliefs on which the Free Church was based. There had been within the Highlands an increasing dissatisfaction with the direction and management of the Free Church. This created the climate within which the Declaratory Act was considered to be the final offence against those who were determined to defend the principles of the Disruption Free Church and who have been thus likened to the Spartans who held the pass at Thermopylae, yet with more success. From the outset they have attracted a measure of scorn. The members of the Free Presbyterian Church have, however, continued to see themselves as being the legitimate heirs of the Disruption tradition.

The Free Presbyterians faced a daunting task. With minimal resources, a handful of ministers had to make provision for congregations that were scattered throughout the Highlands and Islands. They faced hardship in the task that was set before them and also in weathering the antagonistic response which they received from their former colleagues in the Free Church.

In this adversity they were sustained by their belief in the crucial importance of the stand they were taking. To a great extent the hostility and hardship they encountered was matched by the strength of their belief that they were holding to the truths of

*Donald MacFarlane, Free Presbyterian Minister of Raasay and Dingwall. On the fiftieth
anniversary of the Disruption, MacFarlane protested and severed his connection with the Free
Church. (Source: by kind permission, Free Presbyterian Archive, Inverness)*

Scripture when all around them others were falling away. A sense
of their place in history sustained them. Those whom the Free
Presbyterians parted from, however, might not have shared their
view of the importance which they attached to their movement.

The Free Presbyterian Church was predominantly a Highland
and Island development. Its leaders and nearly all of its supporters
belonged to the Highland church. It was, however, developments
outwith the Highlands that led to the formation of the Free
Presbyterian Church in 1893. It is, therefore, necessary to consider
some of the larger national developments against which the Free
Presbyterian secession must be understood.

UNION DISCUSSIONS

❖

In the nineteenth-century most of the developments in Highland
church history involved the Church of Scotland and the Free

Donald MacDonald, Free Presbyterian Minister of Shieldaig. A former colleague said of MacDonald that 'he had no great grasp of mind . . . but he was a man of rare attainments in the life of godliness.' (Source: by kind permission, Free Presbyterian Archive, Inverness)

Church.   The other main Scottish presbyterian church was the United Presbyterian Church, formed in 1847 from the union of the United Secession Church and the Relief Church.   Both of these seceding churches had emerged from earlier divisions in the Church of Scotland and by the 1840s opposed all links between church and state.   Furthermore, the United Presbyterian Church was predominantly Lowland and urban.

In the 1860s and early 1870s the Free Church and the United Presbyterians explored the possibility of union.   Although the Free Church was founded on the establishment principle (state support for religion) and Chalmers had stated that those who had left the establishment in 1843 would be willing to return to a pure establishment, in practice they acted from the start as a voluntary church.   Not surprisingly, as the memory of Chalmers commitment to state connection faded, many in the Free Church found that they had much in common with their voluntary partner.

Union negotiations took place between the two denominations from 1863 to 1873. By this period many in the Free Church had already relaxed their commitment to establishment as a fundamental principle of the Free Church and now joined in condemning the 'advantage' given to the Church of Scotland by its establishment. This move was accelerated when, in 1874, the Church of Scotland abolished patronage and the Free Church formally gave its support to the disestablishment campaign. This reinforced the Free Church's drift away from holding to the necessity of state support for religion.

In this period, 1863 to 1873, there had been considerable opposition from within to the perceived dilution of Free Church principles and especially to the proposed merger with another denomination which was thoroughly antagonistic to any state connection. Although the majority had voted for union, a significant minority in the Free Church, led by Dr James Begg, opposed union with the United Presbyterians and defended the principles upon which they believed the Free Church had been founded in 1843. They maintained that union required the renunciation of certain Free Church principles and they considered that sacrificing principles central to the church of 1843, or leaving them as 'open questions', was too great a price to pay for ecclesiastical union. This minority in the Free Church who were opposed to union regarded the questions at stake of sufficient importance to justify their threatening the extreme course of separation. In addition to the matter of state connection there were a number of other areas of doctrine and practice that they felt were under threat in the changing church of the late nineteenth-century.

When the majority in the Free Church found themselves confronted with their own disruption, they backed down. It had become apparent by 1873 that the union contemplated could be brought about only at the cost of a devastating division within the Free Church itself. Thus the painful consequence of further division, resulting from union, caused the majority to retreat and suggest alternatively the mutual eligibility of Free Church and United Presbyterian ministers to each other's churches.

The initial opposition to union in the 1860s and 1870s was not simply a Highland phenomenon. It found support in many regions in Scotland. When union was again being considered in the 1890s, anti-unionism had become a Highland phenomenon. In less than twenty years the anti-union impulse had been marginalised to the Highland and Island parishes.

CHURCH OF SCOTLAND

❋

The union discussions between the Free Church and the United Presbyterians from 1863 to 1873 also contained implications for the Church of Scotland. In the first place the union discussions revealed a dissatisfied section within the Free Church that was not interested in union with the United Presbyterian Church nor in the compromises which would flow from this. They also had a firm commitment to the establishment principle and had little enthusiasm for a campaign to disestablish the Church of Scotland. Secondly, the union being considered would create a much larger church and put greater pressure on the Church of Scotland to defend its claim to be the established and endowed national church. Even without union, Robert Rainy, Principal of the Free Church's New College, argued that the Church of Scotland had a rather tenuous claim to be a national church as in some areas of Scotland 'no sensible difference would be made by its entire and immediate dissappearance'.[1]

In May 1874 the Church Patronage (Scotland) Bill was introduced to abolish patronage in the Church of Scotland and to place the right of electing a minister of the parish in the hands of the communicant members. This was introduced at the request of the General Assembly of the Church of Scotland and as a measure to strengthen and to perpetuate the establishment. It was also hoped that it would attract other presbyterians back to the established church. In particular this had the anti-union congregations of the Free Church in the Highlands in mind. Here was the great issue of the Disruption again being debated, but this time in a changed context which produced a rather paradoxical response. In 1874 the Church of Scotland favoured the abolition of patronage while the Free Church was opposed to the Bill.

As far as the Free Church and the United Presbyterian Church were concerned this bill did not change anything. The established church was still operating within the limitations laid down by the state. The Free Church and the United Presbyterian Church

THE REASON WHY?

Why has a Conservative Government brought into Parliament a Bill to abolish Patronage?

THE DUKE OF RICHMOND SAYS:—Because "it will strengthen and perpetuate the Establishment."

THE EARL OF ROSSLYN SAYS:—Because "it would lead to a great advancement in the Established Church of Scotland."

THE EARL OF ABERDEEN SAYS:—The measure will have the effect "of strengthening the Church of Scotland."

Why should this Bill be opposed?

1. Because it is intended thereby to "strengthen and perpetuate the Established Church."

2. Because it is Erastian for the State to confer a right on the people which they already possess from the Head of the Church.

3. Because the Bill proposes to make a present of £75,000 to the Established Church (the value of the Crown patronages), and to confiscate the patronages of Burghs, &c., to the extent of at least other £25,000.

4. Because in the Highlands the Established Church has no substantial existence. (Ministers draw their stipends from the State, but in some cases they have no communicants, and in numerous parishes they have no congregations worth the name.)

2

5. Because it does not redress the wrongs of the men and Churches, who for generations have testified against Patronage.

6. Because, while the abolition of Patronage is, in itself, a good thing, Disestablishment and Disendowment is a better. (The Bill leaves all the anomalies and the injustice of the present state of things untouched!)

Why should this Bill be met by a demand for Disestablishment?

1. Because nothing else can make the Church free. What Parliament can give to, Parliament can take from, a State Church.

2. Because Established Churches have neither kept "the faith," nor kept the people.

3. Because the history of Scotland and all other nations proves that Free Churches cannot now be looked for in connection with the State.

4. Because the Endowments (at least £300,000 a-year) are national property, and should not be appropriated by a mere section of the community.

5. Because the Church of Scotland is fettered in its action, and impeded in its testimony for truth, by being Established.

FELLOW CITIZENS!—The present Government, in asking Parliament to alter the subsisting arrangements between the Church and the State, really asks YOUR opinion.

Let your answer be, through your Representatives in the House of Commons,—Give the Church her freedom by separation from the State. Legislate in the interests of justice.

This is an uncharacteristically brief leaflet for the nineteenth-century stating the reasons why many in the Free Church and the United Presbyterian Church opposed the Bill to abolish patronage in the Church of Scotland. These arguments, however, were not popular throughout much of the Highlands.

argued that the state was still regulating its ecclesiastical affairs and therefore the established church could not claim spiritual independence. The Disruption was being redefined as essentially a campaign for spiritual independence rather than a campaign against patronage.

In the Church of Scotland it was argued that the Patronage Bill would simply acknowledge what had come to be current practice in that church. Patrons seldom exercised this right, it was claimed, and it was much more common for communicant members to choose the minister. By 1874 patronage, it was claimed, was virtually dead. *The Daily News* described the Bill as a 'tardy concession to necessity' as statute struggled to keep up with practice. In his speech to the House of Lords, the Duke of Argyll offered no opposition to the Bill to abolish patronage. He claimed that the people were much better qualified to select their ministers and he added that he could no more present any man he liked than he 'could fly to the moon'.

Such a Bill revealed the tensions in the Free Church at this time. In 1875 the Lowland-dominated Free Church Assembly supported the United Presbyterian Church's demand for the disestablishment and disendowment of the Church of Scotland. This, however, alienated those in the Free Church, especially those in the Highlands and Islands, who had opposed union and were strongly in favour of establishment. In 1874 there had been signs that the repeal of patronage was welcomed in the north and some sections of the Highland Free Church clearly felt that they had more in common with the established church than with the United Presbyterians. John Kennedy commented, following the abolition of patronage, 'it does seem a strange thing that any Free Churchman could be found who would not rejoice in this'.

In the 1880s and after, the established church began to take a fresh look at certain aspects of its work. In 1888 a special enquiry was set up into non-church-going and in 1890 a commission was asked to consider the religious condition of the people. The latter was under the convenership of Marshall Lang, minister of the Barony Church, Glasgow. Following these developments and the troubles within the Free Church, the Church of Scotland became more confident about its future in the Highlands. They would have to wait until 1929 before the Church of Scotland could again be strong in the Highlands but for the moment they felt that a better day was dawning.

By the 1890s there had, therefore, been a remarkable resurgence within the Church of Scotland. Press reports referred to the popularity of some Church of Scotland ministers in the Highlands and Islands and noted that their communion services were drawing the largest crowds since the Disruption. Such reports were coming from areas such as Snizort, Rogart and Farr which were renowned for their strong Free Church traditions. The opposition to state connections and endowment that had been developing within the Free Church was not welcome in the Highlands and had the effect of increasing Highland sympathy for the established church.

The established church, to an extent, responded to this

changing mood in the Highlands. Mr William Sutherland, Church of Scotland minister of Tobermory, delivered 'church defence' lectures throughout the Highlands and Islands to what were described as popular and enthusiastic gatherings. He spoke against voluntaryism and argued strongly in favour of national religion. Even in Lewis large crowds were reported to have attended Church of Scotland meetings.

The Church of Scotland took another step towards improving its appeal when in 1896 church courts were permitted to make all decisions affecting church matters without appeal to the civil courts. This gave the Church of Scotland a greater degree of independence and improved its appeal in Highland parishes. Dr Marshall Lang regarded the 1890s as the right time to appeal to the Highlands. Church of Scotland ministers were now more popular, numbers were slowly growing and many in the north still held strongly to the principle of national religion. In 1896 Lang said if 'only some prejudices could be removed and some constitutional objections could be met, the Church of Scotland – whose fundamental principle of national religion, the great majority of the Free Church and the entire body of the secessionists strongly hold - might be a mediating and unifying influence'.[2]

THE DISTINCTIVE PRINCIPLES
OF THE FREE CHURCH

❊

The pressures for change in the churches were many and varied in the last quarter of the nineteenth-century. A number of areas of Christian belief and practice were being challenged by new ways of thinking. The Free Church was not immune to these pressures and the collective consequence was the emergence of a new religious mood which meant that many new ways of thinking, in doctrine and practice, were accommodated within the late nineteenth-century Free Church. In many of the Highland parishes this new mood was resisted and the forces for change were less welcome. By 1890 many Free Church people in the north were suspicious of the changes which were being discussed and introduced in theology, in the status of the Westminster Confession, in interpretation of scripture and in worship. They were firmly persuaded that these changes had no place in the Free Church as they knew it

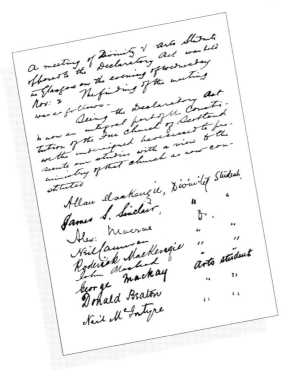

A group of nine students committed themselves to leave the Free Church on account of the Declaratory Act. (Source: by kind permission, Knox Press, Free Church of Scotland, Edinburgh)

and more than that they believed that they violated the distinctive principles of the Free Church as laid down in the 1840s.

In 1881 Dr John Kennedy, minister of Dingwall, was quoted as saying of the Free Church that 'it had ceased to be the church of the Disruption'. There was an ever widening schism between those who wanted to adhere rigidly to their understanding of the origins of the Free Church and those who were not convinced that their Christianity should be bound to the forms of the past. As the nineteenth-century moved on, this division seemed to be increasingly represented by the Highlands and the Lowlands. Those who clung to Free Church origins were known as constitutionalists. They had little sympathy with the progressive plans of the predominantly Lowland Free Church majority.

Their grievances were regularly expressed in the Highland press where they came across as a group that were being marginalised within their own church and disregarded by the Edinburgh headquarters of the Free Church. Highland constitutionalists believed that the Bible was the inspired, infallible Word of God. They held that the Westminster Confession of Faith defined the doctrines of the Christian faith. They also believed in the state support of religion and that hymns and musical instruments should not be used in public worship. For the constitutionalists these were not simply matters of individual belief and preference. These were the standards upon which the Free Church had been securely based and adherence to them was not optional.

In the last quarter of the nineteenth-century these beliefs were being challenged from within the Free Church. There was much support for the campaign to disestablish the Church of Scotland in the Free Church Assembly. More distressing was the fact that the principle of establishment also found little support. The Assembly in 1878 supported the view that 'the connection subsisting between the church now established and the state is wholly indefensible'. The constitutionalists were also disturbed by Free Church ministers who had begun to question the divine inspiration and inerrancy of Scripture. In addition the purity of public worship was being undermined by the introduction of 'hymns of human composition' and instrumental music.

In the 1860s there was some support for introducing hymns into the Free Church. This met with considerable opposition. The pressure was strong enough by 1866 for the General Assembly to appoint a Committee on Paraphrases and Hymns to consider these matters. This Committee reported in 1869 and although not entirely of one voice the Committee was asked to prepare a collection of hymns. This was presented in 1872 and approved. In 1881 a hymn book was formally sanctioned for public worship. The question of instrumental music was raised in 1882 and after a committee, set up to review the matter, reported in 1883, the Assembly gave congregations the liberty to decide on this issue.

Constitutionalist concern centred on those in Free Church colleges who seemed to be questioning the Christian faith. Many in the north were distressed by the appointment of Drs Dods and Bruce to Free Church colleges in 1889 and 1890 respectively. Both were regarded as being unsound in their views on the inspiration of scripture and the divinity of Christ. In 1890 the Synod of Argyll overtured the General Assembly, saying the views of Dods and

Bruce were not in harmony with scripture or the Confession of Faith. Following a debate on this in 1890, the Assembly voted not for censure but for toleration. With reference to the problems perceived in the Free Church colleges, Murdo MacAskill said 'if they persist in their evil doing, they must occupy some other building for their unholy work. If they want a new Bible – a new Confession of Faith – a new theology, they had better look for new lodgings, for the present premises were never intended for them'.[5]

THE DECLARATORY ACT

❋

The constitutionalists opposed the Free Church's move to adjust the Confession of Faith. In 1889 the Assembly appointed a committee to inquire into the Confession and advise. This was in order to 'meet the difficulties and relieve the scruples' that some office bearers were experiencing with regard to the Westminster Confession of Faith. It was the Report of the Committee on the Confession of Faith in 1891 that resulted in the proposed Declaratory Act which distanced the Free Church from strict adherence to the Confession and allowed it to determine for itself what was the substance of the reformed faith.

Much of the Highland constitutionalist dissatisfaction with developments in the Free Church was supported by their belief that the wrongs they saw had no place in the Free Church and were wholly inconsistent with its principles. The shock of the Declaratory Act of 1892 for the constitutionalists was that it gave legitimacy to all the errors and flaws of the previous years. John R MacKay, minister of the Free Presbyterian congregation in Gairloch, later remarked that 'it was not alone the Declaratory Act that led him and his friends to assume the position they had taken up. The purport of the Act was the legalisation of the backslidings that had characterised the past twenty years of the Free Church, the errors of the past were not only condoned by it, but made legal and as no errors or departure from the original standpoint'.[4]

The Declaratory Act provided a focus for the discontent of Highland constitutionalists in the 1890s. Its aim had been to clarify the church's relation to the Westminster Confession. It was proposed as a necessary step which would better reflect the changing mood in the Free Church. In 1891 the Declaratory Act was sent to presbyteries of the Free Church under the Barrier Act. This act was devised to prevent any sudden alteration or innovation in either doctrine, worship or discipline. Any piece of legislation under the Barrier Act had to be remitted to the presbyteries of the church and reported on at the following Assembly. In the 1892 Free Church Assembly it was reported that a majority of the Free Church presbyteries voted in favour of the Declaratory Act becoming the law of the church.

The controversy surrounding the Declaratory Act divided opinion within the Free Church in the Highlands. They divided on the question of whether the Declaratory Act was perceived to be a relieving or imposing act. Did it simply provide relief for those who were unable to reconcile individual belief with the standards of the church? This would allow them to remain Free Church with a clear conscience. Alternatively, did the Declaratory Act change the fundamental principles on which the Free Church was based and thus impose a new arrangement on all those who belonged to the Free Church?

Those who strongly opposed the Declaratory Act regarded it as an imposing act which significantly changed the principles upon which the Free Church had been based and thereby altered the standards to which ministers and elders were required to subscribe. For those who considered the Declaratory Act a relieving act, the basic principles of the Free Church remained unchanged and office bearers could continue to believe as they had always done with greater latitude now available to any who might entertain scruples concerning certain points in the Westminster Confession.

Constitutionalists can be found on both sides of this divide. There was no exclusive correlation between constitutionalism and the view that the Declaratory Act was an imposing act. All who saw the Declaratory Act as an imposing act were constitutionalists but it did not follow that all constitutionalists regarded the Declaratory Act as an imposing act. In addition, there were Free Church people in the Highlands who took the view that the Declaratory Act was a relieving act but still remained convinced that it had no place in the Free Church.

It was an issue that both focused opposition but, when action was demanded, badly fragmented it and left the constitutionalists divided. At first the proposal to introduce the Declaratory Act was

THE BOND OF UNION OF THE SECESSIONISTS.

THE following are the terms of the Bond of Union which the Free Church Secessionists adopted yesterday week, and which is to be circulated for signature :—

"BOND OF UNION BETWEEN THOSE WHO ADHERE TO THE PRINCIPLES AND CONSTITUTION OF THE FREE CHURCH OF SCOTLAND.

"We, the undersigned ministers, elders, deacons, members, and adherents of the Free Church of Scotland, hereby bind ourselves to adhere to the principles and constitution of the said Church as these are set forth in the Confession of Faith, Larger and Shorter Catechisms, the Claim of Rights of 1842 and Protest of 1843, and the First and Second Books of Discipline; and in particular we declare our belief in the absolute infallibility, inerrancy, and supreme authority of the Scriptures of the Old and New Testaments; also in the whole doctrine of the Confession of Faith as approved of by the General Assembly of the Church of Scotland in 1647, and in the Larger and Shorter Catechisms, which are all founded upon and conformable to the Word of God.

"We feel called upon, in the circumstances in which we are placed in the Providence of God, to assert anew (1) the duty of this nation, as a nation, to profess, own, and support the Protestant and Presbyterian religion; (2) that, in accordance with the Confession of Faith, the Book of Psalms is the only manual of praise in the public worship of God recognised in this Church; (3) that instrumental music ought to have no place in New Testament worship; (4) that to all those for whom Christ has purchased redemption, He doth certainly and effectually apply the same; and (5) that no one believes upon Christ to the saving of the soul without being regenerated by the Holy Spirit.

"Also, we protest against the Declaratory Act of 1892, and reject it wholly; especially because it denies (1) the sovereignty of the love of God (2) that death has passed upon all on account of the sin of our first parents; and (3) the absolute necessity of the means of grace for the salvation of the heathen.

"And further, we protest against the power assumed by the Courts of the Church which has ceased to represent the creed and principles of the said Free Church of Scotland, by passing the Declaratory Act, inasmuch as by the said Act they have substituted for the whole doctrine contained in the Confession of Faith, what they may regard as 'the substance of the Reformed Faith therein set forth,' thus largely dispensing with most solemn vows.

"On all these grounds, we, in humble dependence on God's grace, and the presence and blessing of the Holy Spirit, for the advancement of His glory, the extension of the Gospel of our Lord and Saviour, and the administration of the affairs of Christ's house according to His Holy Word, desire to adhere to all the doctrines of the Word of God and the principles and constitution of the Free Church of Scotland as held in 1843; and we renounce that General Assembly which has permanently placed upon its records the Declaratory Act of 1892, as well as all other Courts in subjection to the said Assembly."

The Bond of Union was agreed on 13 June, 1893. Those who seceded from the Free Church signed it in the Inverness Music Hall.. It was then distributed and read and signed in many more Highland communities.

consistently condemned by constitutionalists. Murdo MacAskill
said, 'This movement on the part of our opponents means - Bible or
no Bible, Confession of Faith or no Confession of Faith. Let Dr
Rainy and his party put their fingers on the Confession and the
whole thing is done'. On another occasion MacAskill warned that
'if the Declaratory Act becomes part of our constitution, what
remains of our former principles is wholy obliterated, and anyone
who pleases may pronounce the funeral oration of the once noble
Free Church of Scotland, she is no longer the Free Church of our
earthly love and loyal adherence'. Hector Cameron from Back in
Lewis also used harsh words to describe the Free Church following
the adoption of the Declaratory Act. He claimed that the 'function
of every church is to witness for the truth of God and when she
ceases to discharge that function she is no longer a church of Christ
but a synagogue of Satan'.[5] Yet these strong words did not lead to
secession; both MacAskill and Cameron remained with the Free
Church after 1893.

RESPONSE TO THE DECLARATORY ACT

❋

At a constitutionalist convention in Inverness in June 1892, those
present agreed that the Declaratory Act should not be binding on
those who choose not to adhere to it. A similar convention in
Glasgow the following month adopted the same position.
Constitutionalists were not a united group and this became painfully
apparent at a conference in Inverness in February 1893. Despite
the fact that both ministers and elders had gathered there from
many parts of the Highlands and Islands, the decision was taken to
have a 'ministers-only' session. The ministers who attended said this
had been the original intention. The elders, however, did not share
this view. For many who had travelled considerable distances to
attend, this decision created a degree of bad feeling.

It was a most uncharacteristic step given the normal
composition of presbyterian courts. Yet, various regional elders
meetings had already shown their strength of feeling and, if
ministers were at all nervous about being committed to secession,
they needed to find a way of limiting the influence of Highland
elders. Thus a 'ministers-only' session went ahead and accepted
the position that had previously been taken by the meetings in

Inverness and Glasgow. The question of separation was not considered necessary and they ruled that the Declaratory Act was not an imposing but a relieving act. The ministers agreed that the Declaratory Act did not impose beliefs on Free Church members and adherents and so constitutionalists could remain in the Free Church with a clear conscience.

This apparent collapse of opposition was viewed with amazement by those who had listened to the stirring speeches of ministers who had now qualified their position when secession appeared as an imminent possibility. John MacLeod, who was then a Free Church student, commented that 'here was the point at which the friends of the church expected decisive action on the part of their leaders. A disruption was looked upon as inevitable. The people were doomed to disappointment.'[6] In the remaining years of the decade a number of letters expressing this sense of betrayal can be found in Highland newspapers. These events may well have informed Free Church leaders that a significant secession of constitutionalist clergy at the 1893 Assembly was unlikely.

The reaction to the passing of the Declaratory Act in May 1892 resulted in meetings being organised and statements of opposition being issued. There were a number within the Free Church, however, who were looking for more decisive and radical action than was being discussed in the meetings in the summer of 1892. This was provided in November 1892 when nine students signed a bond stating that 'as the Declaratory Act is now an integral part of the constitution of the Free Church, we, the undersigned, have ceased to prosecute our studies with a view to the ministry of that church as now constituted'.[7]

One of the nine was John MacLeod, later to become principal of the Free Church College in Edinburgh. In 1893, however, he was urging Free Church members to 'cut their connection with an apostate church'.[8] His advice was being adopted by Free Church elders in the Highlands and Islands who were organising meetings of protest. Many of these resulted in the agreement that if the Declaratory Act was not repealed in 1893 then they would sever their links with the Free Church.

The position which was adopted at the Inverness meeting in February, 1893, however, did not weaken the resolve of Free Church elders. In the following months a number of meetings, mostly led by elders, were held in Skye and on the mainland, to declare opposition to the Declaratory Act. Highland newspapers reported a number of such meetings in March, April and May 1893 at which those attending frequently concluded by committing themselves to leave the Free Church unless the Declaratory Act was repealed at the 1893 Assembly. In March 1893 a Free Church congregation at Millhouse-Kames, in Argyll, also took this step. In May 1893 a meeting of elders and laymen in a schoolhouse at Achnasheen took a similar decision. This was done in the knowledge that their ministers were unlikely to go with them. One group of Skye elders stated that 'the constitutionalist ministers were evidently afraid to lead the people out of a church which has so manifestly backslided from the truth. They were to be greatly blamed for the way in which they had acted at the Inverness conference in not allowing the elders, who came from different parts, to take part in the proceedings'.[9]

THE FREE PRESBYTERIAN CHURCH

❊

At the General Assembly in 1893 there were ten overtures for the repeal of the Declaratory Act. Rainy's proposal that the Assembly should pass from them was supported. However, the students and elders who had adopted the more militant position were not totally abandoned of ministerial support as they had feared. At this Assembly, Rev Donald MacFarlane protested and severed his connection with the Free Church. He advanced and laid his protest on the clerk's table, stating that 'neither my conscience, nor my ordination vows, allow me to act under what has been made law in the church'. He thus separated from the Free Church. MacFarlane was originally from North Uist but had ministered at Strathconon, Moy, Kilmallie and was at this point minister of Raasay.

Following his protest and withdrawal, MacFarlane began immediately to consolidate Free Church dissent. He travelled to Glasgow where he addressed a group of sympathetic students, then to Greenock and on to the Cowal peninsula where the Millhouse-Kames congregation left the Free Church. MacFarlane then placed an advert in the 31 May edition of the Northern Chronicle announcing that a secession meeting would be held in the Inverness Music Hall on 13 June 1893. At this meeting he was joined by Rev

Free Presbyterian open-air meeting. There is some uncertainty about this gathering, but it has been claimed that it is a gathering of seceders in Stornoway. Every area of the Isle of Lewis was troubled by secession activity. In 1895, Lady Matheson granted some land for a Free Presbyterian Church in Stornoway. The church was completed and opened in 1899.

(Source: by kind permission, Mr J. MacQueen, Stornoway)

Donald MacDonald, Shieldaig, and a number of elders and students. There were also representatives from Skye and Lewis, from Wick and from many parts of Ross and Sutherland and from Argyll and other parts of Scotland.

Mr Donald MacDonald, was also a native of North Uist and had worked in a number of Highland areas as a teacher and probationer before accepting a call to Shieldaig in 1872. MacDonald was without a church building until 1877 and as a result of making common cause with MacFarlane he found himself facing the same situation again. At Inverness they produced a Bond of Union and this served as the basis for the Free Presbyterian Church. In January 1894 eviction notices were served by the presbyteries of Lochcarron and Skye on MacDonald and MacFarlane. In addition, the sum of £280 was arrested at the Lochcarron branch of the Caledonian Bank. This included money which MacDonald's congregation had put aside for a new church as well as personal gifts.

In the following month the first presbytery of the Free Presbyterian Church was constituted at Raasay on 28 July 1893. At this meeting in Raasay the first two Free Presbyterian ministers, John R MacKay and Allan MacKenzie were licensed. MacKay took over the Gairloch congregation and MacKenzie, that of Inverness. Another important event which happened at this time was the Raasay communion. A large number of people were present including people from Skye and the mainland. This gathering was addressed by MacFarlane and the majority indicated their willingness to quit the Free Church.

At a further meeting of the presbytery in Portree on 14 August a Deed of Separation was drawn up explaining their reasons for separating. The Deed of Separation re-stated the Free Presbyterians link with the Disruption tradition and listed their grievances. These included the Free Church support for the separation of church and state and the fact that the Free Church sanctioned the use of uninspired hymns and had authorised instrumental music in the public worship of God. This violated the purity of worship. The Free Church now tolerated and supported office bearers who did not hold to the whole doctrine of the Confession of Faith and entertained dubious views on the origin and reliability of scripture. Moreover in the Declaratory Act, the church, by a majority of the

Following his departure from the General Assembly of the Free Church in May 1893,
Donald MacFarlane placed an advert in the Northern Chronicle, *31 May 1893, inviting*
people to a public meeting. This meeting was in Inverness and was of great significance
for the development of the Free Presbyterian Church.

members of its courts was made the sole judge of doctrine in the Free
Church. The Deed of Separation claimed that the Free Church now
'lays its creed at the feet of an irresponsible majority'. The Free
Church had also embraced voluntaryism and turned away from the
original commitment to the establishment principle.

FREE PRESBYTERIAN CONGREGATIONS

❉

In November, 1893 the secession announced that their movement
in the Highlands was progressing rapidly and 'already twenty-
seven congregations have separate organisations and services'.
When they met in Inverness in July, 1895, the Free Presbyterians
claimed that they had seven ministers, eighteen students, forty
missionaries and 20,000 people in connection with the church. On
the other hand the Free Church calculated that the secession
amounted to no more than 6,756 elders, deacons and communicants above the age of eighteen. Yet the secession was clearly large
enough to worry the Free Church leaders. In order to avoid
further losses, Rainy carried a resolution in the Free Church
General Assembly in 1894 stating that the provisions of the
Declaratory Act were not binding on any who declined to take
advantage of them.

By 1900 the Free Presbyterian Church, which had initially

been known as the Free Church Presbytery of Scotland, stood at seventy-five charges and mission stations. Of these seventy-five, seventy were in the Highlands. Of these, sixteen were in Ross and Cromarty, twelve in Skye, eleven in Sutherland, seven in Inverness-shire, thirteen in Lewis, Harris and the Uists, five in Caithness, five in Argyll, one in Aberdeenshire. A further five were in the Lowlands; Glasgow, two, Greeenock, one, Edinburgh, one, and Dumbarton, one.[10]

Free Presbyterian strength was mostly located in areas of Scotland that were most remote from the Free Church headquarters. If control of the Free Church was being increasingly centralised in the colleges and committees, these were the areas that would have felt this most keenly. Equally, these were the areas most likely to be immune to the influence that flows from close attachment to the predominant group in the Free Church. The Free Presbyterian secession was, to an extent, an attempt to redress the increasing estrangement which they felt within their own church. Unable to influence the direction of the church they belonged to, the Free Presbyterians had taken steps to ensure a greater measure of theological and ecclesiastical control.

The movement of the people from the Free Church to the Free Presbyterian Church appears to have taken place as a slow process rather than a sudden event, a slow process that was encouraged by the frequent visits and lecture tours of leading seceders and by key meetings in the churches. In some areas congregations did not decide to secede or stay until they had an opportunity to have the issues clearly explained to them. The early ministers and students of the Free Presbyterian Church were in great demand for communions and pulpit supply.

At the beginning of 1894 the secession remained a major concern of the Highland and Island Free Church. Ministers and elders in Lewis spoke of dissatisfaction, dispeace and division 'almost universally within the bounds of the presbytery'.[11] Consequently, the Lewis Free Church presbytery requested that the Assembly repeal the Declaratory Act and Lewis ministers and elders for their part continued to denounce forcefully the Declaratory Act. Some of this disquiet must have been attributable to the preaching of Neil Cameron. At the meeting in the Inverness Music Hall in June 1893 it was decided to send secession leaders throughout the Highlands and Islands to explain their message to the people. Neil Cameron shared in this task and travelled and preached extensively throughout the north west and the islands. He was later ordained as the first Free Presbyterian minister of St Jude's in Glasgow in January 1896.

In Harris, the strength of the secession was quite remarkable given their relative isolation from the main events. When MacFarlane called the meeting in June 1893 in the Inverness Music Hall to consolidate the secession, the Harris Free Church did not attend but sent a telegram with a simple request, 'Deputation wanted to enlighten Harris on Declaratory Act'. Enlightenment clearly had arrived by some means as it was reported in the following year that there were seven secession gatherings in Harris with an estimated 1400 adults attached to the new church. Another report refers to a secession communion in Harris to which over 1000 attended. This strength of support was not without a measure of bad feeling between Harris people. On one occasion a tent, erected for a Free Presbyterian communion, was badly knifed. This disrupted the proceedings and required that alternative accommodation had to be found.

The remaining months of 1893, following MacFarlane's protest, witnessed considerable secession activity. There were reports of new congregations being formed in both remote areas and in Highland towns. In Ardineskain, Lochcarron, a Free Church congregation resolved on 2 June to leave the Free Church. They decided that they had 'no alternative but to yield to the unbearable yoke or to leap over the traces and get rid of the yoke'.

There was also secession activity in Skye. On 7 June 1893, in Arnizort, a meeting was chaired by local elders who complained of the 'tyrannical and despotic power exercised by the Free Church Assembly'. They left the Free Church and declared themselves proud to follow in the footsteps of Roderick MacLeod who had made similar sacrifices at the Disruption. Also in Braes in Skye, there was a strong movement out of the Free Church, in Glenhinisdale the people supported the secession and in Portree a strong congregation of seceders was formed.

In Gairloch the Free Church was vacant and in July 1893 over 400 turned out for a meeting at a familiar open-air site, *Leabaidh na Bà Bainne*, for a secession meeting. The Free Church Presbytery of

Lochcarron attempted to exercise some discipline by sending a member of presbytery to preach in the church. He was, however, ignored and the majority of the people listened instead to Mr John R MacKay, who was a secession student at that time. Many left the Free Church and MacKay remained with the new secession congregation in Gairloch. He was later ordained at Gairloch with over 500 in attendance. Again this took place in the open-air at *Leabaidh na Bà Bainne*. At this same place at Gairloch, Duncan Matheson had been inducted in 1843. In 1893 Donald MacFarlane preached at the same place and from the same text as had been used in 1843. In 1893 MacKay's call was signed by 480 people and another 200 to 300 in Melvaig also supported this call and invited Mr MacKay to preach to them once a month.

The attempt to impose Free Church discipline did not succeed in Gairloch. It appeared, however, to be slightly more successful in Ness in Lewis. There had been reports that this entire congregation was considering secession and was ready to appoint a leader of the secession as their minister. In response the Lewis Free Church presbytery met with the Ness kirk session and warned that 'any office bearer giving any help or countenance whatever to separatist tactics, subversive of the Free Church was guilty of ordination vows and liable to be summarily dealt with'.[12] The presbytery then elicited from the elders a declaration of loyalty.

The secession was also strong in the Moy and Daviot area. Donald MacDonald and Allan MacKenzie spoke here and many signed the Bond of Union which was taken from house to house for signatures. In 1893 secession congregations were also formed in Wick, Inverness and Newtonmore.

By 1896 Free Presbyterian support had thus been consolidated in a number of areas. There were churches in Kames, Glendale, Ullapool, Shieldaig and Inverness. Church building was also in progress in Oban, Portree, Lochinver, Harris, Applecross and Stornoway. There were also plans for more in Fearn, Gairloch and Halkirk. In addition, there were a number of small meeting houses such as those at Inverasdale, Melvaig, Port Henderson, Beauly, Moy, Aviemore and Kishorn. The Kishorn meeting place had the distinction of possessing the pulpit that Lachlan MacKenzie had preached from.

It is also possible to gain an indication of the size of some of the secession congregations from reports at the time. In 1896 the call for Roderick MacKenzie to the Portree congregation was signed by 626 people. At the opening of the Shieldaig church there were over 700 in attendance. A newspaper report said that 800 attended the Stoer congregation. The church that was being built at Tarbert was said to be for a congregation of several hundred. In Raasay the secession congregation was said to consist of five-sixths of the entire population of Raasay and Rona. Despite this, all applications for a site for a church and manse in Raasay were refused and MacFarlane had to travel to and from Broadford for some time.

The extent of the Free Presbyterian secession is in itself not a reliable indication of the strength of opposition to developments in the Free Church at this time. Many who were critical of the management of the Free Church did not express their disapproval in secession. There are a number of reasons that can be advanced to explain why Highland people and ministers did not join the Free Presbyterians in greater numbers. In the first place joining the Free Presbyterians involved considerable upheaval as it required that the people leave the churches that their families had built and supported. To an extent congregational feuds must have limited schism as one faction was unlikely to join the Free Presbyterians if a former opposing faction had already taken that action.

The hostility of ministers who did not secede, to the Declaratory Act must have contributed to limiting secession as the people would have felt united in opposition with their ministers who were remaining in the Free Church and believed that the Declaratory Act would be defeated from within. Poor organisation, lack of information and distance from the main meetings must also have limited the number of people who seceded after 1893. Finally, there is evidence of the quick action and discipline of presbyteries to crush signs of secession in 1893. These factors, to varying degrees, must have limited the Free Presbyterian schism.

Those who seceded held that if they had remained in the Free Church then they would have to accept these 'objectionable' changes in worship and doctrine. They quit because, in their view, the church they belonged to was no longer the church they had joined. In order to remain loyal to their beliefs they considered they were now obliged to form a new church to embody the principles that had been contended for successfully in 1843. In a number of Highland villages two churches now claimed to have their origin in the Disruption. One was founded in 1843, the other in 1893, yet the latter now claimed to represent more accurately the origins of the former.

CHAPTER 11

Union

*'Though I do not approve of Union, though I do not approve of the steps taken
in connection with Union, I say that as a Free-Churchman, I submit to the
Supreme Court of my church. I deny myself for the sake of peace.'*

Dr Ross

FREE CHURCH ELDER, BARVAS, LEWIS

The United Free Church came into being on 31 October 1900. It
resulted from the union of the Free Church and the United
Presbyterian Church. Both denominations had been considering
this step for some time. In the mid 1890s interest in union again
gained momentum and was this time followed through to a
successful conclusion but this was not without difficulties and
opposition.

To a great extent the difficulties faced by the Free Church in
1900 were a repeat of those experienced in 1893. A Highland
minority again felt that the dominant majority was taking the
church in a direction that was contrary to its origins and a direction
for which the minority held little enthusiasm. Many of the same
themes were present in 1893 and 1900. These included the erosion
of Free Church principles, the marginalisation of the Highland
Free Church and the inability of the constitutionalists to agree on a
programme of action to combat the union proposals.

Resistance to union came principally from the Highlands and
Islands. It was from those who felt alienated from the direction and
management of the church. The division that resulted in the Free
Church in 1900 is often perceived as a Highland-Lowland division.
This is true in one sense, in that the ministers and congregations
that stayed outside the United Free were mostly found in the
Highlands. Yet, on the other hand, most of the ministers and many
of the people in the Highlands joined the United Free Church. As

with the Free Presbyterian secession in 1893 it is an untidy period in Highland church history. Constitutionalists were badly divided in 1900 with some going into the United Free Church and some remaining as a 'remnant' Free Church. Thus, neither the Free Presbyterian secession nor the members who in 1900 remained in the 'Free Church continuing' were an accurate expression of constitutionalist strength.

In 1893, Murdo MacAskill, Free Church minister of Dingwall, said that not one in ten in the Highlands would support the schemes of what was termed the progressive party. Whereas, by the time 1900 came along, not one in ten of MacAskill's ministerial colleagues, including himself, could resist throwing in their lot with the United Free. This does not suggest that their constitutionalism was discarded but that they found other reasons for making common cause with the triumphant United Free Church and were content to take their constitutionalism with them.

Throughout the 1890s many in the Highland Free Church were disturbed by the erosion of what they considered to be the principles on which their church was based. There were also structural and management issues that compounded their grievances. They felt that they were cut off from the decision making centre and mechanisms of the church. The Assembly, the colleges and the Assembly committees offered them little influence and seemed to be consistently working contrary to their interests.

MARGINALISATION OF THE
FREE CHURCH IN THE HIGHLANDS

❊

In 1895 when Rev Peter MacDonald was leaving St Columba's, Edinburgh, to go to Stornoway Gaelic Free Church he was honoured with a farewell breakfast in Edinburgh. At this impressive gathering of eminent gentlemen a number of speeches were made praising MacDonald. Rev Dr White of St George's Free, Edinburgh said that 'what the Highlands required was the right men moved into the right place'. How should we understand this statement? It could be considered as the benign hope that the Highlands would benefit from a high quality of spiritual leadership or alternatively it could be regarded as a policy to deliver, through men like MacDonald, the pacification of the anti-unionists. This would ensure that union could be achieved with minimal losses. The growing perception in the Highlands favoured the latter interpretation.

Even initiatives that were directly aimed at extending the work of the Church in the Highlands were viewed with deep suspicion. By the 1890s the activities of the Highland Committee fell within this category. It was seen by some as a vehicle of the progressive party in the church. The Free Church Highland Committee had been set up in 1849. It consisted of ministers chosen trienially from different parishes with Robert Rainy, Convener in the 1890s and Alexander Lee as Secretary. Mackintosh MacKay and Thomas McLauchlan had been previous Conveners. Among some constitutionalists the Highland Committee had a poor reputation in this period. It was seen as working contrary to the interests of Highland Christianity and subversive of Highland spirituality.

In 1894, following the Free Presbyterian secession from the Free Church, Rev Alexander Lee, left his church at Nairn and was appointed as the visiting agent of the Highland Committee. This was a full time appointment and came with a salary of £500. In addition, John MacKay, minister of Cromarty Free Church, resigned from his church to become a Highland evangelist. MacKay was appointed by Rainy at a salary of only £70 per annum. The Free Church Assembly of 1894 also set aside Rev William Ross, Cowcaddens and Rev J MacPherson, Findhorn, to train Highland missionaries. These lay missionaries were appointed by the Highland Committee, were trained in Glasgow in the summer months and sent to work in the Highlands to consolidate the work of the Free Church in that region. The missionaries were paid by the Highland Committee and were under the direction of Lee.

This new departure aroused a measure of suspicion. It was felt by some that godly old catechists and elders were deliberately being replaced by new missionaries who were under Lee's command. Catechists had previously trained under ministerial supervision in the Highlands and, therefore, had not been exposed to the 'questionable' teachings of Edinburgh and Glasgow. Catechists were also paid less. Coming so soon after the secession of 1893 the introduction of the new missionaries seemed like a poorly concealed attempt to influence the outcome of future developments by getting the Free Church in the Highlands to conform to the predominant ethos.

If the training and commissioning of these lay missionaries was viewed with suspicion, the appointment and activity of Lee as travelling agent of the Highland Committee was viewed with contempt. Archibald MacNeilage, a leading Free Church elder described Lee as 'Rainy's hench-man' and MacAskill of Dingwall, although eventually going into the Union, was no less critical. MacAskill regarded the appointment of Lee as a piece of 'gross ecclesiastical jobbery', describing it as 'part of the spirit of favouritism which prevailed in the church' and adding that, 'for a man who served his party, some niche had to be found'. The Highland press in the 1890s and particularly in 1900 and 1901, around the time of the Union with the United Presbyterians, regularly contained letters that were critical of Lee.

Along with being the full time secretary of the Highland Committee, Lee was also appointed as the superintendent of the Home Mission Committee. This was regarded by some in the Highlands as an unsuitable and unnecessary choice. One letter complained about the partisan nature of this appointment. 'He is now recognised as one of the party's (Rainy's) leaders in the North and in the present divided state of the church, would it not be more desirable to have an entirely neutral gentlemen filling the offices of superintendent of the Highland Committee and Home Mission?'.[1] Presbyteries were invited to suggest what duties the superintendent of the Home Mission Committee should have. At a meeting of the Dingwall Free Church Presbytery in February 1893 they surveyed the Highland parishes and concluded there was no need for such an appointment. What emerged was a statement of ecclesiastical independence. They were managing fine and 'in their case home-rule was perfectly defensible'. No 'bishop' was needed to lord it over them; the message was clear, there was nothing to superintend.[2]

Moreover, the Dingwall Presbytery was confident that if this appointment had been put to a vote in the Highlands not one in ten would have given their support to Lee. When some Highland presbyteries did welcome this appointment, MacAskill derided their actions with a very obvious astronomical reference: 'Jupiter nodded and the minor planets began to revolve at his bidding'. A motion asserting that there was no need for a superintendent of Home Mission was, therefore, unanimously carried by Dingwall Free Presbytery.

The view was expressed frequently that the Highland Committee was serving the purposes of the Free Church establishment and ignoring the Free Church people in the Highlands. Ten years before the Union in 1900, before Lee's appointment and introduction of the lay missionaries, a Free Church Highland elder complained that the Highland Committee was dealing badly with Free Church probationers, students and missionaries. The result of this 'tyranny' was that the Free Church in the Highlands was being deprived of her best sons and the Highland Committee was encouraging men for the ministry in the Highlands that were quite unsuitable. Many saw the Highland Committee as a tool of Rainy and Lee, reflecting their interests and not those of the north.

Mr Donald MacLean, minister of Moy and later principal of the Free Church College, also agreed with this assessment. In a short biographical sketch of Rev John Noble he wrote that 'the influence of the ruling power in the church tended to crush the efforts of a minority struggling to maintain their right of choice in the calling of a minister. Probationers, whose views on current questions of policy and creed do not coincide with those of the prevailing party, found the access to vacant congregations sometimes awkwardly barred by the influence of interim moderators'.[3] This situation was further compounded when congregations claimed that they were sometimes denied the interim moderators of their choice.

The activities of the Highland Committee was not the only complaint of the constitutionalists. Free Church journals were not above suspicion, whether in Gaelic or English. They were attacked as being contrary to the interests of the Highland constitutionalists and it was claimed that they were one sided and contained only the views of the 'advanced' party in the Free Church.

THE FREE CHURCH MACHINE
❉

The sense of anger and disappointment that some Highland Free Church people felt was sharply reflected in the letters to Highland newspapers in the 1890s. For many in the Highlands, both those who entered the Union and those who would stay out, the Free Church machine had effectively marginalised anti-union constitutionalism. This group now felt themselves to be cast adrift within

*Dr Robert Rainy, Principal of New College, Gladstone said he was unquestionably
the greatest of living Scotsmen, but for many in the Highlands he was 'black Rainy' –
the unprincipled Principal.*

their own denomination. A denomination which they believed
passionately had come into being because it had been based on
certain principles which were now, at best, of rapidly declining
relevance.

It was a predicament that was considered by some to be worse
than that faced by their forefathers at the Disruption. Highland
Christians were feeling progressively isolated within a Free Church
which they felt was being managed and controlled from
Edinburgh. Wherever they turned they saw evidence of this; in the
Assembly, the Colleges, appointments, committees and journals all
conspired against the constitutionalists. In 1890, following the
Assembly debate on Dods and Bruce, one commentator asserted
that evangelical Highland Christians were 'at the greatest struggle
which has taken place in this country since the civil and ecclesias-

Dr James Begg. In May 1874, The Spectator *described Dr James Begg as a 'vigorous political agitator rather than a theologian, a debater who would have become the equal of any man in the House of Commons in the power of sheer hard hitting. If he had been caught young enough, a born pugilist, an incarnate denial of the precept 'Blessed are the meek'.*

tical tyranny of the Stuarts was brought to an end in 1688'.

Following the earlier union discussions with the United Presbyterians from 1863 to 73, Dr Robert Buchanan observed that 'death will have a good deal to do among us before the set time for union comes'.[4] This was undeniably true. Many who had resisted union in the 1870s had died by the 1890s; but along with the losses by death can be added the effects of the relentless operation of the Free Church machine.

In accounting for the difficulties that troubled the Free Church in the late nineteenth-century there is a curious focus on two individuals. For those who would throw in their lot with the United Free Church, the troubles could be blamed on the malicious influence of James Begg, minister of Newington Free Church. For those who remained Free Church, the villain was Dr Robert Rainy.

Rainy had long been regarded by constitutionalists as the driving force behind the so-called progressive group in the Free Church. This group were accused of being too ready to distance themselves from Free Church principles. Rainy thus attracted uncomplimentary titles such as 'the unprincipled principal' or 'black Rainy'. He was likened to 'Jeroboam, the son of Nebat, who made Israel sin' and his action was described as 'the sickly despotism of a single individual'. Highland constitutionalists accused him, perhaps not always fairly, of exploiting his power and position in the Free Church for his own advantage and for that of his party within the church. He was, therefore, held responsible by constitutionalists for the troubles which unsettled the Free Church.

In his defence it could be argued that where union was concerned his options were limited. As the dominant mood of the Free Church was pro-union, Rainy felt himself obliged to secure this as smoothly as possible with minimal dissent. However, his outstanding abilities as a church leader and the constraints within which he operated did not entirely impress northern constitutionalists. For them he had control of all the centres of influence in the Free Church and used them consistently for the advancement of one group and the marginalisation of the other. From the constitutionalists' perspective Rainy's actions were an abuse of power and privilege. The conflicting views about Rainy are almost impossible to reconcile. On the one hand he was described as the greatest living Scotsman of his day and on the other as an unscrupulous autocrat.

James Begg died in 1883, but for many Free Church people who went into the Union he was the cause of the trouble in the Free Church both in the 1860s and 1870s and in the 1890s after his death. He has been accused of single-handedly provoking the constitutionalist reaction in the Highlands and nurturing it for his own ends. It has been claimed that this was achieved by Begg's influence over Kennedy of Dingwall and that from Dingwall, Begg's influence spread and came to disturb the whole of the Highlands.

Certainly the analysis that Begg made of the Free Church in the 1860s and 1870s was similar to that expressed by many in the Highlands in the 1890s. Begg had also spoken of Free Church 'despotism' and argued that a 'limited number of men notoriously manage our affairs in any way they please'. Begg had described Free Church leadership as an 'irresponsible prelacy' and accused them of a 'true reign of terror' over all those who disagreed with them. The result of this despotism, he remarked, was that 'few churches, perhaps in the world have been more truly enslaved'.

From the point of view of the pro-union Highlanders this was all misrepresentation and mischief making. Peter MacDonald, minister of St Columba's Free Church, Edinburgh, and Stornoway Gaelic Free Church referred to 'misrepresentation made to simple minded people by those who ought to know better'.[5] For those favouring union with the United Presbyterians, such as Peter MacDonald, Rainy was simply endeavouring to guide the Free Church with the consensus, yet defuse the influence of Highland trouble makers at the same time.

UNION

✼

At the Free Church General Assembly in May 1900, Rainy submitted the report of the Union Committee containing the proposed basis and arrangements for union with the United Presbyterians and he moved its adoption. This had been sent to the lower courts of the church for comment. Seventy presbyteries out of seventy-five had indicated their approval.

Mr Angus Galbraith, minister of Lochalsh, moved the rejection of the report and a re-affirmation of the testimony of 1843. Galbraith argued that the Union Committee's proposals contained provisions which were at variance with and violate the standards of the Free Church which were established when the church was founded at the Disruption. He recommended that no further steps be taken towards union. In this, Galbraith was expressing the views of those who had been called to a meeting at Achnasheen earlier that year, in March, and had committed themselves to 'maintain inviolate the Free Church of Scotland and its testimony'. The Assembly voted 589 for Rainy and twenty-nine for Galbraith; and then agreed to hold a special Assembly in October 1900 for the purpose of finalising the union arrangements.

There was considerable opposition to the actions of the Assembly throughout the Highlands and Islands. In many ways it had been another decade of conflict and those favouring union

The General Assembly of the Free Church of Scotland
on 31 October 1900. On this day their numbers were cut
from over 1000 ministers to twenty-seven.
(Source: by kind permission, Knox Press,
Free Church of Scotland, Edinburgh)

were well aware of the unrest in the Highlands. There was
particular concern with the mood of anger and disappointment in
the Highlands. In Arran, a deputation of ten pro-union ministers
plus elders arrived. This resulted in a very lively meeting which did
not favour the pro-union ministers who were heckled and a
significant portion of the Arran people decided to continue their
opposition to the union.

The island of Lewis was also an area of particular concern
which received a large and impressive deputation of pro-union
ministers. This was in October, 1900, the month of the Union.
This comprised a careful selection of Free Church ministers: Revs
A Lee, D J Martin of Oban, D MacDonald of Kilmuir Easter, J
MacMillan of Ullapool, R Dingwall of Poolewe, J Lamont of
Snizort, M MacLennan of Edinburgh, R MacKenzie of
Maryburgh and D MacLeod of Avoch. Most of the Lewis pro-

General Assembly of the Free Church of Scotland, October 1900. On the afternoon of 31 October the Free Church General Assembly began the task of organising the congregations that had refused to enter the Union. (Source: by kind permission, Free Church College, Edinburgh)

union ministers were also in attendance. This team held meetings throughout the country districts of Lewis, explaining and trying to persuade the people of the benefits of union. Their number is perhaps a reflection of the concern that the new church would not carry the Lewis people with it into the Union. Dr Charles MacRae, a Free Church elder and son of Rev William MacRae, Barvas, who had remained in the established church in 1843, suggested that the 'union question was causing a great deal of anxiety in Lewis, more so than in any other place'.[6]

This deputation of clerical celebrities agreed with Donald John Martin that the 'Free Church was taking all its distinctive principles into the Union without adding anything or detracting anything'.[7] They were, however, having some difficulty in getting this message over to the people of Lewis. This concern over the mood of the people in Lewis is further demonstrated in the Lewis Free Church presbytery's overture to the Assembly, in which they suggested that the Assembly 'make an authoritative declaration that Free Church people who may enter the Union carry all their distinctive Free Church principles with them'.[8]

Lewis also received anti-union deputations consisting of Revs MacCulloch of Glasgow, Galbraith of Lochalsh, MacDonald of Raasay and Campbell of Creich. On 21 September they arrived in Stornoway and held a service in the Drill Hall. This meeting attracted people from town and country and all shades of religious opinion in the island.

Galbraith was the first to speak. As he commenced his address, Peter MacDonald, minister of Stornoway Gaelic, interrupted and asked if the people could hear both sides of the argument. The chairman at this meeting, MacCulloch, said it was a meeting for those opposed to union. MacDonald then demanded to be heard and despite the chairman telling him to sit down, he continued to speak while others in the meeting were shouting at him to organise another meeting and demanding that he 'sit down' or that someone should 'put him out'. The meeting was soon out of control. While the chairman called for the 'protection of the civil powers', others were appealing for Peter MacDonald to speak. A former provost of Stornoway blamed these events on the Free Presbyterians. He claimed that 'the people making the disturbance are seceders, they have no right here at all'.

The journalist to whom we are indebted for this colourful account described the scene at this stage as being 'beyond description. Several gentlemen were on their feet speaking at one time and the rough element were howling'.

In one corner, Mr MacAskill, pro-union Free Church minister of Dingwall, who was trying to get an audience for himself, was exhorted to 'allow the people who came here to speak, to do so'. MacAskill's quick response was, 'And who are you?' This gentleman then introduced himself as the superintendent of police whose protection others were appealing for. However, superintendent Smith was informed of the temporal and limited nature of his authority which apparently gave him no right to interfere. MacAskill continued, 'I know the authority and power under which you act, and you had better take care'. After some time Peter MacDonald led the Free Church pro-union contingent out of the meeting stating, 'I leave this meeting and let your blood be on your own conscience'. MacAskill, however, persisted and requested 'one word' to which the chairman replied 'not one'.

The meeting thereafter continued as it had been planned as a platform for an explanation of the anti-union position and an appeal for support. At the end of the meeting the chairman asked Free Church members to stand and raise a hand if they were opposed to union. 'Considerably more than half of those in the body of the hall stood up'. It was later reported that the chairman next asked for a similar expression from those present who were in favour of union. The account tells us 'there was no response'. This is not surprising as most pro-union people had probably left with Peter MacDonald.[9]

UNION AND DIVISION

❊

A special Free Church Assembly, called to approve the union with the United Presbyterian Church, was held in Edinburgh on October 30, 1900. At this Assembly, Rainy tabled the report of the Union Committee which had been before the Assembly at its usual meeting in May. A number of constitutionalists again spoke against the report; Mr Kennedy Cameron, minister of Brodick, Mr Bannatyne, minister of Coulter, Mr Murdo MacKenzie, minister of Inverness and Mr MacNeilage, a Glasgow elder. In addition a petition was presented containing a request by over 500 elders that union be delayed until kirk sessions and congregations, and not only presbyteries, had been consulted. Despite these efforts the Act of Union was carried by 616 votes; 643 for and 27 against. At this point Mr Kennnedy Cameron presented a protest saying that those who had voted for union had withdrawn from the membership of the Free Church and he and his friends would continue the Free Church Assembly.

Those who resolved to continue as the Free Church moved into a side room. They agreed to meet the following day at the Assembly Hall, but when they tried to obtain access to the Assembly Hall the following morning they were refused. They were informed by the janitor, Mr Temple, that the hall was being cleaned. Mr Kennedy Cameron said that they could have done without the hall being cleaned. To this Mr Temple responded, 'I believe that quite well, you are among dirt anyway'. Despite being locked out and thwarted in their objective of obtaining access to the Assembly Hall, they constituted the Free Church Assembly on the pavement and adjourned to meet in a hall in Queen Street in the afternoon. In this session they elected Mr Bannatyne as their moderator. They repealed the Uniting Act and decided to meet in private in order to avoid the unwelcome attention of United Free supporters who were heckling and disturbing the proceedings.

On 31 October the experience of their former colleagues was very different. They assembled at New College, marched down the Mound and met up with the United Presbyterian Synod that had marched from Castle Terrace. At this point they joined up and continued to the Waverley Market. Together they approved the Uniting Act, it was signed, and Rainy was elected as the first Moderator of the United Free Church.

The Free Church ministers that stayed out of the Union were Bannatyne of Coulter; J Kennedy Cameron of Arran, W MacKinnon of Gairloch, N Campbell of Creich, J MacLeod of Glasgow, M MacQueen of Kiltearn, J Noble of Lairg, D MacLean of Moy, F MacRae of Knockbain, M MacKenzie of Inverness, A Auld of Olrig, J MacCulloch of Glasgow, E MacLeod of Oban, A Galbraith of Lochalsh, H Cameron of Back, W Fraser of Sleat, J MacDonald of Raasay, D MacLeod of Coigach, R Finlayson of Daviot, D Munro of Ferintosh, N Nicolson of Garve, K MacRae of Glenshiel and J MacIver of Resolis.

In addition two retired ministers remained in the Free Church, R Gordon and D MacAllister both from Edinburgh. In Glasgow, J Geddes, who was ill remained Free Church and H Kennedy of Park, although he joined the United Free Church in 1900, returned to the Free Church within the space of a couple of months. It was initially estimated that well over ninety congregations wanted to maintain their links with the Free Church and this number made great demands on the Free Church ministers remaining.

The United Free also acted to consolidate their support and encourage depleted congregations. Many of the reports which were sent into the Highland Committee of the United Free Church spoke of revivals and converts and of many young people being attracted to the church. In the years after the Union the tireless work of two of its ministers drew frequent praise. John MacKay and William Ross operated as United Free evangelists throughout the Highlands. MacKay had been working as an evangelist for some years and Ross had been the Free Church minister of Cowcaddens in Glasgow. Both men travelled throughout the Highlands and Islands where they conducted special evangelistic services and assisted at communions. They had further assistance from lay assistants who helped with this evangelistic work.

In 1900 the four Highland synods of the Free Church had 239 ministers. In this area nineteen remained in the Free Church and 220 went into the United Free Church. United Free estimates for 1901 suggested that in Scotland, as a whole, 30,000 people were connected with the Free Church and over 600,000 with the United Free Church.

An accurate picture of how the Union of 1900 affected Highland congregations is, in some areas, difficult to obtain. It was quite common for one issue of a newspaper to report a congregational division with some figures attached indicating the strength of the two factions. In the following week's newspaper this would be disputed and further corrected in subsequent editions. Those offering their comments all seemed to claim to be eye-witnesses.

The United Free estimated that in the Highlands about one third of the people stayed with the Free Church. The post-1900 Free Church had its greatest strength in Sutherland and Ross-shire and also had a substantial presence in Caithness and Inverness-shire. Free Church records for 1905 list 112 congregations in the Highlands. These were located in the presbyteries of Lorn, nine;

*John MacLeod, Principal of Free Church College, was intimately connected with Highland
church life and was held in great esteem and affection. In 1905 he proposed closer links between
the Free Church and the Free Presbyterian Church. At this point he was a minister of the
latter church yet had accepted a professorship with the former. His proposal was rejected
by the Synod of the Free Presbyterian Church. He then left the Free Presbyterians
and returned to the Free Church. (Source: by kind permission, Knox Press,
Free Church of Scotland, Edinburgh)*

Inverness, twenty-five; Chanonry, five; Dingwall, thirteen;
Lochcarron, thirteen; Skye and Uist, eleven; Lewis, eleven;
Dornoch, fifteeen and Caithness, ten.

In Sutherland the people of Lairg and Creich were mostly anti-
union and remained with the Free Church. In the north and west
of Sutherland, in areas such as Tongue and Lochinver, there was
strong opposition to the Union. Rosehall was divided but had a
pro-union majority. Rogart, Golspie, Brora and Helmsdale were
also divided communities but with anti-union majorities.

A Free Church report also produced some rough figures
indicating United Free adherence in Lewis. In Lochs, with a
population of 4,000, only 100 adhered to the United Free Church.

In Carloway, out of a population of 2,000, about sixty went into the United Free Church. In Shawbost the population was around 1,000, but only the minister's family and one or two individuals joined the United Free. The Barvas congregation was 1,800, out of which the United Free Church gained only eighty adherents. In Ness the congregation was 1,800 and between 100 to 120 were described as 'following the minister' into the Union. The Knock congregation was 2,000, of whom only 100 were also described as following the minister, Mr MacLeod into the United Free Church. Finally, the report mentions the Stornoway Gaelic congregation of whom 100 had joined the United Free Church in Lewis.[10]

According to this source no more than 600 people in Lewis had left to join the United Free Church. The Free Church figures, however, ignored the two congregations where most of the people entered the Union. These were Uig and Stornoway English with congregations somewhere in the region of 600 and 400 respectively. This figure includes both members and adherents over the age of eighteen. A rough estimate of the numbers that joined the United Free Church can thus be obtained by combining the numbers in the *Monthly Record of the Free Church of Scotland* with the congregations of Uig and Stornoway English. This gives a figure of about 1,600 who joined the United Free Church out of a pre-union Free Church total of almost 20,000.

DISTURBANCES

❧

Following the Assembly of October 1900 the new United Free congregations tended to hold onto the churches and manses which they already occupied, and the Free Church had to find alternative accommodation. A variety of locations were used including halls, barns, store-rooms and open-air locations. The preferred meeting-places, however, seemed to be schools. The fact that the United Free Church retained most of the church property created diffi-culties in many Highland communities where a majority of the people had determined to stay with the Free Church. There were reports of hostility, name-calling, intimidation, but it was only in a few communities that there were serious disturbances. These were Evanton, Whiting Bay in Arran, Ness in Lewis and Renton in Dumbartonshire.

In November 1900, in Evanton, a unionist meeting was attacked by people throwing stones and turf. There was only a small United Free gathering and the police were required to restore order. In Whiting Bay, the minister entered the Union but the majority of the congregation opposed it, and the people felt they had a right to the church which they had built. In November 30, 1900, a group of men went to take the building. Some United Free supporters who had blockaded it from within were overpowered when the Free Church people entered by a skylight. The United Free gave in and quit the building, leaving the Sherriff to make subsequent arrangments for its joint occupation.

The Renton congregation was a Gaelic-speaking congregation in Dumbarton. At the time of the Union it was vacant and the congregation remained in possession of the church building. Shortly after the Union in October 1900, the congregation was addressed by two United Free ministers, Mr Lee and Mr Howie. During the service the congregation became aware that the locks were being changed on the church door by pro-union supporters. This realisation brought a prompt end to the persuasive attempts of Howie and Lee; the meeting ended in uproar and this outcome confirmed the Renton congregation's attachment to the Free Church.

In Ness in Lewis there was a much more serious dispute over church possession in which the ability to negotiate a settlement broke down and force was used to take possession of the church. The attempt to arrive at a suitable arrangement for the mutual use of the Cross church in Ness broke down in February 1901 when a Free Church crowd took the church keys from the United Free church officer. One account claimed that about 700 anti-unionists took forcible possession of the church, roughly pushed the United Free minister and worshippers out, took the keys and occupied the church. A subsequent letter to the *Highland News* denied this version of events.

At the point when negotiations broke down the United Free minister, MacDonald, was in possession of the church and claimed that he had offered reasonable terms for the joint use of the Cross church to the Free Church majority. His opponents in the Free Church claimed that six approaches had been made to MacDonald requesting that he consider Free Church requests for the use of the church. The Free Church party claimed that MacDonald had been warned that the Ness people were becoming impatient and restless and that many wanted to take the building by force. MacDonald denied this version of events.

Following these events the church building remained in the hands of the Free Church. By July 1901, Mr MacDonald, had appealed to the civil powers to re-open the Cross church and to 'suggest arrangements for its joint use'. This included the proposal that the keys should be passed to the police and then to the United Free church officer in Cross. This did not take place. With no keys produced a small party consisting of the sheriff's officer, police, Mr MacDonald and a tradesman arrived to open the church. A crowd of about 100 barred their way to the door and the sheriff's officer, who was denied access, was unable to carry out his duty. He returned to Stornoway and in due course seven men from Ness were charged, of whom six were convicted and fined £10 each. This provoked an angry reaction in Ness. When police arrived to change the locks in December 1901 they had to take refuge in the church until they managed to negotiate a safe departure from Cross. These disturbances were considered to be so serious that the authorities sent a warship and a number of mainland police to secure order in what was considered to be a troubled community.

There were a number of additional disturbances in Ness. Both the police station and the United Free Church manse were reported to have been attacked by stone-throwing crowds. Some of the elders who joined the United Free Church had their barley and corn stacks set alight.   The United Free minister, Mr MacDonald, was also singled out for attack and abuse. There are stories which describe his windows being smashed in the night and large stones landing on the bed where he was sleeping. Ness people also refer to an attempted attack on Mr MacDonald. Slightly different versions of this incident exist. One account describes how a group of men were planning to attack the minister as he made his way home one night. As the men were about to do him harm a bright light surrounded MacDonald and the men were unable to carry out their deed. Another account of the same incident is not quite so dramatic and attributes MacDonald's escape to a horse and cart rather than supernatural illumination.

The Ness people, both Free Church and United Free, made

much use of the Highland press to present their versions of these events. Their accounts are fascinating but frustrating in terms of establishing the sequence of events. There was even disagreement over the financial contribution which before 1900, those who were now in the Free and United Free churches had previously made to the Ness church. After he entered the Union, MacDonald, minister of Cross, claimed, 'those who paid highest in the church are with us, and that the great majority of those who follow them (Free Church), paid nothing in it or next to nothing'. This was directly challenged by Murdo Gunn, who before 1900 had been collector of church funds for the Ness Free Church congregation. Gunn said the church had cost £2,400 and over £1,800 had been paid. Of that £1,800 the anti-unionists had paid over £1,600 and those presently in the Union had only paid over £100. Disagreements of such an extreme kind were typical of the debate in Ness. The Highland press contain a number of letters on this subject and it is a fascinating episode of claim and counter claim.[12]

Elsewhere, if there were not such serious disturbances, confrontations between pro-union and anti-union supporters were widely reported. For example, at the Free Church in Dunvegan a pro-union probationer was prevented from entering the pulpit by the elders and turned out of the church. The elders remained in the Free Church and took the service. In Skerray, near Bettyhill, the anti-union congregation were unhappy with their minister, Mr J R MacNeill as he used a Sunday service to give his congregation his views on the benefits of union. One report said 'if it had been a week day it is quite possible that he would have been interrupted more than once; however, as it was the Sabbath, they kept silent, but their silence did not mean their consent'. This congregation later, at a midweek meeting, declared their loyalty to the Free Church and people decided to hold their services in the mission station at Skerray. The locks on this building were changed by both parties, with the Free Church people retaining eventual control. When a United Free assistant minister was sent along to take the service on a Sunday he was stopped from entering the mission by six men and the local constable refused to come to his assistance.

In one church at Arnisdale and Corran the Free Church people were determined to retain possession of the church building. A

Free Church deputation had been informed that the church was firmly locked. However, as they approached the church, one member of the group gently turned the handle and apparently the door flew open. This was explained in supernatural terms and a report said 'the opening of the door in such a mysterious manner to a waiting, anxious and zealous flock of worshippers should indeed be very encouraging'.[11]

Free Church official sources were usually very quick to disassociate themselves from any incidents in which the people took the law into their own hands. Yet in many communities the old minister, now in the United Free Church along with his family and a handful of others retained the property while the majority were denied its use. Mr Kennedy Cameron of Brodick, asked 'is it any wonder that the people should be exasperated by such provocation'?

It was understandably a period of inter-church rivalry and hostility. In communities that were predominantly Free Church, there were reports of United Free supporters claiming to be socially ostracised and frequently intimidated. The same was true in reverse when the Free Church were in the minority. Both parties were also quick to describe the words and deeds of their opponents as being underhand and unworthy of members of a Christian community. The new United Free ministers also complained about the way that their former congregations misrepresented them.

The division between the Free Church and the United Free Church in the Highlands and Islands also had implications for the Free Presbyterians. Following the 1900 Union there were a number of reports of improved relations between the Free Church and the Free Presbyterians. Newspaper reports spoke of Free Presbyterians attending Free Church meetings in Fort William, Spean Bridge, Banavie and Kilmallie. In Skye and Assynt there were also reports of seceders attending Free Church services and communions.

Such initiatives and gestures were not only from the people. The Free Church Synod of Ross noted that Free Church and Free Presbyterian ministers were exchanging pulpits and in 1902 the Free Church Synod of Ross and the Free Church Synod of Sutherland and Caithness overtured the Free Church Assembly

Lochcarron United Free Congregation. This congregation had to meet outside the church following the House of Lords' decision to award the property to the post 1900 Free Church.

(Source: SLA, NMS)

on the desirability of union between the Free Church and the Free Presbyterians.   This was widely supported but in 1902 the Free Church had not yet repealed the Declaratory Act and the Free Presbyterians felt unable to consider closer relations with the Free Church because of this.   The Free Church repealed the Declaratory Act in 1905.

In November 1905 when the Free Presbyterian Synod met in Glasgow, John MacLeod proposed a committee to discuss union with the Free Church.   His proposal was defeated by a counter proposal from Neil Cameron.   The Free Presbyterians considered that there were two sticking points; one was in the wording of the Free Church act repealing the Declaratory Act and the other related to the question of the inerrancy of Scripture.

The Free Church endeavoured to reassure the Free Presbyterians on these points of difficulty and expressed deep regret at the treatment of the first two Free Presbyterian ministers, MacDonald and MacFarlane, by the Free Church Assembly. The Free Presbyterian Synod, however, warned against mixing with the Free Church and instructed presbyteries and kirk sessions 'to maintain order and discipline in the several congregations under their charge'. Following this, three Free Presbyterian ministers moved back to the Free Church in December 1905.   These were John MacLeod of Kames, Alexander Stewart of Edinburgh and George MacKay of Stornoway.

This must have been a great loss to the Free Presbyterian Church.   Donald MacFarlane, Free Presbyterian minister of Raasay, however, commented optimistically that 'by this sifting the Lord is purifying our church – throwing away those whom he knows would be of no use in maintaining a faithful testimony for his truth'.[13]

THE PROPERTY QUESTION

✤

As the Free Church regarded themselves as the legitimate repre-sentatives of the Disruption tradition they believed they had a right to the property of the old Free Church.   In the earlier union discussions of 1860 and 1870, James Begg and others threatened to claim all the property of the Free Church for those opposed to union. This factor contributed to the failure of those negotiations.

Following the Union of 1900 this threat was tested in the courts between 1900 and 1904. The Free Church first took their case to the Court of Session in 1900. They argued that the United Free Church had not preserved intact the whole principles of the constitution of the Free Church. They argued that they had abandoned the establishment principle and in the Declaratory Act had altered the Church's relationship to the Westminster Confession of Faith. The United Free, they argued, therefore, had no claim to the lands, property or funds of the Disruption Free Church.

In their defence the United Free Church argued that they had not changed their principles. The establishment principle, it was claimed, was not central to the constitution of the Free Church and the Declaratory Act had been sent down to presbyteries and had received approval. The church had, therefore, acted in accordance with its constitution.

The Free Church lost their case to the Court of Session, but appealed to the House of Lords. At the House of Lords seven judges heard the case and five decided in favour of the Free Church. This judgement was delivered in August 1904. The Lords, therefore, reversed the judgement of the Court of Session and said that the Free Church was 'entitled to have the whole of the said lands, property and funds applied acording to the terms of the trust'. Of the United Free Church it was said that they had 'no right, title or interest in any part of the lands, property, sums of money and others which stood vested at the 30th day of October 1900 in the Free Church'. Thus, twenty-seven ministers found themselves in the legal possession of 1100 churches and 1000 manses.

It was plain to Government, however, that something had to be done to resolve the issue in a more equitable manner. A Royal Commission was set up to secure the redistribution of church property and was followed by the Churches (Scotland) Act of 1905. The Commission had suggested that the post-1900 Free Church was entitled to the congregational property if one third of the members and adherents had remained in the Free Church on 30 October 1900.

It took until 1909 before all the pre-1900 Free Churches were investigated and their properties allocated. Of the ministers who remained Free Church most were from Highland parishes and this

*There was a cruel irony in the fact that the post-1900 Free Church, which
stood by the principle of spiritual independence, found itself dependent on the state
to settle the question of the ownership of the property and assets of the pre-1900
Free Church. These two cartoons are from a series that mocked the House of Lords'
decision to give the entire property of the pre-1900 Free Church to
the post-1900 Free Church.
(Source: SLA, NMS)*

was also true of the properties assigned to the Free Church between 1905 and 1909. Most of these properties were in the Highlands, 110, as opposed to twenty-two outside the Highlands. In a number of other parishes, throughout the Highlands, the property was divided between the Free Church and the United Free Church.

Church records were allocated on the same basis as property. If the Free Church retained over one third of the people it secured the records. The Free Church, therefore, obtained the records for the pre-1900 Free Church Synods of Ross, Sutherland and Caithness, Glenelg, Moray and Argyll. They also secured the records for seventeen presbyteries all of which were in the Highlands and Islands.

In many places the United Free congregations made it very difficult for Free Church congregations to retake the buildings to which they now had a legal right. Legal assistance was employed in order to obtain possession and there were also a number of enforced re-possessions following the Lords' decision. For their part the United Free Church regarded the re-possessions as unjustified evictions.

A DISRUPTIVE UNION

❋

The movement towards the Union of the Free Church and the United Presbyterian Church was disruptive of the consensus that existed in the Highlands. As the Free Church moved towards union and adjusted its standards, it contributed to division in the north. At some points the categories of constitutionalist and progressive are of little use in explaining the divisions that followed the 1900 Union in the Highlands. Many who were regarded as constitutionalists entered the Union. The categories of constitutionalist and progressive, used widely in the Lowlands, were less relevant to the religious culture and climate of much of the Highlands. Yet, as a result of pressure from the Free Church majority, in the 1890s, two contending factions emerged in the Highlands; pro-union and anti-union. These, of course, do not equate with progressive and constitutionalist.

The demand for change and the movement towards union had put pressure on the Highland Free Church and created an unnatural division. It was not necessarily a theological division since the alignments that resulted from 1893 and 1900 did not reflect the views held. Many Highland Free Church people remained bitterly opposed to the Declaratory Act after 1893 and in 1900 many constitutionalists entered the Union. Theological ideas and theological background do not provide an adequate explanation for the division in 1900. Neither can geography or language.

It is undeniable that the constitutionalists who remained in the Free Church after 1900 were predominantly Highland and Gaelic-speaking, but many more from this region joined the United Free Church. Both constitutionalism and pro-union sentiment were firmly rooted in the Highland church and had the support of Gaelic-speakers. In the attempt to account for the adherence of many Highlanders to the Free Church it has to be acknowledged that many would have followed this course for deeply personal reasons. However, in order to provide a common explanation, reference must be made to the legacy of evangelicalism in the Highlands.

Evangelicalism as it was mediated through the pre-1900 Free Church had a profound effect on a number of Highland communities. It was more than just a series of beliefs that required assent. Evangelicalism shaped the culture, provided institutions, and re-defined social arrangements. These elements were clearly more than belief yet they stemmed from belief. If particular beliefs were called into question then the particular social and cultural arrangements that flowed from belief would also be at risk.

Evangelical religion had made a significant impact on Highland society both before and after 1843. It had provided a range of institutions and structures; from family worship to communion and from kirk session to Assembly, it had provided its ministers and elders with enhanced status and its church people with the prestige of being attached to a major social institution. Evangelicalism had provided a code of what was culturally acceptable along with a system of beliefs.

This was seen as the legacy of the Disruption Free Church to much of the Highlands. To all this union with the United Presbyterians was perceived as a threat. It was perceived, rightly or wrongly, that it would introduce a form of religion that would undermine the culture, social structure and institutions of Highland communities. Given the origin and associations of the

*As an itinerant preacher, Neil Cameron did much to consolidate the Free Presbyterian
Church in the north west Highlands and Islands and as minister of St Jude's Free
Presbyterian Church in Glasgow he opposed closer links with the Free Church in 1905.
(Source: by kind permission, Free Presbyterian Archive, Inverness)*

pro-union party it was understandable why some would regard union in this way. The pro-union Free Church was seen by some to have its origins in the Assembly committees and in the colleges of the Free Church that were loosening their attachment to the principles of 1843 and introducing changes in belief and practice that were unacceptable to Highland constitutionalism. Pro-union spirituality, it was felt, would not sustain the culture, the social arrangements and the particular character of the institutions that evangelicalism in the Free Church had produced.

However, not all who held to these things remained with the Free Church after the Union. There are perhaps many reasons why Free Church people in the Highlands joined the United Free Church. Undoubtedly some cared little for a rigid adherence to Westminster Calvinism and felt more at home with a more inclusive spirituality. Some went into the Union because they continued to respect and adhere to the decisions of the Free Church Assembly and some opted for union in order to avoid further religious conflict.

Yet others were persuaded by the assurances they received that they could enter the United Free Church and take all their distinctive Free Church principles with them. Some Free Church people went into the Union because of the influence of Free Church leaders both at a local and a national level. Indeed, when many evangelical Highland ministers opted for union they provided a model for Free Church people who were impressed by their example. Again there were those who entered the Union for reasons associated with family and community traditions.

Examples for all of the above can be found. The many varied and individual decisions to accept union in 1900, did not necessarily coincide with an adoption of liberal evangelicalism and a rejection of constitutionalism.

A further question that merits some consideration is the extent to which the political developments of the 1880s moderated the constitutionalism of some Highland Free Church ministers and people. In the 1880s there was a remarkable upsurge of political activity in which many Highland Free Church ministers were very directly involved. This involvement provided them with other priorities and this would carry the potential for easing their grip on constitutionalism.

In many ways the nineteenth-century Free Church machine had succeeded. By adhering to a new tone and temper of spirituality and relentlessly identifying these with the prestigious elites in the Free Church, considerable pressure was exerted on both ministers and people. In the Highlands the Free Church dominance of the mid nineteenth-century was badly shattered in 1900. The union agenda was determined outwith the Highlands and many Highland communities that had demonstrated a remarkable attachment to the old Free Church were pulled in different directions. Those in the Highlands who joined the United Free Church, found themselves making common cause with those with whom they had less in common and leaving behind those with whom they had more in common.

CHAPTER 12

Conclusion

There is little that needs to be added at this point. The previous chapters have dealt with distinct issues and have contained their own discussion and conclusions. The aim throughout has been to provide a wide-ranging survey that sets the church firmly within the context of Highland culture and society.

The role of the church is one of the great themes in Highland history. It shaped many aspects of Highland society, it exercised considerable social control, it was intimately associated with social change, it provided opportunity for certain social groups to adjust their position in Highland society and any discussion of Highland themes requires consideration of the role of the church.

It is perhaps inevitable that such an institution in such a period of history should attract both strong attachment and fierce antipathy. The history and role of the Highland church remains a source of debate and contention and this does no more than reflect its divided past and its ambivalent legacy.

The preceding account has included considerable detail, yet has also endeavoured to highlight the main developments in Highland church history. The detail has ranged from poetry to human sacrifice, from famine to shinty and from sheep-farming to the House of Lords. The main developments have been identified as presbyterianism, evangelicalism, the Free Church and its late nineteenth-century fragmentation.

Presbyterianism and evangelicalism were of crucial significance in shaping both the Highland church and Highland society. Although there was some opposition to these in this period, in the long term, the Highlands and Islands did not have the means to resist them.

In 1690 presbyterianism became the lawful form of church organisation in Scotland. This was put in place with not a little pain and with considerable assistance from a variety of agencies. It was slowly but successfully extended and consolidated throughout the Highlands and Islands. This arrangement was barely in place when the structure and mood of the Church of Scotland was challenged by the forceful appeal and triumphant activity of evangelicals both inside and outside the church.

The Free Church benefited from the success of both presbyterianism and evangelicalism in the Highlands. Although the Free Church was a national institution it also provided a structure for traditions that were distinctly Highland and was the natural home and culmination of the dramatic religious changes of the early nineteenth-century in the Highlands. Evangelicalism had provided the Highland church with leadership, traditions and a distinctive character. Thus when the Free Church nationally began to move in a different direction the Highlands had the confidence to resist. Their resistance, however, was at great cost to the unity of the church.

The main developments in Highland church history, identified above, can be linked in a fascinating interplay between external forces and marginal and dominant groups in Highland society. In 1689 presbyterianism was largely an external influence to, and a marginal group in Highland society. The dominant form of religious expression in the Highlands was episcopalianism. This dominant group was, however, weakened by the legal force given to presbyterianism. Thus the success of the combined force of presbyterianism as an external influence and as a marginal group in Highland society was assured. Consequently, Highland presbyterians were able to adjust their position and status in Highland society.

One hundred years later the evangelical impulse was both an external influence and a marginal group in Highland society. The prevailing spirituality in the Highlands in the late eighteenth-century and early nineteenth-century did not have the strength or confidence to resist the forceful appeal of evangelicalism.

Thus we again find a similar set of circumstances in the period 1790 to 1830 as is found from 1690 to 1730. Both occasions involved the successful combination of a strong external influence and a marginal Highland group and this force was fortunate enough to find the majority Highland expression to be weakened and unable to offer any meaningful resistance. On both occasions what resulted in the Highlands was an indigenous spirituality that, although distinct, shared much in common with the Lowland church.

In the late nineteenth-century the same factors were operating again but there were crucial changes which produced a different outcome. Again there was a combination of external influence and marginal Highland group in those favouring a more liberal progressive evangelicalism. What was fundamentally different in the late nineteenth-century was the strength of the majority evangelical church in the Highlands and its consequent unwillingness to accept progressive Free Church evangelicalism. Thus, the outcome was noticeably different, fragmenting the Highland Free Church and introducing a measure of discontinuity between Highland and Lowland spirituality.

The ecclesiastical developments at the end of the nineteenth-century were crucial for the pattern of church provision that characterised the Highlands in the twentieth-century. Almost one hundred years after the Union of 1900, the Free Church and the Free Presbyterian Church are still predominantly Highland churches. Both have had periods of difficulty, with the Free Presbyterian Church dividing in 1989 and the Associated Presbyterian Churches being formed. The majority of the United Free Church moved into the Church of Scotland in 1929, providing the Church of Scotland with a considerable Highland following.

All of these churches can claim to descend from the reformed presbyterian tradition, to some extent from Disruption principles and also from the small despised groups that Neil Douglas and others encountered in the 1790s and described as 'The People of the Great Faith'.

Notes

CHAPTER 2 – THE PRESBYTERIAN SETTLEMENT

✿

1. J MacInnes, *The Evangelical Movement in the Highlands of Scotland*, (Aberdeen, 1951), p.13
2. H Scott (ed), *Fasti Ecclesiae Scoticana* (FES), Vol VII (Edinburgh, 1928)
3. G E MacDermid, *The Religious and Ecclesiastical Life of the North West Highlands*, 1750-1843, PhD thesis, University of Aberdeen, 1967, p.45
4. J MacInnes, *Evangelical Movement*, p.34
5. FES, Vol VII
6. J MacInnes, *Evangelical Movement*, p.27
7. *The Statistical Account of Scotland*, D J Withrington & I R Gray (eds), (1981) XVII, p.573
8. W MacKay, *Urquhart and Glenmoriston*, (Inverness, 1893), p.372

CHAPTER 3 – THE EXTENSION OF PRESBYTERIANISM

✿

1. J MacInnes, *Evangelical Movement*, p.41, W Ferguson, The Problems of the Established Church in the West Highlands and Islands in the Eighteenth Century, *RSCHS*, XVII, 1969, A MacLean, *Telford's Highland Churches*, (Inverness, 1989), p.4
2. *Statistical Account of Scotland*, XVII, p.285
3. The Fourth Report of the Commissioners of Religious Instruction, Scotland 1838, Appendix No1, p.459, *Parliamentary Papers*, 1837-38, XXXII
4. *Statistical Account of Scotland*, XVII, 563
5. quoted in MacDermid, *Religious and Ecclesiastical Life*, p.219, and in, Accounts of the Population of Certain Parishes in Scotland with the Capacity of their Churches and Chapels, Appendix by Dr J Inglis, *Parliamentary Papers*, 1819, XVII
6. PP, 1837-38, XXXII, 275

7.   MacDermid, *Religious and Ecclesiastical Life*, p.50
8.   J MacInnes, *Evangelical Movement*, p.198-199
9.   PP, 1819, XVII
10. CWJ Withers, Education and Anglicisation, The Policy of
     the SSPCK Towards Gaelic in the Highlands, 1709-1825, *SS*, 1982
11. J MacInnes, *Evangelical Movement*, p.11

CHAPTER 4 – MISSION

❊

1.   T M Devine, *Clanship to Crofters' War, the Social
     Transformation of the Scottish Highlands*, (Manchester,
     1994), p.105
2.   J Greig (ed), *Disruption Worthies of the Highlands*,
     (Edinburgh, 1877), p.224
3.   J Kennedy, *The Apostle of the North*, (Glasgow, 1978), p.40
4.   J MacInnes, *Evangelical Movement*, p.126
5.   J A Haldane, *Journal of a Tour Through the Northern
     Counties of Scotland*, (Edinburgh, 1798), p.17
6.   J Kennedy, *The Apostle of the North*, p.42
7.   J Kennedy, *The Apostle of the North*, p.57
8.   J MacKay, *The Church in the Highlands*, (London, 1914),
     p.225 & 227
9.   A I MacInnes, Evangelical Protestantism in the Nineteenth-
     Century Highlands, in, G Walker & T Gallacher (eds),
     *Sermons and Battle Hymns, Protestant Popular Culture in
     Modern Scotland*, (Edinburgh, 1990), p.54
10. T M Devine, *Clanship to Crofters' War*, p.106
11. T C Smout, *A History of the Scottish People, 1560-1830*
     (London, 1983), p.436

CHAPTER 5 – THE DISRUPTION

❊

1.   GNM Collins (ed), John MacLeod, *By-Paths of Highland
     Church History*, (Edinburgh, 1965), p.41
2.   T Brown, *The Annals of the Disruption*, (Edinburgh, 1893), p.665
3.   T Brown, *Annals*, p.379
4.   The Third Report for the Select Committee on Sites for
     Churches, (Scotland), 1847, *Parliamentary Papers*, XIII, p.123
5.   SRO, CH2 473/2 Lewis Church of Scotland Presbytery
     Records, 4 March, 1845
6.   N MacLean, *The Life of James Cameron Lees*, (Glasgow, 1922), p.15
7.   C MacNaughton, *Church Life in Ross and Sutherland from the
     Revolution (1688) to the Present Time*, (Inverness, 1915), p.395

8. T Brown, *Annals*, p.416
9   Select Committee on Sites, p.199

CHAPTER 6 – THE FREE CHURCH
❋

1. Home and Foreign Missionary Record of the Free Church of Scotland, May, 1845, and Proceedings of the General Assembly of the Free Church of Scotland, 1850
2. Letter from James Loch to Golspie Elders on behalf of the Duke of Sutherland, in, J MacKay, *Memoir of Rev John MacDonald, Minister of the Free Church at Helmsdale*, (Edinburgh, 1861), p.98
3. T Brown, *Annals*, p.135
4. Select Committee on Sites, p.33
5. Select Committee on Sites, p.iv
6. Select Committee on Sites, p.199
7. CWJ Withers, *Gaelic Scotland, the Transformation of a Culture Region*, (London, 1988), p.119
8. A I Macinnes, *Evangelical Protestantism*, p.57
9. Select Committee on Sites, p.129
10. M MacPhail, Notes on Religion in the Isle of Lewis, *Oban Times*, 10 September, 1898
11. Lay Member of the Established Church, *An Account of the Present State of Religion Throughout the Highlands of Scotland*, (Edinburgh, 1827), p.48
12. J Noble, *Religious Life in Ross*, (Inverness, 1909), p.viii
13. R MacCowan, *The Men of Skye*, (Glasgow, 1902), p.vii
14. GNM Collins, *Princpal John MacLeod* (Edinburgh, 1951), p.43
15. N C MacFarlane, *Apostles of the North*, (Stornoway, nd), p.15 & 40

CHAPTER 7 – EDUCATION
❋

1. CWJ Withers, *Education and Anglicisation*, p.38
2. D J Withrington, Schooling, Literacy and Society, in, *People and Society in Scotland*, vol I, 1760-1830, T M Devine & R Mitchison, (eds), (Edinburgh, 1988), p.165
3. D J Withrington, Schooling Literacy and Society, p.165
4. D Sage, *Memorabilia Domestica*, (Wick, 1899), p.276
5. D Sage, *Memorabilia Domestica*, p.112
6. CWJ Withers, *Education and Anglicisation*, p.39
7. V E Durkacz, *The Decline of the Celtic Languages*, (Edinburgh, 1983), p.65
8. W MacKay, *Urquhart and Glenmoriston*, (Inverness, 1893), p.403
9. CWJ Withers, *Education and Anglicisation*, p.45

10. CWJ Withers, *Education and Anglicisation*, p.47

11. quoted in, A W Harding, *Sgoilean Chrìosd*, M Litt thesis,
    University of Glasgow, 1979, p.37

12. *First Annual Report of the Edinburgh Society for the Support of
    Gaelic Schools*, Resolution on the Formation of the Society on
    Wednesday, 16 January, 1811, Resolution VII, (Edinburgh, 1811)

13. A W Harding Gaelic Schools in Northern Perthshire,
    TGSI, 1980-82, p.15

14. Select Committee on Sites, p.47

15. Anonymous letter from a correspondent in Bayble, Lewis, in,
    *The Twenty-Sixth Annual Report of the Edinburgh Society
    for the Support of Gaelic Schools*, p.29 (Edinburgh, 1837)

16. Circular to Gaelic School Teachers, 26 February, 1844, from
    Mr Alex Hutchison, Assistant Secretary of the Edinburgh
    Society for the Support of Gaelic Schools, *Thirty-Third
    Annual Report*, (Edinburgh, 1844)

17. W K Leask, *Dr Thomas M'Lauchlan*, (Edinburgh, 1905), p.164

CHAPTER 8 – SPIRITUALITY

❋

1. J MacInnes, *Evangelical Movement*, p.294

2. K Ross, Calvinsts in Controversy, John Kennedy, Horatius Bonar
   and the Moody Mission of 1873-74, *SBET*, Spring, 1991, p.52

3. M Campbell, *Gleanings of a Highland Harvest*,
   (ed D MacMillan, (Tain, 1989), p.18

4. quoted in, D E Meek 'Falling Down as if Dead', Attitudes
   to Unusual Phenomena in the Skye Revival of 1841-42,
   SBET, Autumn, 1995, p.118

5. J Kennedy, *Days of the Fathers in Ross-Shire*,
   (Inverness, 1861), p.111

6. J Kennedy, *Days of the Fathers*, p.80

7. J MacLeod, *North Country Separatists*, (Inverness, 1930), p.7

8. J MacLeod, *North Country Separatists*, p.4

9. W MacKay, *Urquhart and Glenmoriston*, p.392

10. quoted in G E MacDermid, *Religious and Ecclesiastical Life
    of the North West Highlands*, p.273

11. N MacLean, *Life of J C Lees*, p.89

12. N MacLean, *Life of J C Lees*, p.67

13. D Beaton, *Memoir, Diary and Remains of
    Rev D MacFarlane*, Dingwall, (Inverness, 1929), p.46

14. quoted in G E MacDermid, *Religious and Ecclesiastical
    Life of the North West Highlands*, p.273

15. W Gillies (ed), *Ris a' Bhruthaich, the Criticism and Prose
    Writings of Sorley MacLean*, (Stornoway, 1985), p.297, 298

CHAPTER 9 – LAND

❊

1. D Smith, *Passive Obedience and Prophetic Protest, Social Criticism and the Scottish Church*, 1836-1945, (New York, 1982), p.137

2. A MacKenzie, *A History of the Highland Clearances*, (Inverness, 1883), p.37

3. A I Macinnes, *Evangelical Protestantism in the Nineteenth-Century*, p.60

4. T M Devine, *Clanship to Crofters' War*, p.106

5. J MacInnes, *Evangelical Movement*, p.294

6. J Hunter, *The Making of the Crofting Community*, (Edinburgh, 1976), p.105

7. E Richards, *A History of the Highland Clearances*, vol II, (London, 1985), p.357

8. E Richards, *A History of the Highland Clearances*, vol II, p.357

9. V E Durkacz, *The Decline of the Celtic Languages*, p.129

10. IMM MacPhail, *The Crofters' War* (Stornoway, 1989), p.3

11. D E Meek, The Land Question Answered from the Bible, *Scottish Geographical Magazine*, vol 103, 2, 1987, p.84 & D E Meek, The Bible and Social Change in the Nineteenth-Century Highlands, in, D F Wright (ed), *The Bible in Scottish Life and Literature*, (Edinburgh, 1988), p.186

12. quoted in G E MacDermid, *Religious and Ecclesiastical Life of the North West Highlands*, p.143

13. E Richards, *A History of the Highland Clearances*, vol I (London, 1982), p.321

14. T M Devine, *The Great Highland Famine, Hunger, Emigration and the Scottish Highlands in the Nineteenth-Century*, (Edinburgh, 1988), p.33-40

15. T McLauchlan, in, *The Witness*, 11 Jan, 1851

16. Petition from the Highland Destitution Committee of the Free Church in, *The Witness*, 2 August, 1851

17. W K Leask, *Dr Thomas M'Lauchlan*, p.110

18. J Kennedy, *Days of the Fathers*, p.28

CHAPTER 10 – SECESSION

❊

1. R Rainy, Report of the Committee on Legislation Regarding Patronage, *Free Church Pamphlet*, No XXXII, (1874)

2. *Northern Chronicle*, 27 May, 1896

3. K Ross, *Church and Creed*, (Edinburgh, 1988), p.186

4. *Northern Chronicle*, 11 October, 1893

5. *Northern Chronicle*, 22 June, 1893
6. *Northern Chronicle*, 22 February, 1893
7. GNM Collins, *Principal John MacLeod*, p.36
8. *Northern Chronicle*, 22 February, 1893
9. *Northern Chronicle*, 29 March, 1893
10. J L MacLeod, The Influence of the Highland- Lowland Divide on the Free Presbyterian Disruption of 1893, *RSCHS*, XXV, 1995
11. *Northern Chronicle*, 7 January, 1894
12 *Minute Book of the Free Church Presbytery of Lewis*, 8 August, 1893

CHAPTER 11 – UNION

❀

1. *Inverness Courier*, 20 January, 1893
2. *Inverness Courier*, 17 February, 1893
3. D MacLean, A Biographical Sketch of Rev John Noble, In J Noble, *Religious Life in Ross*, p.xlix
4. GNM Collins, *Principal John MacLeod*, p.33
5. K MacDonald, *Social and Religious Life in the Highlands*, (Edinburgh, 1902), p.241
6. *Highland News*, 27 October, 1900
7. *Highland News*, 27 October, 1900
8. *Minute Book of the Free Church Presbytery Of Lewis*, 17 October, 1900
9. *Highland News*, 29 Setember, 1900
10. *Highland News*, 16 March, 1901 & *Minute Book of the Free Church Presbytery of Lewis*, 27 March, 1895
11. *Free Church Monthly Record*, May, 1901
12 *Highland News*, 11 May, 1900 & 16 Nov, 1901
13. D Beaton, *Memoir, Diary and Remains of Rev D MacFarlane*, Dingwall, (Inverness, 1929), p.54

Bibliography

ABBREVIATIONS

❖

RSCHS Records of the Scottish Church History Society
TGSI   Transactions of the Gaelic Society of Inverness
IR   Innes Review
SHR   Scottish Historical Review
SS   Scottish Studies
SBET   Scottish Bulletin of Evangelical Theology

The following bibliography contains the books and articles that have been consulted in the preparation of this study. There are, however, a number of sources that have not been included in this list. These include Parliamentary Papers, contemporary newspapers, presbytery, synod and Assembly records, personal letters and estate papers.

I M Allan   *West the Glen, A History of the Free Church
                 Just West of the Great Glen,* (Inverness, 1997)
D B A Ansdell   The 1843 Disruption of the Church of Scotland
                 in the Isle of Lewis, *RSCHS,* XXIV, 1991
D B A Ansdell   The Disruptive Union, 1890-1900 in a
                 Hebridean Presbytery, *RSCHS,* XXVI, 1996
A Auld   *Ministers and Men in the Far North,* (Wick, 1896)
D Beaton   *Memoir, Diary and Remains of Rev D MacFarlane,
                 Dingwall,* (Inverness, 1929)
D Beaton   *Memoir Biographical Sketches, Letters, Lectures and
                 Sermons (English and Gaelic) of the Rev Neil
                 Cameron,* (Inverness, 1932)
D Beaton   *Diary and Sermons of Rev Alexander MacLeod,*
                 (Inverness, 1925)
D Beaton   Fast Day and Friday Fellowship Meeting
                 Controversy in the Synod of Sutherland and
                 Caithness, *TGSI,* XXIV, 1916-18
D Beaton   *Some Noted Ministers of the Northern Highlands,*
                 (Glasgow, 1985)
D Bebbington   *The Baptists in Scotland, A History,*
(ed)   (Glasgow, 1988)

A Beith   *Three Weeks With Dr Candlish, A Highland Tour,* (Edinburgh, 1874)

D M Boyd   *Popular History of the Origins of the Free Presbyterian Church of Scotland,* (Inverness, 1988)

D M Boyd   *Halkirk, Free Presbyterian Church of Scotland, 1897-1997,* (1997)

C G Brown   *Religion and Society in Scotland Since 1707,* (Edinburgh, 1997)

C G Brown   Religion and Social Change, in, *People and Society in Scotland, vol I, 1760-1830,* T M Devine & R Mitchison (eds), (Edinburgh, 1988)

C G Brown   Religion, Class and Church Growth, in, *People and Society in Scotland, vol II, 1830-1914,* W H Fraser & R J Morris (eds), (Edinburgh, 1990)

C G Brown   *The People in The Pews,* (ESHSS, 1993)

S J Brown   Martyrdom in Early Victorian Scotland, Disruption Fathers and the Making of the Free Church, in, Diana Wood (ed), *Studies in Church History, vol 30,* (Cambridge, 1993)

T Brown   *The Annals of the Disruption,* (Edinburgh, 1893)

S Bruce   Social Change and Collective Behaviour, the revival in Eighteenth Century Ross-shire, *British Journal of Sociology,* XXXIV, 1983

J Buchanan   *The Lewis Land Struggle, Na Gaisgich* (Stornoway, 1996)

J H S Burleigh   *A Church History of Scotland,* (Oxford, 1960)

W Calder   *After 70 Years, A Historical Sketch of the United Free Congregation, Stornoway,* (Stornoway, nd)

A D Cameron   *Go Listen to the Crofters,* (Stornoway, 1986)

M Campbell   *Gleanings of a Highland Harvest,* (ed) D MacMillan, (Tain, 1989)

A Carmichael   *Carmina Gaedelica,* (Edinburgh, 1900)

A C Cheyne   *The Transforming of the Kirk, Victorian Scotland's Religious Revolution,* (Edinburgh, 1983)

G N M Collins   *Men of Burning Heart,* (Edinburgh, 1983)

G N M Collins   *Donald MacLean,* (Edinburgh, 1944)

G N M Collins   *Principal John MacLeod,* (Edinburgh, 1951)

G N M Collins   *Big MacRae,* (Edinburgh, 1977)

G N M Collins   *The Heritage of Our Fathers,* (Edinburgh, 1976)

G N M Collins (ed)   *John MacLeod: By Paths of Highland Church History,* (Edinburgh, 1965)

W J Couper   *Scottish Revivals,* (Glasgow, 1918)

J Darragh	The Catholic Population of Scotland in the Year 1680, *IR*, IV, 1953
D Davis	Contexts of Ambivalence, Folkloristic Activities of the Nineteenth Century Scottish Highland Ministers, *Folklore*, vol 3, no 2, 1992
T M Devine	*Clanship to Crofters' War, the Social Transformation of the Scottish Highlands*, (Manchester, 1994)
T M Devine	*The Great Highland Famine, Hunger, Emigration and the Scottish Highlands in the Nineteenth Century*, (Edinburgh, 1988)
T M Devine	Highland Migration to Lowland Scotland, *SHR*, 62, 1983
T M Devine & R Mitchison (eds)	*People and Society in Scotland*, vol I, 1760-1830, (Edinburgh, 1988)
N Douglas	*Journal of a Mission to Part of the Highlands of Scotland*, (Edinburgh, 1799)
A L Drummond & J Bulloch	*The Scottish Church, 1688-1843*, (Edinburgh, 1973)
A L Drummond & J Bulloch	*The Church in Victorian Scotland, 1843-74*, (Edinburgh, 1975)
A L Drummond & J Bulloch	*The Church in Late Victorian Scotland*, (Edinburgh, 1978)
V E Durkacz	*The Decline of the Celtic Languages, A Study of Linguistic and Cultural Conflict in Scotland, Wales and Ireland from the Reformation to the Twentieth Century*, (Edinburgh, 1983)
W Ferguson	The Problems of the Established Church in the West Highlands and Islands in the Eighteenth-Century, *RSCHS*, XVII, 1969
F Forbes & W J Anderson	Clergy Lists of the Highland District, 1732-1828 *IR*, XVII, 1966
W H Fraser & R J Morris (eds)	*People and Society in Scotland, vol II, 1830-1914* (Edinburgh, 1990)
Free Presbyterian Publications	*100 Years of Witness*, (Glasgow, 1993)
P Gaskell	*Morvern Transformed, A Highland Parish in the Nineteenth-Century*, (Cambridge, 1968)
W Gillies (ed)	*Ris a' Bhruthaich, the Criticism and Prose Writings of Sorley MacLean*, (Stornoway, 1985)
F Goldie	*A Short History of the Episcopal Church of Scotland*, (Edinburgh, 1976)

I F Grant   *Highland Folk Ways*, (London, 1961)

M Grant   *Free St Columba's, A History of Congregation and*
                   Church, (Edinburgh, 1991)

M Gray   *Scots on the Move*, (ESHSS, 1990)

J Greig (ed)   *Disruption Worthies of the Highlands*,
                   (Edinburgh, 1877)

I F Grigor   *Mightier Than a Lord, the Highland Crofters'*
                   Struggle for the Land, (Stornoway, 1979)

J. Haldane   *Journal of a Tour Through the Northern Counties of*
                   Scotland, (Edinburgh, 1798)

A W Harding   *Sgoilean Chrìosd*, M Litt thesis,
                   University of Glasgow, 1979

A W Harding   Gaelic Schools in Northern Perthshire, *TGSI*,
                   LII, 1980-82

G D Henderson   *The Church of Scotland*, (Edinburgh, 1939)

G D Henderson   *Heritage, A Study of the Disruption*, (Edinburgh, 1943)

P Hillis   The Sociology of the Disruption, in, S J Brown
                   & M Fry (eds), *Scotland in the Age of the*
                   Disruption, (Edinburgh, 1993)

J Hunter   *The Making of the Crofting Community*,
                   (Edinburgh, 1976)

J Hunter   The Emergence of the Crofting Community,
                   The Religious Contribution, 1798-1843, *SS*, 1974

J Hunter   The Politics of Highland Land Reform,
                   1873-1898, *SHR*, 55, 1976

J Hunter   *On the Other Side of Sorrow*, (Edinburgh, 1995)

J G Kellas   The Liberal Party and the Scottish Church
                   Disestablishment Crisis, *English Historical*
                   Review, vol 79, 1964

J Kennedy   *The Days of the Fathers in Ross-shire*, (Inverness, 1861)

J Kennedy   *The Apostle of the North*, (Glasgow, 1978)

Kilmuir . . .   *Kilmuir Church, North Uist, 1894-1994*, (np, nd)

B Lawson   *St Kilda and its Church*, (Stornoway, 1993)

Lay Member   Lay Member of the Established Church,
                   An Account of the Present State of Religion
                   Throughout the Highlands of Scotland,
                   (Edinburgh, 1827)

W K Leask   *Dr Thomas M'Lauchlan*, (Edinburgh, 1905)

B Lenman   The Scottish Episcopal Clergy and the
                   Ideology of Jacobitism, in, E Cruikshanks
                   (ed), *Ideology and Conspiracy; Aspects of Jacobitism,*
                   1689-1759, (Edinburgh, 1982)

M Lundie   *A History of Revivals of Religion in the British Isles*,
                   (Edinburgh, 1836)

D MacArthur	The Breadalbane, *TGSI*, LV, 1986-88	*Bibliography*
J MacAskill	*A Highland Pulpit, Being Sermons of the Late Rev*	✻
	Murdoch MacAskill, (Inverness, 1907)	*225*
M MacAulay	*Aspects of the Religious History of Lewis*, (Inverness, nd)	
M MacAulay	*Hector Cameron of Lochs and Back*, (Edinburgh, 1982)	
M MacAulay	*Burning Bush of Carloway*, (Stornoway, 1984)	
T P McCaughey	Protestantism and Highland Culture, in, J P Mackey (ed), *An Introduction to Celtic Christianity*, (Edinburgh, 1989)	
J McCosh	*The Wheat and the Chaff*, (Dundee, 1843)	
R MacCowan	*The Men of Skye*, (Glasgow, 1902)	
G E MacDermid	*The Religious and Ecclesiastical Life of the North West Highlands, 1750-184*, PhD thesis, University of Aberdeen, 1967	
D MacDonald	*Lewis, A History of the Island*, (Edinburgh, 1978)	
D MacDonald	*Tolsta Townships*, (Stornoway, 1984)	
I R MacDonald	The Beginning of Gaelic Preaching in Scotland's Cities, *Northern Scotland*, 1989	
I R MacDonald	*Glasgow's Gaelic Churches* (Edinburgh, 1995)	
K MacDonald	*Social and Religious Life in the Highlands*, (Edinburgh, 1902)	
R MacDonald	The Catholic Gaidhealtachd, *IR*, XXIX, 1978	
R MacDonald	The Highland District in 1764, *IR*, XVI, 1965	
R MacDonald	Bishop Scott and the West Highlands, *IR*, XVII, 1966	
D MacFarlane	*Memoir and Remains of Rev D MacDonald, Shieldaig*, (Dingwall, 1903)	
N C MacFarlane	*The Men of the Lews*, (Stornoway, 1924)	
N C MacFarlane	*Apostles of the North*, (Stornoway, nd)	
N C MacFarlane	*Donald John Martin*, (Edinburgh, 1914)	
D MacGiliosa	*An Eaglais Shaor Ann An Leòdhas*, (Edinburgh, 1981)	
M McHugh	The Religious Condition of the Highlands and Islands in the Mid-Eighteenth Century, *IR*, XXXV, 1984	
A I Macinnes	Evangelical Protestantism in the Nineteenth Century Highlands, in, G Walker & T Gallacher (eds), *Sermons and Battle Hymns, Protestant Popular Culture in Modern Scotland*, (Edinburgh, 1990)	
A I Macinnes	*Clanship, Commerce and the House of Stuart, 1603-1788*, (Tuckwell, 1996)	
J MacInnes	*The Evangelical Movement in the Highlands of Scotland*, (Aberdeen, 1951)	
J MacInnes	The Origin and Early Development of the Men, *RSCHS*, VIII, 1944	

J MacInnes	Religion in Gaelic Society, *TGSI*, LII, 1980-82
J MacInnes	Baptism in the Highlands, *RSCHS*, XIII, 1959
E MacIver	*Memoirs of a Highland Gentleman, Being the Reminiscences of Evander MacIver of Scourie*, (Inverness, 1893)
I F MacIver	Unfinished Business, The Highland Churches Scheme, 1818-1835, *RSCHS*, XXV, 1995
J MacKay	*Memoir of Rev John MacDonald, Minister of the Free Church at Helmsdale*, (Edinburgh, 1861)
J MacKay	*The Church in the Highlands*, (London, 1914)
W MacKay	*Urquhart and Glenmoriston*, (Inverness, 1893)
A MacKenzie	*A History of the Highland Clearances*, (Inverness, 1883)
D W MacKenzie	The Worthy Translator, How the Scottish Gaels got the Scriptures in their Own Tongue, *TGSI*, 1992-94
K M MacKinnon	The School in Gaelic Scotland, *TGSI*, XLVII, 1971-72
K M MacKinnon	Education in Argyll and the Isles, 1638-1709, *RSCHS* VI, 1936
A MacLean	*Telford's Highland Churches*, (Inverness, 1989)
C MacLean	*Going to Church*, (NMS, Edinburgh, 1997)
C I MacLean	*The Highlands*, (London, 1959)
D MacLean	*Duthil, Past and Present*, (Invernesss, 1910)
D MacLean	*The Counter Reformation in Scotland, 1560-1930*, (London, 1931)
D MacLean	The Presbytery of Ross and Sutherland, 1693-1700, *RSCHS*, V, 1935
D MacLean (ed)	*The Spiritual Songs of Dugald Buchanan*, (Edinburgh, 1913)
D C MacLean	Catholicism in the Highlands and Islands, 1560-1680, *IR*, III, 1952
M MacLean C Carrell (eds)	*As An Fhearann, From the Land*, (Edinburgh, 1986)
N MacLean	*The Life of James Cameron Lees*, (Glasgow, 1922)
J MacLennan	*From Shore to Shore*, (Edinburgh, 1977)
D MacLeod	*Gloomy Memories in the Highlands of Scotland*, (Glasgow, 1892)
D MacLeod	*The Gospel in the Highlands*, (Inverness, 1995)
D W MacLeod	*Knockbain Free Church of Scotland, Past and Present*, (Inverness, 1993)
J MacLeod	*North Country Separatists*, (Inverness, 1930)
J MacLeod	*Scottish Theology in Relation to Church History*, (Edinburgh, 1995)

J MacLeod	*No Great Mischief if You Fall,* (Edinburgh, 1993)
J MacLeod	*Highlanders,* (London, 1996)
J L MacLeod	*The Origins of the Free Presbyterian Church,* PhD thesis, University of Edinburgh, 1994
J L MacLeod	The Influence of the Highland Lowland Divide on the Free Presbyterian Disruption of 1893, *RSCHS,* XXV. 1995
N MacLeod	*Reminiscences of a Highland Parish,* (London, nd)
R MacLeod	The John Bunyan of the Highlands, The Life and Work of the Rev Robert Finlayson, 1793-1861, *TGSI,* 1984-86
R MacLeod	*Progress of Evangelicalism in Western Isles, 1800-50,* PhD thesis, University of Edinburgh, 1970
R MacLeod	Ministearan an Arain? A Profile of Nineteenth Century Hebridean Moderates, *TGSI,* LII, 1980-82
R MacLeod	The Bishop of Skye, *TGSI,* LIII, 1982-84
C MacNaughton	*Church Life in Ross and Sutherland From the Revolution (1688) to the Present Time,* (Inverness, 1915)
I M M MacPhail	*The Crofters' War,* (Stornoway, 1989)
A MacPherson	*Glimpses of Church and Social Life in the Highlands in Olden Times,* (Edinburgh, 1893)
A MacPherson (ed)	*History of the Free Presbyterian Church of Scotland 1893-1970,* (Inverness, nd)
A MacRae	*Revivals in the Highlands and Islands in the Nineteenth Century,* (Stirling, 1905)
T Maxwell	Presbyterianism and Episcopalianism in 1688, *RSCHS,* 13, 1957
A B Mearns	The Minister and the Bailiff, A Study of the Presbyterian Clergy in the Northern Highlands During the Clearances, *RSCHS,* XXIV, 1990
D E Meek	Gaelic Poets of the Land Agitation, *TGSI,* XLIX, 1974-76
D E Meek	The Bible and Social Change in the Nineteenth-Century Highlands, in, D F Wright (ed), *The Bible in Scottish Life and Literature,* (Edinburgh, 1988)
D E Meek	Evangelical Missionaries in the Early Nineteenth-Century, *SS,* 28, 1987
D E Meek	Dugald Sinclair, The Life and Work of a Highland Itinerant Missionary, *SS,* 1990
D E Meek	The Gaelic Bible, in, D F Wright (ed), *The Bible in Scottish Life and Literature,* (Edinburgh, 1988)

D E Meek	The Land Question Answered from the Bible, The Land Issue and the Development of a Highland Theology of Liberation, *Scottish Geographical Magazine*, vol 103, 2, 1987
D E Meek	Scottish Highlanders, North American Indians and the SSPCK; Some Cultural Perspectives, *RSCHS*, XXIII, 1989
D E Meek	*Tuath is Tighearna, Tenants and Landlords*, (Edinburgh, 1995)
D E Meek	Saints and Scarecrows, The Churches and Gaelic Culture in the Highlands Since 1560, *SBET*, 14, 1996
D E Meek	Evangelicalism and Emigration; Aspects of the Role of Dissenting Evangelicalism in Highland Emigration to Canada, in, G W MacLennan, *Proceedings of the First North American Congress of Celtic Studies*, (Ottawa, 1988)
D E Meek	Baptists and Highland Culture, *Baptist Quarterly*, XXXIII 4, October 1989
D E Meek	The Baptists of Ross of Mull, Evangelical Experience and Social Change in a West Highland Community, *Northern Studies, 26*
D E Meek	The Independent and Baptist Churches of Highland Perthshire and Strathspey, *TGSI*, 56, 1991
D E Meek	'Falling Down as if Dead', Attitudes to Unusual Phenomena in the Skye Revival of 1841-42, *SBET*, Autumn, 1995
D E Meek	The Preacher, The Press Gang and the Landlord, The Impressment and Vindication of the Rev Donald MacArthur, *RSCHS*, XXV, 1994
D E Meek	*Island Harvest, A History of the Tiree Baptist Church 1838-1988*, (Edinburgh, 1988)
D E Meek	*The Scottish Highlands, The Churches and Gaelic Culture*, (Geneva, 1996)
R Middleton (ed)	N Cameron, *Ministers and Men of the Free Presbyterian Church*, (Settle, 1993)
I R M Mowat	*Easter Ross, 1750-1850*, (Edinburgh, 1981)
T M Murchison	The Synod of Glenelg, 1725-1821, Notes From the Records, *TGSI*, vol 38, 1936-38
N Murray	*Back Free Church, 1891-1991*, (np, nd)
J Noble	*Religious Life in Ross*, (Inverness, 1909)
J B Orr	*Scotch Church Crisis*, (Glasgow, 1905)
G Parsons	*Religion in Victorian Britain*, vols I & II (Manchester, 1988)

D M Paton	Brought to a Wilderness, Rev David MacKenzie of Farr, *Northern Scotland*, 13, 1993	*Bibliography* ❋ 229
N T Phillipson & R Mitchison (eds)	*Scotland in the Age of Improvement*, (Edinburgh, 1970)	
J Prebble	*The Highland Clearances*, (1969)	
J Prebble	*Glencoe*, (1968)	
E Richards	*A History of the Highland Clearances*, I & II (London, 1982 & 85)	
E Richards	How Tame Were the Highlanders During the Clearances, *SS*, 1973	
L A Ritchie	The Floating Church of Loch Sunart, *RSCHS*, XXII, 1985	
G Robb	Popular Religion and the Christianisation of the Scottish Highlands in the Eighteenth and Nineteenth Centuries, *Journal of Religious History*, 1990	
J M E Ross	*Ross of Cowcaddens*, (London, 1905)	
K Ross	*Church and Creed*, (Edinburgh, 1988)	
K Ross	Calvinists in Controversy, John Kennedy, Horatius Bonar and the Moody Mission of 1873-74, *SBET*, vol 9,1, Spring, 1991	
D Sage	*Memorabilia Domestica*, (Wick, 1899)	
P C Simpson	*The Life of Principal Rainy*, vol I & II (London, 1909)	
A Smith	*An Eaglais Mhòr*, (np 1992)	
D Smith	*Passive Obedience and Prophetic Protest, Social Criticism and the Scottish Church 1836-1945*, (New York, 1982)	
T C Smout	*A Century of the Scottish People*, (London, 1986)	
T C Smout	*A History of the Scottish People 1560-1830*, (London, 1969)	
A Stewart & J Kennedy-Cameron	*The Free Church of Scotland, The Crisis of 1900* (Edinburgh, 1989)	
J A Stewart	Clan Ranald and Catholic Missionary Success, 1715-1745, *IR*, XXXV, 1994	
D S Thompson	*The Companion to Gaelic Scotland*, (Oxford, 1983)	
D H Whiteford	Jacobitism as a Factor in Presbyterian-Episcopal Relations in Scotland, 1689-90, *RSCHS*, XVI, 1969	
N M Wilby	The Encrease of Popery in the Highlands, 1714-47, *IR*, XVII, 1966	
C W J Withers	*Gaelic Scotland, The Transformation of a Culture Region*, (London, 1988)	

C W J Withers   Education and Anglicisation, The Policy of the
                 SSPCK Towards Gaelic in the Highlands,
                 1709-1825, *SS*, 1982
C W J Withers   *Gaelic in Scotland, 1698-1981*, (Edinburgh, 1984)
D J Withrington The SPCK and the Highland Schools in the
                 Mid-Eighteenth Century, *SHR*, XLI, 1962
D J Withrington *Going to School*, (NMS, Edinburgh, 1997)
D J Withrington The Free Church Education Scheme, *RSCHS*,
                 XV, 1964
D J Withrington The Disruption; A Century and a Half of
                 Historical Interpretation, *RSCHS*, XXV, 1993
D J Withrington Non Church Going, Church Organisation and
                 the Crisis in the Church, c1850-c1920, *RSCHS*,
                 XXIV, 1991
D J Withrington Adrift Among the Reefs of Conflicting Ideals?
                 Education and the Free Church, 1843-1855, in
                 S J Brown and M Fry (eds), *Scotland in the Age*
                 of the Disruption, (Edinburgh, 1993)
D J Withrington Schooling Literacy and Society, in, *People and*
                 Society in Scotland, vol I, 1760-1830, T M
                 Devine and R Mitchison (eds), (Edinburgh, 1988)
D J Withrington Education and Society in the Eighteenth
                 Century, in, N T Phillipson and R Mitchison
                 (eds), *Scotland in the Age of Improvement*,
                 (Edinburgh, 1970)
D J Withrington Scotland, a half educated nation in 1834?
                 Reliable Critique or Persuasive Polemic?, in,
                 W M Humes and H M Paterson (eds), *Scottish*
                 Culture and Scottish Education, 1800-1900
                 (Edinburgh 1983)

Index